RURAL EDUCATION

RURAL EDUCATION

DR. (MRS.) SANGH MITTRA
Dy. Director (Research)
ICHR

KALPAZ PUBLICATIONS
DELHI–110052

RURAL EDUCATION
(Education Rural Development)

Rs. 890

ISBN: 81-7835-144-7

Published in 2002 in India by
Kalpaz Publications
C-30, Satyawati Nagar
Delhi-110052
E-mail: kalpaz@hotmail.com

Laser Typesetting at: A.S. Printers
Printed at: Mehra Offset Printers, New Delhi

Contents

Preface

In primitive societies children learned chiefly from watching, listening to and imitating their parents, their neighbours, and older children, and by their own experience. Little by little people learned that some special skills or knowledge can best be taught by formal, organized education. Thus schools and universities came into existence. Yet always there remain the informal skills, disciplines and judgments of everyday life, which are not included in formal education, but must be picked up by the child from informal, everyday experience.

The parts of the child's development which are formally planned cam to seem important to those who plan and administer the schools, while the parts which are left to informal contacts are overlooked as of small importance, or are forgotten. Yet they continue to be very important, perhaps more important than all the matter included in formal education. Rural education, like all education, should not limit itself to the processes of the schoolroom, but at every stage from primary school to university should insist that pupils and students shall learn also from the great traditions of common life.

Since rural education must evolve its own distinctive pattern, there is no need to follow traditional forms in educational administration. One general policy should be observed, namely, that rural education should be administered in the main by persons who have been directly concerned with rural education movement.

Our education must find its guiding principle in the aims of the social order for which is repares, in the nature of the civilization it hopes to build. Education is the great instrument of social emancipation by which a democracy establishes, maintains and protects the spirit of equality among its members. In the past it has been assumed that men who are successful in the professions and in business are justified in acquiring as much wealth as they can without dishonest means, and to live on whatever scale of expenditure such wealth makes possible. A democratic society requires a very different spirit.

All universities, urban and rural, should share in bringing about such a change of spirit of business and the professions. Yet it is the part of practical wisdom not to lose any opportunity afforded by favourable conditions. The creation of rural universities, inheriting the spirit with which Gandhiji infused the basic education movement, offers opportunity for giving a fresh impulse to such a change.

The present work contain valuable relevant account on diverse aspects of rural education. Students, teachers, educationists and educational administrators besides policy planners and teacher-trainers will find this book most useful and informative.

Editor

1

Nature of Rural Education

At this fateful moment in our history, we have the extreme good fortune to have had presented to us a pattern and philosophy of education of such universal and fundamental worth that it may well serve as the type of bringing into being the new India which is the desire of many of us. We have no sympathy with hero worship, and feel that there should be no with-holding of criticism of an educational plan because it was presented by our great leader. With some details of Gandhiji's programme of basic education we may not agree.

However, taking his concept as a whole it presents the seeds of a method for the fulfilment and refinement of human personality, and wisdom and excellence of which will become more apparent through the years, and will stand the test of time and of criticism. Year of time and vast effort will be required to insure this movement against warped and mistaken expression, and to develop effective skills and methods; yet inherently the concept is one of the world's great contributions to education. The methods outlined in its rudiments by Gandhiji is not just a way of meeting the educational needs of little children. He has stated the essential elements of a universal method of education, from the time a little child shares in its mother's work, through the whole process of growth of personality to the time when the mature man of disciplined mind and character works at the side of the master in the achievement of a great design.

The essence of this philosophy is that education should combine practice in the everyday processes of living and working, with more formal training. This a fundamental concept which is steadily gaining support and application in the educational world. Gandhiji was not the first to have this vision. Aristotle, Francis Bacon, Milton and Louis Agassiz are among the world's great man who specifically expressed a similar conviction. But in one important respect he differed from most of the others.

While their minds caught the vision of a new day, the bookishness of their lives held some of them captive. Therein is Gandhiji's pre-eminence. No sooner was a conviction matured in his mind than he acted on it.

The "basic education" programme—To see rural higher education in good perspective it is desirable to have a glimpse at the elementary and secondary education out of which it should emerge. As to the programme of Basic National Education for grades one to five, the revised syllabus published by Hindustani Talimi Sangh about 1947 may be taken as a representative statement.

A we have seen this programme in practice in several parts of India it seems to us in the main to be justifying the expectations of those who gave it form. A possible criticism of actual practice is over-emphasis on the one process of producing fabric and cloth. This is highly valuable as a centre of correlation of learning, since clothing, like food and shelter, is a basic human need. Also it provides opportunity for children to experience skillful achievement, and to have first hand familiarity with an economic process from start to finish. However in some cases it seems that a more distributed interest and attention to varied processes of rural life would be desirable. Basic education should introduce children to all the chief issues and interests of living, it should not become a routine with spinning and weaving as its main expressions.

These first steps of the basic education programme have been clearly defined and, in some cases at least, given able and inspiring expression. The "post-basic" secondary school programme has been less fully worked out, while that of higher education has not been clearly formulated. Therefore these will be considered in some detail.

The extreme poverty and lack of cultural opportunity of our population is a common factor. The course of wisdom is not to deny or to ignore this glaring lack, but rather to create the types of educational opportunity which are appropriate to Indian rural life, and to give a quality and range to that life which will remove the disparity which is now a reality. There should be no feeling of conflict between existing and new type universities, any more than between engineering education and medical education.

However, because the pattern and spirit of existing universities is so distinctly urban centred, and because of the tendency of an old and dominant institution to impose its type upon any new institution in a similar field, it is a matter of practical necessity that new universities aiming at extending educational opportunity to the great mass of rural India, and to give vitality and quality to rural life, should have their own independent design and programme. They will have qualities and methods in common with existing universities, and as they become established there will be general co-operation and interaction. To a large degree the European university, with the offspring institutions in India and America, will be indispensable to the new rural university, but their services should be those of consultation, friendship and advice, and not of authority and direction.

The significance of the indian village—As free India begins to plan its course, a great increase of interest in village welfare is in evidence. This is important, not only for the sake of the villages, but for the destiny of India as a whole. In the course of world history, seldom has the greatness of a nation long survived the disintegration of its rural life. For untold ages man by nature has been a villager and has not long survived in any other environment. Almost every study of the subject which has been made in Europe and America has revealed that as a rule city families survive for only a few generations.

Cities grow and thrive only as they are constantly replenished from the rural population. So long as a nation's rural life is vigorous it possesses reserves of life and power. When for a long time cities draw the cream of life culture from the villages, returning almost nothing, as has been the case in India during the last two centuries, the current village resources of culture and energy become depleted, and the strength of the nation is reduced.

India must decide whether to aim at a widely distributed population, making the villages such prosperous, interesting and culturally rich places, with such range of opportunity and adventure that young people will find more zest and interest, more cultural advantages, and more opportunity for pioneering there, than in the city; or whether to run to vast centralized industries, with masses of labour taking direction either from the state or from private corporations.

Natural drift will not change existing trends. Definite governmental and educational policy and a change of public attitude are required. Consider the present state of the village. Though there are areas with clean, attractive villages, most of the more than half a million villages in India consist of mud huts with earth floors, with one, two or three rooms, with unprotected open wells. Houses are crowded along narrow crooked paths which serve also as open drains.

These conditions, along with extreme poverty, result in a large amount of water-borne, insect-borne and earth-borne diseases. Less than ten per cent of the villages are literate to the extent of recognizing their own names on a letter. An average day's work in an Indian village produces probably less than a quarter as much wealth as would a day's work by modern methods. The villages are largely isolated from the world, and so have difficulty in getting a world view. Picture the kind of village life which should be aimed at. It must be economically prosperous. Its life must not be wasted in primitive habits of production. Full advantage should be taken of modern technical developments.

Small scale farming by efficient methods will require only a small part of the human labour needed at present, and production may be greatly increased. Much of the village population will be available for work other than agriculture. Each village, and especially each group villages, will have a wide range of economic activity. A large part of the industry of the country should be located in villages and small towns. Every village should have good year round transportation, and should be supplied with electric power. Each one should have a piped water supply under pressure, a sewer system and a telephone system.

With good water supply, drainage and sewage, malaria and intestinal diseases will practically disappear as they have nearly disappeared in certain countries. Health centres and public health care will nearly eliminate communicable diseases. Household vermin will almost wholly disappear as they have disappeared in certain other countries.

The people's college—With adoption of the new Indian constitution the achievement of democracy is only barely begun. Fundamental changes of attitude will be necessary before what is written on paper can become the prevailing way of life. One of the key points at which democracy will fail or succeed is in the kind of education which will be made available to the common people. Even after a vast extension of basic education, a large proportion of Indian rural boys and girls may not attend formal school beyond the seven or eight years of basic education.

How, after that, they will enter into the life and thought of the nation, is not only important to them, but may determine whether or not democracy becomes a reality in India. The university, and especially the rural university, has a vital relation to this problem.

To indicate what that relationship may be, and how the university may contribute to the further education of this great majority of the Indian people, is essential to an understanding of the right place and work of the rural university. For helpful guidance in this matter, we may turn to the programme of the People's Colleges of the Scandinavian countries, especially to those of Denmark. Sir

Richard Livingstone, England's foremost figure in adult education, called the Scandinavian People's College "the only great successful experiment in educating the masses of a nation". When the People's College movement was initiated in Denmark a century ago the Danes were a defeated. poverty-stricken, largely unschooled, privilege-ridden and dispirited people. In considerable degree as a result of the People's College movement the Danish people have risen from ignorance and poverty to about the highest general level of education and well-being of all the peoples of the earth.

Their social legislation has been sane and liberal. Danish agricultural practice has changed form a primitive state to among the most scientific and best organised in the world. All this change has been brought about with an increase, rather than a loss, of the human element. The part which the People's College have played in this transition is suggested by the fact that a third of the rural people attend them, while another third come under their direct influence.

More than thirty per cent of the members of the national legislature, and eighty per cent of the co-operative leaders in a country where co-operatives play a dominant economic role, were educated at the People's Colleges. The principle writers of modern Sweden also were educated at People's Colleges rather than at the universities. A paraphrase of a recent description of the philosophy and method of the Danish People's College will indicate how it might suit Indian conditions, and how the rural university could further its development.

While democracy requires well qualified men and women in positions of importance and authority, yet government by and for the people requires also that fine resources of culture, leadership, and wisdom shall be maintained with good distribution throughout the population. The rank and file of men have often been deprived of their best elements and their potential leadership as a result of a typical attitude toward democracy, which is not that it eliminates privilege, but that it gives everyone an equal chance to "get ahead" of others in the competition to escape from the mass of men and join the more privileged classes. Important as it is to keep open avenues of development for the specially gifted, society has an even more fundamental need. In leavening bread we do not aim to have the gas in the dough escape from the mass and rise to the top, but rather we desire to trap the gas in small bubbles all through the dough, so that the entire mass will rise with uniform light texture.

Our ideal for the gifted person among the common people, that he shall escape into an environment of culture and economic privilege, results in his leaving behind a yet more sodden mass of uninspired and unenlightened people. With this prevailing ideal, the very equality of opportunity of a political democracy accelerates the tendency towards a population composed of subject masses and ruling classes. For a continuing democracy it is essential that our programme of liberal education shall not promote the escape from the common people of the culture which that education generates, but shall inspire able students to remain common people, in and of the people, acting as their servants and leaders, and raising the whole social lump. A familiar attitude among educators calls for a liberal education for a small elite group, and vocational education for the masses. John Dewey wrote, "I cannot think of any idea more completely reactionary and more fatal to the whole democratic out look". Another suggestion is that the shortcomings of such a leadership can be partly cured by liberal colleges drawing potential leaders form all ranks of society. "by making liberal education available to all young people who possess the essential intellectual and personal qualities." Yet, the chief issue is not where young people *come from* to get an education, but where they *go* with their education.

Democracy requires leadership steadfastly loyal to the whole people. Throughout history the people's cause has often been lost by leadership becoming estranged from and even turning traitor to the people, though often it had only recently emerged from the common people. The philosophy of rule by an intellectual elite, which characterised Plato, was the object of criticism by Bishop Grundtvig, originator of the Danish People's College. He wrote: "People in out day shout themselves hoarse about freedom and culture, and that is certainly what we need, but the proposals for attaining them usually have the same fundamental faults as Plato's 'Republic", where the guardians of freedom and culture themselves swallow them both up, so that the people for all their labour get only proud tyrants to obey, to support, and if that can comfort them, to admire and deify."

Leadership which cannot express itself in the shoes of the common man is rather rulership than leadership. Was not that Gandhiji's message? How to achieve intellectual discipline and culture which give quality to leadership , and yet to maintain identity with the common people, is a problem which seldom has been solved. Because the Danish People's College has contributed greatly to that solution, its methods are important. Because that problem in India may profit by a new approach, the rural university may make a significant contribution to its solution here. It is a general assumption of the intellectual elite that a long period of study with conventional "cultural" subject matter in high school and college is necessary to produce liberally educated men.

The People's College challenges that assumption. It holds that education is not identical with formal intellectual training; that men can become educated without being intellectuals, and that intellectuals are not necessarily educated men. Grundtvig wrote: "Scholarship is one thing, and education and fitness for life is another; they must not be hostile to each other. Scholarship will lead scholars astray if it is not confronted by an education of the people which obliges it to take present-day life into consideration, just as education of the people will soon degenerate into a superficial polish if scholarship does not keep it alive."

Einstein commented: "School is not to promote future officials, scholars, lecturers, barristers and authors, but human beings." Whitehead similarly remarked, "The school course of classics mush be planned so that a definite result is clearly achieved. There has been too great a product of failures on a road to an ambitious ideal of scholarship." The People's College aims at helping people to desire and to achieve the primary values of life, from which other values must be derived.

The rural secondary school

A Residence School Village - Doubtless a number types of rural secondary school will emerge as the general principles of basic education find expression in practice. Let us picture one type as a continuation of the basic education programme.

Except where there are good reasons to the contrary, the rural secondary school should be a residence school, with the pupils living in hostels, or if feasible, in such houses as would be suitable for good village life. The grounds and streets should be planned, and the buildings planned and built, as nearly as possible like a well panned modern village. The entire setting should be an example to the students of what their own villages might be life.

Secondary school education should not make boys and girls content with living in the villages as they are. It should, however, make them familiar with practical ways of creating new villages, within the reasonable financial and social resources available. The school village should be an example of what is desirable and practical in village planning, construction and operation. In case an entire family should wish to move to the school village building and managing its home according to the standards of the school, the children of that family might well live at home. In such case that family as a whole might share in the educational process. There have been a few colleges or secondary schools where they young family and not the individual was the unit being educated.

In some cases it would be desired by students or their parents who reside nearby that the boys and girls should live at home and go to the school each day. This probability draws attention to two sometimes conflicting aims in the establishment and administration of residence secondary schools. On the one hand it is desirable that the student be in the school village setting where he can see village life as it might be, can free his mind from rigid village tradition, and can have that kind of living together and intimate relations with his teacher which marked the relations of the old time *guru* with his pupils. On the other hand it is highly important that his school experience shall not so divorce him from his village associations that he cannot and will not return to work with the world from which he came. He should be imbued by his school experience with a desire to improve his village, not to escape from it. For some of the boys and girls to continue to live at home might help the school to keep that desirable association, but it would be unfortunate for the students as a whole to do so.

Residence schools should not be allowed to wither because of supposed economy to the parents or to the government. The People's College programme with its residence schools has been singularly successful in arousing a desire for progress without leading students to abandon their villages. Small units of 150 to 200 students will be far better than mass schools of many hundreds. A school for 150 students should have probably 30 to 60 acres of land, depending on circumstances. Perhaps 10 or 15 acres of this should be for school house, hostels, homes for teachers, playgrounds, workshops and industrial sites. The rest should be for agriculture, forest and pasture. The secondary school village as a rule would serve a group of villages, and should be conveniently located with reference to them.

In case of the reconstruction of villages, as hereafter proposed, in some cases provision may be made in them for secondary school plants, with suitable land and environment. In such cases secondary school students might live at home, or part at home and part in hostels, as as would be desirable. While every normal boy and girl should have opportunity for continued schoolingafter the 7 or 8 years of basic schooling, the provisions suggested are estimated to be adequate for the next one or two decades.

The first cost of small residence secondary schools may be higher than buildings for mass education, but not necessarily so. The buildings may be very simple. Research is finding ways to use local materials and labour to make permanent structures. In so far as possible, the school village should be built by the pupils and their teachers working together, with the help of a person trained in village and school planning.

During construction of the school village pupils and teachers would live in temporary shelters, or return to their home villages at night. The cost of bringing students by bus each day from the several villages would be eliminated. Nearly all the work of maintaining and cleaning buildings and grounds, preparing food and doing other necessary work, could be done by the students as part of their practical education. This is less feasible where the students live at home and attend school in large masses

Learning by living—Residence school students not only profit from their studies but, under the leadership and companionship of teachers of mature character and culture, they may learn a way of life together. It is largely through personal friendships, acquaintances, and mutual trust that society hold together. "The old school tie", a powerful element in social organization, has hitherto been limited to a small social class. The old school ties of residence secondary schools and People's Colleges will be threads of acquaintance and fellowship over larger area than the village, and will help toward widening social understanding and unity.

The life of the school should follow the course of life of a good village, except that about half the working time should be given to study and about half to practical work.

Some work such as cleaning the school village probably should be done by everyone, teachers and pupils working together. There are some kinds of work with which nearly every pupils should become familiar, such as child care, cooking and home keeping for girls, and agriculture and the use of household tools for boys and girls. The school should raise most of its food and should teach boys and girls how to make the land yield as much as possible. The practical work should include farming, building, carpentry and cabinet making, housekeeping, weaving, street cleaning, and other useful village work. It should also include one or more modern industries, manufacturing goods fore sale.

So far as training in a modern industry is concerned, a two to four year period of work in a secondary school industry under skilful teaching, along with related study, should produce highly skilled workers, ready to perform many of the more exacting processes in new industries in new secondary school villages. Some students would continue more advanced training.

As boys and girls grow older, the periods of uninterrupted work will naturally grow longer. Rather than work and study for a part of each day it probably will be well to divide the students into two shifts, each shifts working or study alternate day,s or more probably alternate weeks or fortnights. It would be desirable for some of the part time work of each student during his secondary school year to be away from the school village, to give him a more representative view of practical life.

The rural secondary school programme—Little by little many boys and girls would find desirable callings and would begin to specialize. For many, the secondary school period would complete the schooling and their special training. Other would find it desirable to go to home advanced rural schools or colleges. In their study periods the pupils should be getting an all-round, well proportioned education. Where feasible the subjects of study should be related to or grow out of the practical work and life of the pupil. However, as boys and girls grow older it will be found increasingly desirable to follow some orderly courses of study, sometimes regardless of their own experiences of the moment. They should become acquainted with the physical environment as disclosed by geography, geology and astronomy; with the physical sciences in physics and chemistry, and with the world of living things in biology.

They should get a general knowledge of the history of their own locally, of India and of the world, and should be introduced to some good literature. They should have enough mathematics to serve their practical needs, and a general knowledge of local and national government. Their studies also should help them to understand the theory of their work. Physical education should be universal. To select subject matter and to distribute the available time among the different subjects, so that these fields shall be covered without overcrowding the students' time, will require through preparation by those planning post-basic education.

Even more important than the imparting of information is the development of habits and attitudes of mind and spirit. The habit of openness and honesty is a tremendous source of national strength and so are habits of goodwill and fair play. In training teachers of secondary rural school these qualities should be the first consideration. The scientific attitude, that is, the habit of free, critical inquiry, of looking into actual facts and causes, rather than credulous acceptance of rumour or tradition, would put new life into India. In its industrial work the rural secondary school should aim at creating a new industrial tradition. It has been assumed that the industrialist works chiefly for profit, whereas the teacher works chiefly for service. There is no inherent reason why these different callings should be carried on with different motives.

The tradition should develop that rural industrialists deserve reasonable and decent living and economic security, but that beyond these standards all earnings should go to strengthening the industry, accumulating reserves for expansion or against depression, founding new industries for new secondary schools, improving quality, lowering prices, or raising wages and bettering working conditions. It is a curious delusion that amassing a fortune gives greater satisfaction than does good citizenship. Rural education should aim at changing that tradition.

Even where there are programmes for village improvement which provide for nurses, health advisers, agricultural extension workers and others to live and work in the villages, such plans are handicapped, or even break down, because of the unwillingness of such persons to live in the villages. Secondary school villages, planned and built according to approved standards, would be suitable centres for rural clinics, rural library service, agricultural extension work, co-operative banking, and other village activities. Such services could become parts of the secondary school training programme. Though the school system they should be integrated into a unified process of social education, and should not continue as competing activities of unrelated departments. The secondary school village thus might well become the cultural and service centre of a group of villages, and might go far to insure the success of these various services.

Self-supports in basic education—Basic secondary education can develop a large element of self-support, and can be better education than that which is wholly supported by taxation. A substantial degree of self-support may not be achieved at once, for the methods of that type of education, and competence in economical production, must be mastered. No specific amount of self-support should be made imperative.

The educational development of boys and girls should be the first consideration, but experience in competence and responsible production will be found to contribute greatly to such development. Generally the land, buildings and equipment should be supplied from public funds. If boys and girls do part of the work of building, then their labour should be paid for at a fair rate from public funds, for otherwise, in order to be self-supporting, it may be necessary for them to use all working time to produce for immediate use or sale, and the educational value of building might be lost.

For basic secondary education to be in some degree self-supporting, it is necessary that living standards of great simplicity should prevail. The tradition of our country has largely been of hovels and palaces, with almost nothing gin between. The basic education school should be an example to young people of the truth that simple, inexpensive leaving can be clean, convenient and attractive living. Self-support must come partly by restricting wants to very simple living, and partly by increasing income.

Fear is sometimes expressed that any element of self-support may lead to exploitation of child labour. To provide boys and girls with all-round education, and to train them for specific competence in some field, is a good way to reduce exploitation. The entire spirit and atmosphere of the basic education programme, and the sensitiveness of democratic government to charges of exploitation, can be relied on to protect them form excessive toil.

Division of labour in basic secondary schools— The division of labour in secondary schools should probably be different from that in the first years. Probably some labour should still be shared by all, such as a half hour for general clean-up in the morning. Most work should be divided, with each student having his or her definite duties. The duties of a student may be changed from time to time so that he or she can become acquainted with many kind of work. A convenient way of dividing work perhaps would be to have most students work and study every other week or fortnight. In one such period about half the students would be at work and the other half at study.

During the following period those who had been studying would work and those who had been working would study. Thus one set of teachers would teach two sets of students. Some members of the staff would give their whole time to supervising students' work. This programme has been used successfully in some secondary schools for thirty-five years. In some cases the alternation of work and study might be influenced by the seasonal needs of agriculture and climate.

Every boy and girl in basic and post-basic education should be able to perform almost any common, necessary duty. In line with the spirit of the new Indian constitution every boy and girl in a basic and post-basic education school should make the following resolve: I shall never ask nor accept from any person any menial service that I would not gladly do for him or her, or for others.

Short time technical courses—Perhaps associated with secondary school villages should be provisions for short term technical courses, somewhat parallel with People's College sessions. For practical workers in many fields to have even one or two weeks a year of training and experience in a good shop with good supervision might in many cases quite change the degree of understanding and skill with which they would do their work. If mechanics, craftsmen and technicians of all sorts should develop the habit of attending short courses in their special field for them a week to a month each year or two, receiving instruction and example form the most competent persons in each field, the general quality of technical work and of craftsmanship might be greatly improved. Such short courses might be given at both secondary school villages and at rural universities. Different schools or rural universities might develop reputation for skill and leadership in different fields.

The duration of rural education—The duration of the rural post-basic or secondary school period should be related to the entire span of education. One suitable distribution of this entire span would be:

8 years for basic education,

3 or 4 years for post-basic or secondary education,

3 years for college,

2 years post-graduate university work for the master's degree.

An alternative distribution of time would be 7 basic, 4 post-basic, and 3 for college. As the value of education is better realized, and as the material resources of India increase, there probably will be a tendency to reach a programme of 8 years basic education, 4 years secondary education and 4 years of college to the equivalent of the bachelor's degree.

The expression "college" in this connection refers not only to education leading to an academic degree, but any education beyond the secondary school, whatever may be its form. While it probably is desirable to consider a regular period, as 3 or 4 years, for post-basic or secondary schooling and 3 or 4 years for college, these would be only general guiding standards. Some students entering secondary school may be well prepared for their work in two years, some in three years.

The aim of the school should be to help the student to most effective living, so far as the educational resources justify preparation. In a four year secondary school programme for instance, there should be no sense of failure for the student who comes to the end of his productive period of study in one or two or three years.

(Secondary) education and village industrialization

Industrialization is Inevitable—One of the issues which troubles the basic education movement is the extent to which modern industrial processes shall we welcomed in the villages. India will surely industrialize. To pump irrigation water by muscle power as in India requires more than a hundred times as many manhours for a given result as by modern methods. The difference in labour between hand and machine spinning is very great, and nearly all village weavers prefer the machine spun yarn. The makers of hand made padlocks in India are finding constantly greater difficulty in competing which machine-made padlocks from other countries. The village blacksmith is losing to the big factories in Indian cities his trade of making agricultural implements.

Industrialization is one of the great basic changes in human living, perhaps as fundamental as the change from hunting to settled agriculture. It cannot be stopped, but can be guided into wholesome channels. The energy and devotion needed to guide industrial development in India, so that it shall serve widespread decentralization on a high economic, social and spiritual level, should not to dissipated in trying to prevent it.

The next few years may largely set the pattern of Indian industrial life for a long time. If there is clear and prompt recognition of the need and possibility for distributing much of modern industry through the villages and small town, the prosperity of modern industry may be diffused through the whole country. If there is effective opposition to specialized modern industries in the villages, on the ground that each village should be a self-contained, independent unit, these may concentrate in the cities.

Decentralized industry—A very large amount of small unit industry is feasible, though a part must be in large units. People looking at America from a distance see only the towering industrial giants. Yet there are many thousand of thriving small industries in that country, and there would be more but for the cut of size and power which seeks to grow large, just as a ruler might wish to add to his dominions, even though the administration might not thereby be more efficient.

Over the half the business of America is done by small and medium sized firms. These are on the whole more profitable than the great industries, as is disclosed by several public and private studies. While some industries are growing larger, others are decentralizing, and many are moving from cities to rural areas. Small and medium sized business is very much alive in America, and can be in India.

Industrial inter-relations—In the modern world the village will steadily lose the status of an independent, self-contained economic unit, but at the same time it can become far more important as a basic unit of society, out of which the larger society is built. Village people want books, radios, watches, bicycles, metal goods, electric power, and railway travel, which cannot be produced by each village for itself. The world is becoming constantly more inter-related. That inter-relationship will be best it each of the units has a vigorous, definite existence of its own, while it co-operates with others.

It is a mistaken aim to atomize India into nearly unrelated villages, as though inter-dependence were itself an evil. A better social aim is the growth together of independence and of interdependence, each where it is most appropriate. Not the *greatest* degree, but the *best* degree of local self-sufficiency should be the aim.

If the village does not industrialize, the actual result will be that urban industry will take over all those processes that are most profitable, leaving to the village the unprofitable operations. As industrialization spreads over the earth it becomes increasingly true that handicraft workers receive very small pay for their work, and even then the products are commonly luxury goods, sold to wealthy people.

The development of secondary rural education should presume decentralized, well-balanced, progressive industrialization. In fact a considerable part of the vocational training of post-basic schools should be to prepare boys and girls no longer needed in agriculture for other callings. The industrial development of India is being handicapped by the lack of workers who are skilled in hand and eye to fill positions not requiring full professional training. As rural industries develop, the rural secondary schools should go far to meet the need.

A Programme for the reconstruction of Indian villages

The future of the village—Without some picture of what the future of the Indian village may be, the future of rural education cannot be clear. In trying to understand the problem of secondary and higher education for the people of India who live in its 600,000 villages, we seem at first to come up against a stone wall which makes progress all but impossible. That "stone wall" is the present condition of the Indian village. Anything in the nature of broad, liberal education in the modern spirit will surely make villagers more keenly aware of the inadequacy of the village, and in many cases of the futility of trying to make it livable. Except as some generally effective way is found for dealing with this condition, any plans for rural higher education will in effect be plans for driving more people from the village, and therefore for the further impoverishment of the rural life of India. A clear cut, comprehensive and adequate solution of this problem is imperative. The following statement, we believe, outlines such a solution.

Over a large part of India the village is obsolete, not fit for human habitation. Of the 600,000 villages in India there are probably many thousands to which this statement does not apply. In a few localities villages are reasonably fair places of residence. But in the main it seems to be true. While the destiny of India depends on the vigor, the health, the culture and the intelligence of the villages,,the villages *has* declined and *is* declining. Only if the realities are faced will there be a chance to guide the course of events towards a great destiny for the nation. The problem of the village in most cases requires its complete relocation in reconstruction.

One of the greatest handicaps of the Indian village is the lack on the part of the villager of any clear, full picture of what a good village might be like. If there should be a fine modern village here and there, if the villager should get a clear picture of what a good village would be like, and if he should lean by practical example of the steps he could reasonably take to have such a village, then his day-by-day comparison of that village with his own would lead him to have a powerful desire to get what he has learned to be practical and desirable. As to every phase of village life it should be the business of rural education to develop clear pictures of what are desirable and practical living conditions, and to provide examples of such conditions.

This picture of village life should not be limited to well-planned physical layout and to varied opportunity to make good living. Of no less importance are habits of neighbourliness and good will, of co-operation, and of dependable, fair dealing with one another.

The situation of the village is not hopeless. In fact, we are constantly impressed by the vast potential human resources ready to become alive and to spring into action if they are but freed and encouraged by public policy and by private example. So far as material resources and human energies are concerned, the wholesale relocation and reconstruction of our villages is entirely feasible.

The great material wealth of mankind is not its stored wealth, its hoarded gold, its cities, railroads, ships and factories, but the current year by year production of wealth by the people. The potential wealth-producing capacity of men is almost incredibly great. What are lacking are not natural resources or human energy, but a clear mental picture of what is desirable and possible, and the character, skill, experience and culture necessary to realize such possibilities. These qualities it is the main business of rural education to provide. India has such vast natural and human resources that, given these qualities, the average India might have many times as much wealth at his disposal as he now possesses. If even ten per cent of our potential resources should be realized, India and all her people would be rich.

Reconstruction—The construction of new and fine village throughout India may become a great national movement. Moreover it may be carried through to a considerable extent without the financial help of the central or provincial government. As public fiscal policy can be readjusted, public money received from the taxation of rural lands should mostly be returned for the use of rural education and for village improvement. Except per great undertakings beyond the limits of local control, the carrying through of public projects may usually be more economical and more productive by local initiative. The handling f such projects by local initiative may become a school for democracy, thrift and responsibility. As an example to be generally followed in this particular kind of development, the T.V.A. may be misleading. Despite the widespread publicity of the T.V.A and the use f expressions concerning democracy, the T.V.A is not fully in the line of the democratic tradition.

There is a tradition in the United States which has worked and spread so quietly that its vast achievements have been scarcely realized; even in America. This is the habit of creating local or regional limited governments for special purposes. These little special purpose governments are often in the form of special assessment improvement trusts. They are created by the people interested, for such purposes as reclaiming wet lands, creating parks and recreation districts, and in some cases for developing water supplies for groups of towns.

Following such a method the central or provincial government might provide the laws necessary for such local democratic initiative, so that village or groups of villages may work out their own plans. India provincial governments should use a considerable part of the funds received from land taxes to improve the condition of the villages. The central government may provide samples of good development so that the people can see what is possible. To get such a movement started in any district the central or provincial government may agree to pay half the cost of the first undertakings, and perhaps a quarter or a third of the cost of other undertakings. Also the central or provincial government, and especially the rural university, can carry on research as to the best methods. Governments might well have power to prevent borrowing money for any plan which is not honestly or competently developed, or which would probably be a loss or a disappointment to the people. They could develop a variety of plans and suggestions, and provide skilled advice which might be beyond the reach of local organization. Many villages are too small to provide the range of services. Interests and associations necessary for most satisfactory living. Research to determine the most desirable size might result in consolidation of some of the smaller ones, and the grouping of villages with some services in common.

With proper legislation providing for village trusts for such reconstruction, a village could rebuild itself quickly, and the added, tax, spread through twenty years, probably would be no more than is now paid for various poor services,. The land of the villagers would be security for the cost. Much of the work they could do themselves under skilled direction.

If such a movement is made possible by wise legislation and by a limited number of sample cases, it will spread so fast that for many years there will not be enough village planners, sanitary engineers, house builders etc., to meet the demand in some parts of India dissatisfaction of villagers with present living conditions and desire for radical improvement are becoming strong. Unless they are met by an effective programme they may soon grow into menacing political discontent.

Each year in the natural course of events numerous villages are relocated and rebuilt. This is made necessary by the construction of reservoirs in river control projects, by the caving of river banks, by removal to escape malarial conditions, in constructing new villages for refugees, and for a variety of other reasons. Each such change can be made the occasion for replanning and rebuilding villages on modern lines. The central government and each provincial government should provide in one of its departments a person or a small staff to keep in touch with all such cases, and to advise on plans and methods or relocation. The central government staff should include a research centre for community planning, methods of construction and methods of administering relocation and reconstruction.

The villages of India are a vast reservoir of human energy, intelligence and aspiration, much of it now wasting in futility. Indian boys and girls start out in life alert, curious, eager to live and to learn. The dull hopelessness of their environment kills this spirit in many, so that as men and women they become conservative and inert. Give the villager a picture of a good life, with health, cleanliness, variety of occupation, place and time for recreation, and a feeling that his hopes may be fulfilled, and the energies of the people will make a new rural India, a fit and fine dwelling place for a great people.

Rural colleges and universities

General characteristics—The general advancement of rural India will call for an ever increasing range and quality of skill and training. To supply these and to meet the requirements of an educated citizenship, a system of rural colleges and universities in necessary. A new beginning is desirable, with freedom to create a distinctive tradition as to purposes, spirit and methods.

The crowding together of thousands of undergraduates, as in the case of some existing universities, is highly undesirable. A way should be found to combine the advantages of small resident undergraduate colleges where there are close relations between teachers and students, with the advantages of fully developed universities which offer a wide range of specialized and advanced educational opportunity to advanced students, or to other students with specialized interests.

As a general type of arrangement, it is suggested that a rural university should include a ring of small, resident, undergraduate colleges, with specialized and university facilities in the centre. The suggested number of students for each of the undergraduate, resident colleges is about three hundred, and that of the maximum over-all enrolment for colleges and university combined, about twenty-five hundred.

Each college of about three hundred students would have separate teaching staff and facilities so far as its basic courses are concerned, except that undergraduate libraries, laboratories, gymnasiums and hospital facilities might be shared by as many colleges as should prove desirable. The aim of each college would be to equip its students with a general educational foundation, and to encourage the development of individual aptitudes and interests as they appear.

In some cases undergraduate students would be well qualified to undertake professional or other specialized studies in some particular fields. It should be possible in such cases for them, while still undergraduates, to carry single courses in university or professional school. Each student should have opportunity, without sacrificing the core of general education, to begin specialization at whatever time he is ready for it, even at the risk that he might later change his field of occupational interest. Some Students have clearly defined occupational bents at an early age. They will make better progress, take more interest, and have more normal personal development if such dominant interests find early expression. Similarly, there should be no hard and fast lines between undergraduate and post graduate education. A student might be an undergraduate in most subjects, and yet in some field of special interest he might be doing post-graduate work. The college and university programmes should be flexible enough to serve such cases.

Work and study—In rural colleges, as in rural secondary schools, general studies should be united with practical courses, so that those who attend college shall become cultured, educated men and women, and also persons trained and skilled in some field, or prepared for further advanced training. Probably the greater part of rural college students will not have further schooling, except for "refresher courses", and so their college years should include occupational preparation. Also as with rural secondary students, rural college students may spend about half their time at studies and half at practical work. The working and study periods probably should be longer than in a secondary school, the intervals of work and study being perhaps 5 or 10 weeks each.

A part of the staff of the college or of a group of colleges should be engaged in securing suitable working opportunities, and in supervising students during their working periods. Such working positions might be located anywhere within several hundred miles, in a great variety of fields. This programme of work and study has been developed in some places in Europe and America through more than thirty-five years, and has been successful. In America a steadily increasing number of universities, technical institutes and similar institutions now use it. The colleges as a rule may develop their own industries and other economic activity, which might well be more specialized and more exacting than those of rural secondary schools.

There is a tendency in university circles to look upon alternating work and study, and also upon "practical" courses, especially those calling for manual craftsmanship, as suited to inferior minds, while professional courses are for intellectuals. This separation of skill of hand from skill of mind has greatly retarted the mastery of the physical world and has been a major cause of poverty, especially in India. Practical work should not leave the worker in a "blind alley" without continued opportunity for advancement. Practical skill should be looked upon as equal in dignity and worth to purely intellectual skill. Like scholarship, it should be recognized with ascending grades of achievement and opportunity, so that a man who develops high ability with hand and eye may have an open road to advancement equal to that of the purely intellectual worker.

The curriculum of the rural university—The great cultural values are not peculiarly rural of urban, but are common to all humanity. As described in this report under *General Education*, a common core of liberal education may be assumed for the rural university as for any other, though the methods used in teaching and in learning may be different. This common core would include substantial introduction to the fields of mathematics, chemistry, physics, geology, astronomy, biology, physical education, psychology, the social sciences, philosophy, and language and literature.

As to advanced and specialized subjects, no field of human concern should be foreign to the rural university. The rural setting should seen as a suitable environment for the full sweep of human interests. Yet interests and possibilities especially related to rural life should have explicit attention, and the way should be prepared for their realization. While there should be many common elements for all students, the curriculum should be made to fit the needs of individuals, and not the students made to conform to an arbitrary curriculum. By the time students reach college, if they have been well advised and have had the practical work experience described elsewhere, many of them will have definite ideas of the work they want to do. With the help of their teachers they can combine courses from several fields to meet their individual needs.

For instance, a main planning to direct public water control projects may combine engineering, law, business, and public administration. Lawyers as a rule are quite unable to understand technical engineering matters, while engineers are commonly ignorant of law. Both are frequently unacquainted with business methods. Yet all these elements are needed for effective management of such projects.

A combination of law, engineering and business in some cases has made men exceptionally able to hand important work which involved them all. None of these courses would be standard and conventional, but those elements in each field would be included which taken together would make well-propotioned preparation for the person concerned.

A large number of study possible combinations might be cited. Many students without definite aims would follow more general programmes. However, to become competent in all the chief activities associated with some field is a great help to personal success and to social usefulness.

Rural secondary and higher education should constantly explore the changing needs and opportunities of Indian life, and should make sure that their programmes are planned for the conditions of today and tomorrow and not for those of yesterday. Both the general programme and the combinations of studies of individual students would be influenced by such continuing inquiry. Intelligent appraisal of current needs for men in various callings, and of the prospective supply of such needs, will be generally effective in guiding students' vocational choices, and will be far better than arbitrary limitation of vocational opportunity.

The flexibility and adaptability of the programme outlined above require freedom for creative education. That freedom would be destroyed by any system of uniform, external examinations.

In educational the rural university student can prepare for administration and leadership in primary secondary and higher rural education. In agriculture he can prepare for leadership in production, marketing, breeding, and agricultural co-operation. He can prepare, to participate in agricultural co-operation. He can prepare, to participate in agricultural extension work, in the organization of youth and adult study and working groups, and in agricultural research. He can become skilled in the processes of planning and rebuilding agricultural villages, in the consolidation of small agricultural holdings, and in many other phases of rural life.

The student interested in industry should study the design and improvement of machines and processes. He should study the methods by which many small industries can co-operate in purchasing, research, marketing, in business ownership and management. The curricula of professional and specialized subjects should first of all deal with those fields which are or should be of major concern to rural life. The student of the rural college or university should not be isolated from the life of his time. Should be make a deliberate choice of urban living, no barriers should be put in his way. Rural life should be made so interesting and productive, so full of opportunity and adventure, that it will be preferred. The aim of rural education should be to make it so.

Rural India is a great reservoir of creative life, but the pattern that life shall adopt is not yet determined. The future society may take any one or more of many directions, some better, some worse. The range of possibilities may have few limits except the capacity of men's minds and spirits to create and to live by patterns of excellence. So far as our rural population is concerned, the development, enlargement and refinement of that design should largely be the work of rural education. The curriculum of the rural university should be guided by that responsibility.

Rural universities

Rural professions—In a rural India in process of active development some new or relatively new professions will be useful. Some of these may be peculiarly rural and others common to both urban and rural life. Among professions or branches of professions in the development of which rural universities may well participate are various phases of water control engineering, soil improvement engineering, temperature control engineering, food processing technology, "chemurgic engineering", ocean products technology, mineral processing, rural industrial counselling, rural public administration, rural social welfare, rural land and village planning, social engineering, rural sociology and anthropology, rural arts, and rural medical service.

The social attitudes of the rural professions and of business—Our education must find its guiding principle in the aims of the social order for which is repares, in the nature of the civilization it hopes to build. Education is the great instrument of social emancipation by which a democracy establishes, maintains and protects the spirit of equality among its members. In the past it has been assumed that men who are successful in the professions and in business are justified in acquiring as much wealth as they can without dishonest means, and to live on whatever scale of expenditure such wealth makes possible. A democratic society requires a very different spirit.

While recognizing such factors as the great time and expense required for professional education or for business preparation, and the greater obligations of men in responsible positions which require expenditures, the spirit of democracy will not make these the excuse of justification for a standard of living far beyond the hop e of achievement of the general population, even in a well-ordered society. The tradition should grow among successful men that simple and unostentatious living which is not a burden to society is the only way of life which comports with the spirit of the new India.

All universities, urban and rural, should share in bringing about such a change of spirit of business and the professions. Yet it is the part of practical wisdom not to lose any opportunity afforded by favourable conditions. The creation of rural universities, inheriting the spirit with which Gandhiji infused the basic education movement, offers opportunity for giving a fresh impulse to such a change.

What is a "profession" in rural education?"— Members of some of the older professions may be inclined to take offence when the word profession is applied to many fields of work. The difference between professions, practised primarily for human service, and business and industry followed or profit, has largely disappeared. Also, the time has passed when scholarship and disciplined preparation were the marks of only a few tractional fields. Any useful calling for which a high degree of preparation has been needed and has been made, and which is pursued in a spirit of service to the public, deserves the name of profession.

The spirit of democracy will not tolerate the monopoly of that term by any privileged group. It is mistaken idea that there is any field of necessary human effort which will not respond to a high quality of preparation, and so deserve the name of profession. Just as the despised calling of scavenger has emerged as the honoured profession of sanitary engineer, so can every necessary human work become in truth a profession. The rural university should strive constantly to increase the number of useful occupations which in outlook, skill and spirit of service have been raised to the status of professions.

Rural education and the great traditions— There are several great traditions in human culture, each the product of a long past. Their existence depends on unbroken continuity through the centuries. If the continuity of one of these traditions is completely broke, centuries may be too short a time for its rebirth. Some cases will illustrate this.

The great tradition of agriculture is the accumulation of centuries. No man who is cut off from that tradition becomes a good farmer in one generation, though a business man may succeed in farming by the help of workmen who do have that tradition. Another great-tradition is that of medicine. No person can discover or invent the art of medicine for himself. It is the same with business. Even the self-made business man profits by the experience of those who have gone before. Another great tradition is that of home making. No woman becomes a great home keeper soley from own genius. At the back of a finely managed home are centuries of accumulated tradition of home making.

Scholarship is another of the great traditions. With all their faults, existing universities and other similar institutions are almost the sole carries of the tradition of scholarship. Organised knowledge and disciplined thinking cannot be quickly created a new, no matter how great the native intelligence, nor how strong and sustained the enthusiasm.

Here, then, we have the dilemma of the rural university. It would modernize agriculture, but must work with farmers, often with men burdened by ignorance, credulity and conservatism, while they possess the wisdom of the ages. The rural university would build rural industry in a spirit of good will and mutual helpfulness, and without being controlled by the traditional passion of maximum profit. The rural university would built a health service for the people of rural India in the spirit of social service, moderate income, and a sharing of the common lot, but it must begin with doctors, some of whom have been trained in the doctrine that the physician is a superior person who, if the can, will live in luxury even at the expense of patients who cannot.

Finally, the rural university must have scholarship,

and this it can get chiefly from the existing universities which, along with the great tradition of scholarship, also are full of unimaginative formalism, pedantry, petty ambition, timidity or cowardice, and lack of practical contact with real life. Out of these materials, how is the rural university to realize its aims of building a new and fine rural India, and of releasing the vast creative energies of Indian life, now so tightly bound in the chains of privilege, prejudice, exploitation and ignorance? There are two things the rural university movement can do.

First it can define and clearly express its own purposes. This is one of the primary duties of those who would build a new rural India. Second, it can constantly search all India and all the world for those exceptional persons who, while making themselves masters of one of the great traditions, such as agriculture or medicine or business or scholarship, have nevertheless held to the greatest of all the great traditions, that of committing their live and all they have to the service of their fellow men. As such men find each other and work together they can create the basic elementary school, the rural secondary school and the rural university, and through them the new India.

The great traditions of common life—In primitive societies children learned chiefly from watching, listening to and imitating their parents, their neighbours, and older children, and by their own experience. Little by little people learned that some special skills or knowledge can best be taught by formal, organized education. Thus schools and universities came into existence. Yet always there remain the informal skills, disciplines and judgments of everyday life, which are not included in formal education, but must be picked up by the child from informal, everyday experience. The parts of the child's development which are formally planned cam to seem important to those who plan and administer the schools, while the parts which are left to informal contacts are overlooked as of small importance, or are forgotten. Yet they continue to be very important, perhaps more important than all the matter included in formal education. Rural education, like all education, should not limit itself to the processes of the schoolroom, but at every stage from primary Scholl to university should insist that pupils and students shall learn also from the great traditions of common life.

These great traditions are among the most priceless treasurers of making, of more value than our material possessions. One of the chief criticisms of the present system of education is its tendency to rely on verbal description rather than on actual participation, and thereby partly to lose the essence of the great art of living. The processes of violent revolution, which would destroy the social structure to do away with inequality, may destroy precious, hard-won elements of the great traditions, and set back humanity many centuries toward barbarism.

The method of basic education, from elementary school through the university, on the part of the student calls for intimate participation in the life through which these great traditions are expressed and perpetuated. By such participation, as well as by formal learning, he comes to inherit fully those traditions. It is the part of teaching and leadership to share with the students great traditions, in the process of being inherited, shall be purified, enlightened, enlarged, and made to express the basic aspirations of men for understanding, for justice, liberty, equality and fraternity, and for effective mastery of their environment.

Rural education and research—Just as democracy cannot be maintained by a small educated class, but must be based on the education of the whole people; so the full advantage of modern science cannot be secured by a few able scientists working in a few well-equipped laboratories, but requires also that a spirit of open minded, critical inquiry shall pervade the whole population.

The poverty of India is largely due to the general absence of this spirit. Much work is performed in the same way generation after generation, though the methods might be greatly improved. This is due not to inborn limitation, but to long standing traditions of conformity. Our children have curiosity and active interest. Our scientist have proved their ability. If the spirit of free, critical, objective inquiry becomes general, not only will everyday working methods improve, but from the many boys and girls with open, inquiring minds great scientists in many fields will emerge.

Development of the spirit of free inquiry should be a chief aim of basic education, and of the secondary and higher education which grow out of it. More important than the teaching of any particular subject is encouragement of the spirit of free inquiry in every field.

Our thoroughly trained scientist with their well equipped laboratories are highly important to our country. Many important problems of rural life cannot be solved by simpler means. Rural universities should have such scientists in such laboratories. But that is only part of the story. No all research must wait for university degrees or for scientific equipment. Whatever there is an active inquiring mind there is opportunity for research. Some of the great scientific and practical developments of modern times have been the work of men who had neither university degrees nor scientific equipment. The Wright Brothers built their first airplane in a bicycle repair shop while some world famous scientists were declaring that such flight was impossible.

Gregor Meden whose discoveries of the lays of inheritance place him among the foremost of biological scientists, was a village priest with no laboratory but a garden patch and some pigeon coops. Langstreth, who advanced the art of bee keeping more than all men before him for two thousand years, was a preacher who had to give up his preaching because of serious illness, and who used for research the occasional periods when he was well enough to work. His laboratory was his little workshop, his carpenter tools, and his hives of bees. James Watt, Robert Owen and George Stephenso, pioneers of the industrial age, were men of little or no schooling and without scientific laboratories.

The day is not past for such pioneering. There are many pressing problems, some of them among the most important which face our rural life, which require little or no laboratory equipment or scientific apparatus for their study. Library facilities are generally essential to save waste of time in repeating work other men have already done, but in some cases a few hundred rupees or even less will provide the necessary published material. Some men will let the years slip by as they mourn the lack of research facilities, while others with no more opportunity, but with strong scientific spirit and desire for human service, may be making scientific history. The rural university will do well to accomplish what it can with what it has, even though its facilities seem inadequate. This not a suggestion for reducing public expenditures for research. Much that is highly important for national welfare requires laboratories with complex and expensive equipment. A nation which omits such investment will pay heavily for its neglect. But along with research requiring large investment there are very many opportunities for men of scientific temper, opportunities which need not wait upon large appropriations.

A Distinctive pattern—Since rural education must evolve its own distinctive pattern, there is no need to follow traditional forms in educational administration. One general policy should be observed, namely, that rural education should be administered in the main by persons who have been directly concerned with rural education movement. However, to guard against the tendency for a new movement to become another orthodoxy with its own static dogmas, the administration of rural universities would do well to include a substantial minority from entirely outside its field, to contribute objective judgment and criticism. In the long run it may prove desirable for all education to have a common structure and common direction. Yet, the new rural education should maintain independence and self-direction until it is mature and stands with self assurance and equality. At least for a few decades while it is establishing its own tradition, spirit and methods, it should be free to create its own pattern and organization. The following is suggested as a general way of organization.

Rural education councils—In each province, or in a group of small provinces, there should be a rural education council. This should be made up in the first place of leaders in rural education who should determine the basic of membership. Thereafter the council should have a democratic government. At first this may be an undifferentiated organization. In the course of time, the membership probably would organize into a number of sections, one concerned with pre-basic education, one with basic education, one with post-basic education, one with the college and university level and perhaps one concerned with research.

Also there should be an all-India Rural Education Council. The Hindustani Talimi Sangh now serves that purpose, and could be enlarged. This in time would have sections concerned with the different levels of education, and doubtless would develop other special sections, such as on general education, on vocational and professional education, on work programmes in education, and on student counselling. Quite probably basic education would be chiefly guided by provincial councils, college and university education by the national council, and post-basic education by both. These councils, or their appropriate sections, would be the recognized appraising and accrediting agencies for rural education. They would carry on educational research and would strive to raise the quality of rural education.

Autonomy—No matter how sound the underlying principles are, the development of techniques will take time. While the philosophy and method are being developed, the rural university will be a place of pioneering experiment. Each institution should be autonomous, free to work out its own programme in its own way. Heads of departments, at least, should prepare their own syllabi with the approval of the academic council of that college or university, and should test the achievement of their students in their own way. Each institution should determine what credits or certificates or other evidence of completion of work its students should receive. There should be no external examinations.

To encourage high standards of education, it would be desirable for each level of the rural education programme, primary, secondary undergraduate college, and graduate university, to have one or more appraisal committees, appointed by and reporting to the appropriate section of a rural education council, to make periodical examinations and appraisal of each institution in its class, and to issue a report through the rural education council describing the quality of work being done at each. Such a report should state with reference to each institution:

1. Just what it claims to be doing.
2. How it is succeeding in doing it.
3. What the facilities are in plant, staff, finance etc.
4. What other quality or lack of quality is evident.
5. Whether or not it should be accredited

The report concerning each institution, before it is published should be submitted to that institution so that any errors of fact may be corrected. Only accredited institutions should be eligible for membership on the council. In the long run the periodical publishing of such appraisals would furnish strong incentive for improvement without killing creative initiative in the institution.

The councils or their appropriate sections would determine which schools be accredited, that is, recognized to be of such quality that their graduates, with the approval of the head of the institution, should be accepted as qualified for entrance to schools of the next higher level.

Each accredited school would determine the fitness of individual pupils or students for entrance to institutions of the next higher grade. The Rural Education Council of some backward province might set relatively low standards of for the post-basic (secondary) schools of that province. Such provincial standards might allow students to go from any accredited school to any college or university in that province. At the same time, the national council might have more rigorous standards, so that only a smaller part of the secondary schools in that province would be accredited to approve their graduates for entrance to any university in all India.

Such dual accrediting operates successfully in America. Students from relatively commonplace schools in some states are admitted to colleges and universities in that state, but students from the smaller and more rigorously selected list of the national or regional council have national or regional acceptance. Schools with only state accrediting are looked upon as second class, and constantly strive to qualify for wider recognition. In some progressive states, standards within the state are more rigorous than those for the region or the nation.

Each institution above the basic education school should be free to limit enrolment to the number it can reasonably accommodate, and to select the best of the applicants. The cure for inadequate educational facilities is more facilities, and not the overcrowding of those already existing. It is better to give good educational opportunity to one hundred students than to give a travesty of education two hundred. So long as students are being accepted,the general public will assume that satisfactory education is being provided. Where a large number is refused entrance for lack of accommodation, the public will bestir itself and provide more facilities.

Rural university administration—The rural university might well have two governing bodies. First, a small *academic council,* consisting of perhaps a dozen members of the staff chose by appropriate means, should formulate policies and programme for the academic and related affairs of the institution, sometimes acting through suitable committees. It would deal with educational policies, curricula, inter-relations of fields and departments, student counselling etc., but would not undertake the day-to-day business and administrative management of the institution. Meetings and action of the entire faculty might well be a source of information and of advice for the academic council.

Student participation on the academic council and its committees has in some cases been found to an enlivening, stabilizing and unifying influence. Progressive recognition and encouragement of student participation, as competence and responsibility are demonstrated, is a desirable aim.

The current administration of the university would be in the hands of the vice-chancellor with a few chief academic and business assistants, such as the academic dean, the dean or director of practical work, and the treasurer or bursar. They should meet periodically to clarify plans and programme. Such focusing of day-to-day administration is important. The academic council is poorly adapted to administrative duties.

The second governing body might be called the *executive council.* It would be the over-all authority to direct university policy and to pass on the major acts and proposals of the academic council and administrative staff. It would not handle details of educational or business administration, but would control general policy and programme. It should meet perhaps three to six times a year, a part of each meeting being solely for its own members, and a part in joint meeting with the academic council and the vice-chancellor and his chief assistants. Such joint meetings help all parties to be well informed.

The choice of members of the rural university executive councils will largely determine the quality of the institution. Except perhaps for co-opted members, most members should be persons who for, say five years have been directly concerned with rural life and in most cases with rural or basic education. Such a provision is necessary to prevent rural education from being dominated by existing tradition. However, as already stated, a minority well consist of leaders in other fields who would have outside viewpoints:

The primary aim in selecting members of the executive council of a rural university should be secure:

1. General competence, character, judgment and experience, free from and superior to political or academic cliques, or partisan inclination or influence.
2. Acquaintance with and active interest in rural India and rural education.
3. General, broad cultural and educational interests.
4. Good administrative judgment.
5. Simplicity of personal tastes, habits and expenditure.
6. A variety of types and interests, so that the council shall have universality of outlook.

As to the specific process of choosing members, and as to the specific make-up of the council, the rural university should not be found by precedent.

Except for the vice-chancellor, none of the other usual elements of college governments, such as court or chancellor, will be needed. The entire content of medieval university ceremony, ritual and regalia, much of which emphasizes academic hierarchy, may be omitted in the new universities. They are in some degree incompatible with the new spirit of India. The new university should develop its own traditions which should be outgrowths of its own genius and spirits, and that of the new India.

The new university should develop its own traditions which should be outgrowths of its own genius and spirit, and that of the new India. In the determination of grants by central and provincial governments and in other public relations the procedure recommended elsewhere in this Report may well be followed.

The relations between rural secondary schools, colleges and universities, and the existing universities—It is important that there be no unnecessary barriers between the existing and the new type of institutions. Students who are enable of doing so should be able to move from one type to the other. For this to be possible we will require an attitude of tolerance and adjustment on the part of each, will liberalization of legislation dealing with higher education. Students from the older type of Indian secondary schools may find themselves at great disadvantage in a rural university where most of the students are from rural secondary schools.

The rural university should be reasonably tolerant of such limitations where there is evidence of general character and ability, and desire to overcome such handicaps. Similarly the older universities should acceptable and sincere students from rural secondary schools, even though their education has not followed the prescribed pattern of the older secondary schools. There should be no legislative barriers to such practice.

The actual records in other countries of good students going from one type of institution to another justified such mutual tolerance.

How to get the rural education programme under way—The criticism will be made that while the programme here outlined would be a desirable one, India does not have the resources to put it into effect. Under the programme of the India, university facilities must be increased. The only question is where and how. Similarly facilities for secondary schooling must be very greatly enlarged and extended, with vastly increased opportunity for vocational education. The suggested programme for secondary schools will be an economical and effective means to that end.

Most provinces are already committed to the principles of basic education. Each of them might well establish a number of resident secondary school villages, and they might cooperate in establishing one or more rural universities. Similarly, the central government might well establish several resident secondary school villages and a rural university. The growth of the new system will depend largely on the supply of suitable teachers. The central government or the provinces might establish one or more training schools for teachers for this programme.

The Gandhi Memorial Trust might well establish several secondary school villages over India, and one rural university, staffing them with persons trained in existing training centres and with others who are sincerely committed to the principles of basic education. That might help to insure that the spirit of Gandhiji would find expression. Also it would be appropriate for persons of means to make possible the establishment of a number of such institutions.

It will be no disadvantage for the programme to have varied, independent beginnings. Different men and agencies, working somewhat independently but in co-operation, will give a variety and fullness to the programme which no one of them could provide alone. However, the next few years may largely set the type of Indian education for the next half century. The new type secondary schools and universities should be vigorously developed as an essential element of the educational expansion on which the future welfare of India depends.

Co-operation with other agencies of government—The governments of free India and of the various states and provinces are showing interest in rural conditions, and are considering many plans for improving rural life. These plans include rural health service, agricultural extension work, boys and girls agricultural club work, rural library service, and the promotion of rural industries. If each of these develops independently of the others there will be much duplication of expense, a tendency to conflict and jealousy, and much loss of value.

There would be very great gain if all these agencies should work through the rural educational institutions. The secondary school village might well be the local centre for all these services. In that way suitable housing and living conditions would be provided, secretarial help, transportation etc. could be pooled, and local officials having business with some of the agencies would find them all at one place. More important than these economics would be the fact that secondary school students would be in constant touch with these agencies. The nurses, librarians, agricultural agents and promoters of industry might share in the teaching and in the direction of practical work. Thus the resident secondary school village would be the educational and cultural centre of a group of villages. Similarly, the rural university could be the regional centre for all such rural service agencies.

Rural workers and directors would profit by rural university associations, faculty members of the universities would profit by constant with those directing the field work, and university students in their part time work could assist rural workers and could be in training for similar service. It would be a great loss to India for the varied rural service to develop without such co-ordination suggested will call for some changes in the administrative machinery of the central and provincial governments.

2

Challenges of Rural Education

In 1985, the government of India has released a document titled "Challenge of Education—Policy Perspective". It has identified the maladies confronting our educational system leading to unequal opportunities, production of unemployed and unemployable young men and women, progressive erosion of traditional values in culture, lack of effective links between the world or knowledge and world of working, and has proposed a rethinking to revamp the system so as to generate suitable man-power to meet the ensuing challenges confronting the nation now and that of the 21st century.

The document reveals an in-depth analysis of the problems confronting the overall educational system in the country and lays emphasis on reorientation, reorganisation and rejuvination of the traditional concepts. There is a little mention in its analysis about the situation of agricultural education while dealing with higher education. Some ideas have, however, been thrown about the relevance, importance and organisation of the technical education in the country to meet the emerging challenges. These thoughts can be extrapolated not only for agricultural education but also for other professional education like medicine, engineering etc. Formal agricultural education started about 150 years ago in this country.

The actual fillip came with the establishment of agricultural universities patterned after Land Grant College Model of U.S.A. since 1960. The agricultural universities are the fore-runners in introducing a system which was totally alien to the country and was much different from the British pattern of education followed since several decades by the liberal and traditional universities. This book is restricted in its approach, for it confines to higher education in agricultural sciences as imparted by state agricultural universities (SAUs) and the ICAR institutes. This issue has been widely debated in several agricultural universities sities in the light of the document "Challenge of Education" and the recommendations and individual opinions generated have been included in the present discussion.

Rural higher education in agriculture

The Indo-American team in its reports 1955 and 1960 had suggested for the establishment of Agriculture Universities in different states, based on the model of Land Grant Colleges of the United States while keeping in view the recommendations of the Radhakrishnan Education Commission (1949) about the "Rural Universities". Some of the concepts of Land Grant College system recommended for adoption by the Agricultural Universities were :

- The Agricultural Universities will foster teaching, research and extension activities in agriculture and related sciences with an objective to alleviate the social and economic status people through knowledge leading to greater productivity of land and cattle.

- The education system will be flexible so that the boys and girls coming from rural background are able to receive formal and informal education in various agricultural sciences, depending upon their merit and capabilities.
- The system will be based on a term tenure coupled with internal evaluation by the teachers.
- The teacher will be the key figure in the system responsible for imparting latest knowledge and training to the students through class room, laboratory and field work. He shall also monitor the progress of the students throughout.
- The jurisdiction of the agricultural university will be the state. The state, in turn, would provide enough land and funds for the development of infrastructural facilities. The universities would generate enough resources through the allotted land so as to reduce its financial dependence on the state.

Based on these concepts, the first state agricultural university was established in Utter Pradesh in the rural background at Pantnagar in 1960. Subsequently, in 1962, Punjab Agricultural university was established with headquarters at Ludhiana and with two additional compuses located at Hisar and Palampur.

The departure from rural setting of agricultural university followed by Ludhiana was a negation of the original rural concept. All other agricultural universities that were established subsequently were in the urban areas. Today, there are 24 SAUs and 48 agricultural colleges affiliated to traditional universities in addition to a few ICAR Institutes which are involved in training graduates and post-graduates in agricultural, veterinary and animal sciences, in addition to agricultural engineering and recently introduced home sciences. Basic science units in these agricultural universities were also established with a view to impart basic training in related sciences for the agricultural education.

The undergraduate training, particularly for B.Sc. Agriculture, is thus distributed in the agricultural universities and their campuses plus agricultural colleges affiliated with traditional universities. Initially it was envisaged that the entire agricultural education in a state would be the responsibility of the agricultural universities. Some how there are still a sizeable number of agricultural and traditional universities, following a different system of training.

It is estimated that about 10,000 students are admitted annually to various colleges and SAUs in the undergraduate programmes and more an half get their education from the SAUs. At the postgraduate level, about 3,500 students are enrolled every year in the SAUs, ICAR Institutes and traditional universities.Since the system of education in the agricultural universities is different from the traditional universities, therefore,the standards of the students passing out from these institutions is also likely to be different.

Accomplishments and erosions

The agricultural education,being essentially the responsibility of SAUs, were linked with the state departments of agriculture. The state Agriculture departments, who originally had the responsibility of Agricultural research, passed on their responsibility to these universities while maintaining a close link with the SAUs. The SAUs were, however, not owned by the University Grant Commission (UGC), since these were linked with State agriculture research and extension were the state subjects. Thus, the agricultural education of SAUs only came under the purview of the state agriculture departments.

The enthusiasm of the state governments to develop agricultural universities in their states was often dominated by the state needs and political pressures than the actual requirements. Further, regional interests in some states led to the establishment of more than one agricultural university in the state. In other cases, the concept of having separate campuses in different agro-climatic zones of the state to satisfy regional needs, developed.

Initially the agricultural universities started off well because they obtained qualified persons trained in a similar system from the United States. Some of the SAUs established collaborative arrangements with one or the other university in the United States. The system of education in SAU was based on semester/trimester system, with defined course curriculum, progressive evaluation through the term of the students and internal evaluation system, which made the agricultural universities quite distinct from the traditional universities.

During the process of their development the agricultural universities formed their own norms, rules and regulations, some of which were adopted from UGC while others were taken from the state departments. Each of the SAUs produced graduates and postgraduates which were readily employable and they performed well. Over the years, a great deal of dilutions of the norms and the system of education have occurred due to reasons of diverse regional interests, socio-economic behaviour of the people and the politicians. Since the system was totally alien to this country it needed some amendments.

These were made only after the system had cracked at various places. With time, unfortunately, due to several distortions that had crept into the administrative working of SAUs, the graduate produced by the agricultural universities were not always of desired standards, so much so, some of them were even unemployable. Analysis of the functioning and of the on-going programmes of the SAUs have been made by various committees appointed by ICAR and other agencies. Most of the SAUs have earned laurals on account of their research achievements essentially and/or also for their extension work.

Some of the training programmes in a few of the disciplines at the post-graduates level have also been applauded in the reports of these terms for some universities. Not much has, however, been evaluated critically with regard to the undergraduate teaching programmes of these universities. It is general feeling that the educational standards in the SAUs are not the same as these used to be earlier or as are desired. Obviously, some notable ills and maladies have crept into the system which are eroding the teaching programmes. It is a recognized fact that more than 2/3rd budget of the SAUs is spent on research activities while the remaining is disbursed between teaching programmes and extension work. The resource allocations for teaching programmes, particularly for undergraduate teaching, have not increased proportionately with the requirements time and changing needs.

The out modelled equipments, microscopes etc. badly need replacement with modern machines and audio-visual aids. Post-graduate education has been relatively better sustained because of the gains obtained by the universities and the institutions through the research output of the students. The teaching component, of the postgraduate education, however, has not escaped deterioration. A university, definition-wise, is a temple of learning, with emphasis on teaching.

Agricultural universities on the contrary, have greater role in advancing the research objectives than of teaching. Keeping their present character in view, the SAUs should better be called research institutes than universities because the teaching component has been relegated to a rather lower position, which is contrary to the concepts of a university. Coupled with this, the teacher involved in teaching feels far less important because another teacher involved in full time research is correspondingly much better placed and is being rewarded through his publications and quick promotions that help him in the enhancement of his career. This disparity between the teacher and the research worker has led to lack of motivations and purposefulness in the involvement of teaching. As a consequence of this, the student advisory system has become non-functional, respect of teachers by the students is fast eroding and the teachers response to teaching programmes is becoming a routine.

The situation has reached when the university administration, and particularly the teachers, become silent spectators when the students miss classes on mass or go on strikes. The evaluation and examination are becoming casual and actual working days in a year are much less than prescribed. This erosion in the teaching system has many roots, which differ in their magnitude from state to state. The fault squarely lies with our system and the policy makers and not with the students or teachers alone.

Educational management system

Agricultural education in SAUs is a state subject. ICAR is charged with the responsibility of guiding the developmental programmes in the SAUs. Management of education is SAUs is much different than that of agricultural colleges affiliated to traditional universities governed by UGC. The ICAR has developed a model agricultural universities act as a guideline for the SAUs. Presently, non of the SAUs have adopted the model act in its letter and spirit. ICAR through mutual discussion at various levels, has also developed course curricula for different programmes. Here again, none of the SAUs have followed these guidelines fully. The Indian Agricultural Universities Association meeting held at Andhra Pradesh Agricultural University, Hyderabad in 1985, reviewed the management and educational systems of the SAUs and once again reiterated that the model act be adopted and also that the Dean's Committee Report prescribing the course curricular of various programmes, their duration, system of examination, grading etc. be adopted. These recommendations are yet to see the light of the day. In the ICAR, there is only one Deputy Director General looking after the agricultural education in the 24 SAUs, while there are four corresponding Deputy Director Generals looking after the research components of different agriculture sciences.

The agricultural education being a state subject, the ICAR thus has a little power to enforce the recommendations evolved by various committees. Perhaps, no two agricultural universities have identical system either of management or of execution of teaching programmes. Some of the notable variations which are affecting the academic health of the teaching programmes of different SAUs are listed below:

- Entry tests for graduate and postgraduate admissions in practised by a few and not by other SAUs.
- Both trimester and semester systems with variable number of working days, number of examinations and grading systems are in operation.
- The total credit requirement for the undergraduate and postgraduate students for the degrees vary considerably.
- The diversity in course curriculum is also notable.
- The component of Basic Sciences and Humanities courses in the total undergraduate agricultural programmes varies from 24 to 40% in different SAUs.
- Some SAUs have a strong field oriented training programmes as a component of the undergraduate degree while others a have a little or no such programmes.
- In the postgraduate programmes, the total credit requirements and the requirements of major, minor, supporting courses and research credits vary from university to university.
- The reservation of seats for different categories of people is quite variable among the universities.
- A few universities encourage admission of students from outside the state while others are operating on

closed door system, admitting students from their own state essentially.

- In multi-campus universities the standards of teaching differs from campus to campus.

It is, thus, obvious that each SAU has developed its teaching programmes in a manner that suits them, without keeping in view the national minimum standards. It also points out that graduate and postgraduates produced by these universities are of different standards, Still, each university recognises the degree of the other university, irrespective of the equivalence in the contents of the programmes, more or less out of their mutual respect and appreciation, as they all belong to one freternity.

This also brings out a fact that ICAR, unlike UGC, has not been able to guide, supervise and monitor the educational programmes in different states. It is difficult to say whether these deviations are healthy or unhealthy trend but certainly the disparaties are far too great to be ignored. No doubt, the ICAR has contributed generously to the development of teaching programmes in the form of funds, yet the desired leadership in the form of implementation has been wanting. This, perhaps, may be on account of the fact that ICAR, true to its name, has focussed its main attention to the "research" activities than to the teaching. In case higher education in agriculture is to be brought to any desired minimum standards, the ICAR will have to play a dominant and assertive role in leading the educational programmes in the SAUs.

Nevertheless, it is imperative that unequal development of educational programmes in agriculture must be brought to a level so as to join the mainstream of higher technical and professional education of the country and that it is ready to face the future challenges. This task is enormous. The educational unit of ICAR needs strengthening and it must interact with other professional bodies like UGC, Indian Council of Medical Research, and IITs etc. so that professional ethos of higher education and learning in agriculture is kept at a proper perspective for the socio-economic development of the country as well as the youth.

Student management

True to the concept of rural universities, the agricultural universities have adequate provisions for admitting students from rural areas. The professional education, in general, is very expensive and it has been often suggested that higher technical education should be restrictive and available only to the meritorious students. Agricultural universities have made such provisions that admission of rural youth dominates most other category of people. Further more, this professional education is very highly subsidised because it is assumed that the students coming from rural backgrounds are not capable of supporting themselves in expensive educational institutes.

No doubt, these concepts were of prime importance about two decades ago when higher education in agriculture was not as attractive as it is today. In the formative years of SAUs, teams of teachers used to go around the rural schools of the state to invite bright students for admission to these universities. Added to this was also a concept that these students with rural background after having professional education in agriculture would go back to their villages and thus initiate a chain reaction for all round improvement in the villages.

Unfortunately, later part did not fructify to any desired level. The question then arises, whether higher agricultural education should still be subsidised and reserved for the rural youth who do not prefer to practise their profession on the farm? Or, that the teaching in SAUs has been such that the sting of professionalism to practise at the farm has been taken out during the training programmes. We should pause and think about these basic points seriously,as the answers to these would direct our future strategies.

No doubt, the students coming from rural schools are the most suitable material for training in agriculture because of their rural background and knowledge about the problems surrounding their communities. The rural youth is considered to be relatively more simple, raw in his outlook and hardworking. Therefore, it necessitates a different mode of handling by the teachers in agricultural universities. This unfortunately is not happening.

The experience reveals that the students' problems in SAUs are similar to the traditional universities of the country than to the professional institutes. Perhaps this is the reasons why the professional spirit of agricultural universities and thus their outlook and motivation for practising their profession is lacking. This calls for a different management system for the students in SAUs. It needs to be so geared so as to inculcate in the students the spirit of professionalism as is prevalent in engineering, medical and other professional institutes.

Man-power requirements

The first degree programme is agricultural sciences is of 4 or 5 years duration. The students admitted in one year will thus be ready after 4 or 5 years of training. The admission number of students thus are to be related to the requirements of the state, region or the country, at least five years in advance. Unfortunately, the projections of requirements of agricultural, veterinary or other graduates are not available at the state or national level.

Today, for instance, 25% of the total posts in different disciplines of agricultural sciences are lying vacant, while on the other hand, there is some unemployment of the graduates and postgraduates in different states. The requirement of state governments, research institutes and other organisations are linked with five-year plans of the country and further linked with agricultural policies of the individual states. There are instances that in one year a state may have openings for 200 graduates while in subsequent years, it may dwindle to 10 to 20 annually.

Such erratic employment patterns are not only detrimental to the future of the graduates and postgraduates coming out of the SAUs but such unemployed graduates become a burden to the state and the society. In addition to this, one often hears that several of the graduate and post-graduate degree holders are unemployable because of their poor training or because the requirement in a specific area of a discipline has changed for which employable graduates are not available. This is on account of the arbitrary number of admissions in different professional programmes. While on one side we intend to produce professionally qualified agricultural scientists a huge costs, but on the other, these graduates do not find appropriate jobs and the training is abused as they enter into non-agricultural professions. It is, therefore, very necessary that man-power requirements are adequately worked out with projections on five-year basis, both at the state and national levels. It is not unusual to find various agricultural universities launching new postgraduate programmes in emerging areas. No doubt, this is a healthy trend.

But indiscriminate initiation of such programmes without keeping in view the employment potential of such highly specialised students is waste of scarce resources without much meaningful grains, except the glamour of having such a programme in the University. Further more, it has been experienced that several postgraduate programmes are started even though qualified man-power to run these programmes are not available. The postgraduate teaching programme in several disciplines of home science and some disciplines of animal and veterinary sciences, forestry, agricultural meteorology, etc., are some such areas where this malady is rampant in many universities. It is easy to start a programme or admit a number of students to a programme but it is extremely difficult; to discontinue a programme or to reduce the number of admissions to any programme. Some guiding principles for initiating new programmes keeping in view the man-power requirements is to be evolved at national level if the scarce resources are to be used profitably.

The administrative set up of an institution is responsible for its educational and other programmes. The SAUs are much different from the traditional and professional universities in the manner of their governance. Although the Vice-Chancellor is the highest executive and administrative head of the university but his appointment procedures are different in different SAUs.

Since agriculture is a state subject, therefore, the state governments have a dominant role to play in the appointment of Vice-Chancellor, which more often than not, is guided by the politics of the state. The highest policy-making body in case of SAUs is usually called 'Board of Management', 'Executive Council', or ''Syndicate'. It usually consists of government functionaries, some publicmen and some scientists, etc. Most of the members are either ex-officio government officials or nominated by the state with the formal approval of the Chancellor who is usually the Governor of the state.

The Vice-Chancellors have little role, if any, in nominating persons on this highest executive body. The practice of electing members to this body, which is a common feature of the traditional universities under the control of UGC, is rather rare in SAUs. Contrary to the practice followed in the traditional universities wherein representatives of teachers are either elected or nominated to these bodies, such a system of having active teachers on this body is yet to be adopted by SAUs.

The highest management body of the university is responsible to develop academic policies for the advancement of the education in the SAUs. Unfortunately, this role of some of the vocal honourable Board members has been often exploited by some elements in furthering individual interests or interest of the politics and communities, thus affecting the functioning of the Vice-Chancellors. Although ICAR has prescribed guidelines through a model act for the constitution and functioning of the Board of Management of SAUs, yet most universities differ from each other and from the ICAR model act. Besides, these Boards are not very democratic in their outlook and functioning because of the nomination feature of the members and because of poor representation of teachers.

Therefore, the Vice-Chancellors have little option but to be subservient to the dictates of the members of the Board at most occasions. This ultimately reflects on the academic health of the University. The politics has entered in all the universities to a small or large extent through students, teachers, and or members of the hierarchy. This one factor alone has greatly eroded the functioning of the Vice-Chancellors and the academic standards. No concrete steps by the SAUs are in view to overcome the malady. No long ago, the Vice-Chancellors enjoyed a very high respect and prestige in the society as well as universities because of their great academic stature and leadership qualities. On account of this, they were able to lead and guide the academic destiny of the universities towards excellence.

Over the years, erosion has taken place in their respect and prestige due to a variety of extraneous influences, pressures and other disguised and undisguised rules and regulations governing the universities. As a consequence of this, distinguished academicians of high academic stature usually shun to undertaken the assignment of Vice-Chancellorship. On the other side, the state governments feel it convenient to have persons from civil services, retired judges etc. to shoulder these responsibilities because they have better administrative acumen. Such persons have also proved successful as Vice-Chancellors in several SAUs. No doubt, administrative capability is important in governing the university, but for the teachers to come out with their best academic performance leading towards excellence, the academic leadership from the Vice-Chancellor is, perhaps, more important.

How-so-ever we may deliberate on the issue of appointment of the Vice-Chancellors, the fact remains that their appointment is still vested with the persons administering the education in the country and not the academicians who are starving for academic leadership and excellence. In SAUs, the Vice-Chancellor is assisted by various academic functionaries like Dean and Directors and administrative functionaries like Registrar, Comptroller etc. In traditional universities, the number of assisting functionaries to the Vice-Chancellors are rather few, because Heads of Departments are vested with all the essential powers required to govern the academic communities for their free academic functioning. In SAUs, teachers feel tied down to the bureaucracy of he Deans and Directors, Registrar and Comptroller etc. than Heads of Departments. Further, the paper work for an ordinary teacher in SAUs is 10 to 15 times more when compared with the teacher of equivalent status in traditional universities.

Often the argument is advanced that the traditional universities are vested with main function of teaching and with a little research and no extension, while SAUs have far greater responsibilities for research followed by extension and teaching. To administer the three components, hierarchal system has been necessary for administering integration of teaching, research and extension. It remains to be seen, however, whether the hierarchal system of administering teaching, research and extension and with so much paper work are really directed towards academic excellence or are acting as bottlenecks in functioning of the individual teachers and Heads of Departments. In other words, the Deans and Directors, though academicians, assume the role of 'Managers' of academic staff in the hierarchal system. What actually is needed is the academic leaders and not managers in SAUs.

Perhaps, this part of the system of agricultural universities needs to be compared with the land grant colleges of USA from where the system has been taken. However, it can be safely said that a teacher in agricultural university does not enjoy academic freedom of the status enjoyed by his corresponding teacher in other professional or liberal universities of the country or that the status enjoyed in the land grant colleges of USA in their formative years. Obviously, teacher's autonomy and functioning has a direct relationship with the academic excellence in education. This point,though often deliberated, has not materially helped the teachers in acquiring freedom for his academic pursuits in SAUs.

It can be summed up that the SAUs, have developed a system wherein the focus of activity is centred on various Deans and directors for academic activities as managers, who make Heads of the Departments and the faculty to work in accordance with the norms and guidance obtained from the Board of Management through Vice-Chancellor. In the total system, the teacher has been relegated to a low position, yet, on the other side, he has been charged with the highest responsibility of educating the youth leading them to excellence. The entire governing system of agricultural universities, therefore, needs a rethinking because no system worth the name can attain academic excellence where teacher it not given the highest esteem.

Policy reforms and futuristic approach

The future perspective of agricultural education can be derived from the experience of more than two decades wherein the agricultural universities have operated for advancing the frontiers of agricultural education in the country. The past tells us that the start of all agricultural universities was with a big bang. Anything new is always glamorous. But the galmour of agricultural university for teaching is fast losing lustre because of the ills that have crept into its systems. The future is expected to be more demanding of the agricultural scientists and educationists. It is only through good education that excellence in research and extension can be achieved.

The mediocrity in the present-day agricultural system can hardly sustain growing needs of tomorrow, what to say of the next century. The government of India has brought out "The Challenge of Education" document very timely, because it is expected of us to pause and think as to what have been our accomplishments and short-comings at this crucial juncture after two and half decades of operation. As a consequence of these thoughts the directions which are to be taken in order to face the challenges of the future agricultural needs, will have to be worked out now.

The task is enormous and a dispassionate view shall have to be taken now to evoke certain codes and ethics to guide ourselves for future. The fore-going discussions has highlighted some of the maladies faced by the agricultural universities. Although only generalised issues have been discussed, there are many more faced by the individual universities which need tackling and streamlining at their own level. In order that excellence in highest education in agriculture is achieved, the following are the synthesis of recommendations made by various agricultural universities and individuals who have contributed the papers.

The technical and professional higher education has become very expensive. The State Agricultural Universities have to depend heavily for finances on the state governments for their educational programmes. The SAUs thus mortgage their autonomy to the state government for their effective functioning. This needs early rectification. In order to restore adequate autonomy to SAUs, the agricultural education be shifted from the state to the centre. The ICAR, which has so far the role of providing financial assistance for the teaching developmental programmes at the initial stages, must function more assertively and aggressively not only as funding agency but also as a central supervisory and monitoring agency capable of guiding the destiny of the agricultural universities like UGC.

The present set up of ICAR for education is rather minimal. It should be increased several folds. Or, a separate body like 'National Council of Agricultural Education' parallel to UGC or other professional bodies be formed to look after the functioning, administration and welfare of teachers of the agricultural universities and to bring uniformity in academic standards aiming at excellence.

Each agricultural university has its own rules and regulations for admission, appointments, course curriculum, degree requirements, examination and evaluation system. etc. The disparities are large enough to be ignored. Following points need special consideration:

(a) There should be a compulsory entry test for undergraduate and postgraduate programmes either at the national level or at the state level.

(b) The course curriculum should have uniform component of core courses for all the universities with provisions for addition of a few more courses depending upon the requirements of the state or the region. This should be ensured for both undergraduate and postgraduate programmes.

(c) The minimum and maximum course credit load be fixed for every degree programme.

(d) Whether it is trimester or semester system, the number of working days, number of examinations per term, method of evaluation and grading systems should be made uniform.

(e) At least 25-30% seats under each programme be kept open for out of state candidates both for admissions as well as for recruitment.

(f) The reservations of seats for admissions or employment should not exceed the limit prescribed by the central government. In fact, merit should be the only criteria for admissions, particularly at postgraduate level.

(g) The admission to different programmes should be restricted and related to well worked out man-power requirements based on five year projections.

(h) A uniform policy decision be taken and adopted with regard to medium of instructions at different levels in SAUs.

(i) Subsidizing higher education at the tax-payer's cost should be reduced, if not eliminated.

(j) A thought may be given whether all M.Sc. programmes should have thesis as an essential component or that it could be done with theory only.

(k) Students be discouraged to obtain more than two degrees from the same university.

The research and research workers have assumed prestigious positions in agricultural universities because of their importance, financial support, quick rewards and benefits. On the other hand, the teachers undertaking teaching programmes have far fewer opportunities, scarce finance and other help and with little rewards thus leading to lack of motivation for teaching affecting teaching processes. The teachers in agricultural universities need special consideration for rewards and incentives if their motivation for excellence in teaching is to be retained.

The teacher is one of the last and small digit in the hierarchal system dominated by Deans, Directors, Registrar, Comptroller, Heads of Departments and the Vice-Chancellors in SAUs. His autonomous status needs to be enhanced.

Any education is limited to the accumulated knowledge of teachers which is subsequently passed on to the students. Their knowledge has to be frequently updated. Both junior and senior teachers actively involved in teaching profession need to have advanced training programmes. Such programmes for teachers are absent in the country. A provision is required to be made wherein teachers may go to any institution in India or abroad for advancing their knowledge. System of sabbatical leave for teachers be made Compulsory.

Induction of teachers should be made very carefully at the very beginning. An unworthy teacher is a permanent source of degradation of teaching standards for decades.

SAUs are fortunate that they have a choice to select best teachers out of research or extension units. Carefully selected teachers of proven merit be only allowed to teach. Such teachers should not then be shifted to research or extension, since good teachers having dedication are hard to find. However, their promotional interests should always be kept in proper focus. Inbreeding in the SAUs is becoming a serious menace, particularly to teaching. It should be curbed. There is a top heavy system, which manages the destiny of teachers and teaching programmes without much involvement of the teachers. This needs correction. The governing bodies of the agricultural universities should have more representatives of teachers.

The functioning and administration of agricultural universities is neither on the pattern of UGC nor similar to the state departments. This admixture of rules derived from UGC as well as state departments has eroded the conceptual status of teachers and various other functionaries. The functioning of several SAUs, is more similar to state departments than a university. Codes prescribed for liberal universities be made applicable to SAUs. Or, these be taken over by state governments and called Research Institutes.

The code of conduct adopted by most agricultural universities is that of the government employees. This is quite at variance with the UGC code of conduct for teachers. The agricultural university teachers should have a uniform code of conduct with greater functional autonomy as operative in professional institutes of learning. The administration of SAUs should be in the hands of persons of high academic merit and recognition, having administrative acumen, having an outlook for educational advancements and capable of providing leadership to the academic communities.

- Some SAUs have adopted the system of rotation of Deans, Directors and Heads of the department. The system's working needs a criticals, disspassionate appraisal before it is adopted by other SAUs.

Similarly, the policy of personal merit promotion with reference to pay scales and not the designation, be considered for continuity of work and avoidance of stagnation.

- The interaction between agricultural university scientists and the scientists of traditional and professional universities should be increased and encouraged so as to build up joint programmes for solving problems facing agricultural and other fields. At present, this interaction is minimal and the two are working in isolation from each other.
- The agricultural universities should exercise more autonomy, particularly financial autonomy, if these are to succeed in implementation of their programmes through future policies for the advancement of agricultural education in the country.
- Centres of "Advanced Studies" in different disciplines be planned in different SAUs wherein excellence be the motto.
- A Central Agricultural University as a model for other Universities be established.

All the future strategies of advancement in agriculture depends on the highly knowledgeable manpower capable of tackling the ensuring problems of research and extension, besides teaching. It is, however, the teacher and the teaching programmes developed by him, which can generate capable manpower for fature, depending upon the teachers' capabilities.

3

Rural Development Programmes

Ruarl development programmes have to be viewed in the wider perspective of socio-economic transformation in the country. The programmes for poverty alleviation should be regarded as supplementing the basic plan for overall economic growth, in terms of generating productive assets and skills as well as incomes for the poor. The economic betterment of the poorer sections cannot be achieved without social transformation involving structural changes, educational development, growth in awareness, and change in outlook, motivation and attitudes.

The social framework should be such as to provide opportunities for the poorer sections to display initiative and to stand on their legs. Moreover, such a framework can ensure that the benefits of poverty alleviation programmes really reach the poor and are not frittered away through various leakages. Strict enforcement of land reforms and revamping of credit institutions can provide the necessary access to assets and resources for the poor as well as promote a more equitable social structure.

Greater participation of the poor through the elected institutions at the grassroots level as well as through their own organisations is another means to achieve social change. Improvement of literacy and education, both through formal and non-formal means, and the imaginative use of various mass media for communicating useful information and knowledge as well as for changing the outlook of the people by instilling in them the egalitarian spirit the urge for an confidence in achievement self-betterment through co-operative endeavour, are essential for speeding up the process of socio-economic transformation. Admittedly, there have been various deficiencies in the implementation of the poverty alleviation programme. However, there has been a distinct improvement in the actual implementation of these programmes over the Sixth Plan.

The Approach to the Seventh Plan reiterates the goal of bringing down the percentage of population below the poverty line to less than 10 by 1994-95., Therefore, the special programmes for income generation for the poor through assets endowment and wage employment for them will be continued at an accelerated pace during the Seventh Five Year Plan. In view of the deficiencies noticed in the implementation of the Integrated Rural Development Programme, it has been suggested that greater priority should be assigned to rural development programmes by shifting resources away from IRDP. The argument is two-folds. First the household enterprises of the type visualized are inherently uneconomic and are in any case handicapped for lack of necessary infrastructure. Secondly, owing to the illiteracy and weak economic position of the beneficiaries and the existence or a chain of intermediaries only a small portion of the intended outlay reaches the actual beneficiaries.

Employment programmes on the other hand, it is argued, can prove secure wage-income to the poor, through the creation of durable community assets. However, the experiences of the working of the poverty alleviation programme is by no means uniform in the country. In general, the programme of IRDP has been better in the relatively developed regions which are well provided with infrastructure and where level of awareness among the beneficiaries is high.

Even in the less developed areas, performance has been satisfactory wherever special efforts have been made for undertaking the necessary follow-up measures and for greater involvement of people through their representatives. As to the economic viability of the household-enterprises, it should be noted that such enterprises are already in existence on a wide scale in the developed as well as the less developed regions. In fact, they are a major source of employment and income for the poor in rural areas-next only to land. But they suffer from various handicaps in regard to the supply of raw materials, access to credit, facilities for marketing, etc. As a result, there is considerable exploitation of these households by the middlemen. Public intervention to provide the necessary services to these already existing enterprises would contribute to a substantial increase in their income.

Government-sponsored programmes for the poor, such as dairy and poultry, account for only a small proportion of the total market for such products now, sometimes even less than one per cent. The demand for such products, and for a number of other rural crafts, is highly responsive to increase in income and, therefore, there is no reason for pessimism about the prospects for income generation for the poor from such activities so long as overall economic growth is satisfactory. Besides, the possession of productive assets and skills confers other advantages such as economic security, social status and creditworthiness.

Such activities are labour-intensive and not land-intensive and, therefore, typically suit the marginal holdings and the landless. Even though the capital-output ratios investment per unit of output for some of these activities are higher than that for crop production, they are still very much lower than for many of the small-scale industrial enterprises. In many cases, where traditional skills are available and remain underutilised for want of resources, the capital-output ratio turns out to be much lower than even for crop production. These activities, in general, require government support for resources, training in skills, and marketing. IRDP and employment programmes are not mutually exclusive. As it is, most of the IRDP beneficiaries supplement their incomes through wage earnings in agriculture as well as from projects under National Rural Employment Programme and Rural Landless Employment Guarantee Programme.

These activities supplement one another and together ensure a more stable flow of incomes to the poor throughout the year. The problem of ensuring maximum benefits to the target groups by minimising leakages is common for all the poverty alleviation programmes and indeed for the rural development programmes in general. Apart from the necessary restructuring of the administrative set-up, there is no alternative to raising the awareness of the rural poor and involving representative institutions from below in the formulation as well as implementation of such programmes. Cost-effectiveness of the programmes and minimisation of leakages should be the two guiding principles in the implementation of poverty alleviation programmes.

Economic viability should be understood primarily in terms of cost effectiveness, ie., maximum income generation per unit of total expenditure incurred. This is to be distinguished from economic viability defined as level of investment sufficient to enable a family to cross the poverty line. The ability of a poorer household to cross the poverty line depends on its overall income, i.e., income from the poverty alleviation programmes and other wage and non-wage incomes accruing to them. Cost-effectiveness or efficiency of programmes depends to a considerable extent, on the nature of activities chosen. In view of the significant regional diversities in the country in regard to resource endowments, availability of infrastructure, regard to resource endowments, availability of infrastructure, administrative arrangements, etc., there needs to be sufficient flexibility in the choice of activities in different regions in keeping with the specific circumstances of the area concerned. The total impact of the programme depends on the degree to which the different poverty alleviation programmes, including the Minimum Needs Programme, are integrated with one another and with the overall development of the area.

For example, endowment of land under land reform measures can enable a family to grow fodder for the animal given under the IRDP; development of house sites under MNP can be integrated with the construction of houses under NREP or RLEGP and vice-versa, and both in turn integrated with the IRDP by developing work sheds and production estates around the housing complex. NREP and RLEGP can also be used extensively for raising productivity in agriculture through construction of field channels for irrigation and for drainage.

In India, a Rural Works Programme, started in 1970-71 in areas chronically affected by drought with the principal objective of organising permanent works to obviate scarcity relief and to generate adequate employment through labour-intensive schemes such as major, medium, and minor irrigation, works, soil conservation, afforestation, and village and district roads necessary to open up the area for agricultural production.

Integrated rural development programme

The programme of asset-endowment under IRDP was designed to develop self-employment ventures in a variety of activities like seri-culture, animal husbandry and land-based activities in the primary sector; waving handicrafts, etc., in the secondary sector; and service and business activities in the tertiary sector. With a view to diversifying the occupational structure, it had been stipulated that 33 per cent of the beneficiary coverage should, as far as possible, be in the secondary and tertiary sectors.

The assets provided to the selected households were financed through a mix of Government subsidies and institutional credit on an average subsidy credit ratio of the 1:2. The capital cost of the assets was subsidised to the extent of 25 per cent for small farmers, 33-1/3 per cent for marginal farmers, agricultural labourers and rural artisans and 50 per cent for the scheduled tribes. A family could receive up to Rs 3,000 by way of subsidy. In drought prone areas, the limit of subsidy ceiling was Rs. 4,000 while for tribal beneficiaries it was RS. 5,000. The Programme Evaluation Organisation of the Planning Commission. RBI, NABARD. Institute of Financial and Management Research, Madras, and a number of other institutions have conducted studies in respect of IRDP. Most of these studies were based on the experience of the first one or two years of the programme, when it had yet to stabilise when the per household investment levels were very meagre. The number of persons who would have crossed the income level of Rs. 3500 according to these studies would not exceed around 40 per cent, although additional incomes have accrued in the case of 55 to 90 per cent of the beneficiaries, and the relative consumption expenditure of households assisted under these programmes has been found to be generally higher than for comparable non-beneficiary households.

The Sixth Plan had assumed an ICOR of 1.5 and resources had been allocated in such a manner as to enable average investment per household of around Rs. 3000. The studies made so far indicate the ICOR assumptions were too optimistic and the investment levels per household were inadequate, in quite a few cases, to generate enough additional income to carry the beneficiaries, particularly those with a large income gap, above the income level of Rs 3500. Some of the other significant issues brought out by the evaluation studies are as follows:

(i) The financial allocations and physical targets under the programme were determined on a uniform basis per block, without regard to the incidence of poverty, or even the size of population, which in some cases also, resulted in the selection of ineligible families.

(ii) The extent of wrong identification was quite high at around 15-20 per cent. The main reasons for wrong identification were: (a) reliance on lists of households identified under the SFDA where the identification was based on land holding rather than income; (b) non-involvement of people's institutions in the survey and selection process; (c) better bankability of those having an asset base; and (d) collusion between the government functionaries and vested interests in some cases.

(iii) There have also been complaints of outright leakages through corruption and malpractice which, however, have not been quantified by any of the studies. Some factors which could have promoted this are: (a) non-involvement and lack of awareness among the beneficiaries; (b) methodology of administration of subsidy; and (c) insufficient investment in terms of project cost norms resulting in purchase of substandard assets.

(iv) The selection of schemes under the Programmes has shown an overwhelming bias towards animal husbandry, more particularly milch cattle. While this activity has considerable employment and income generation potential, this was vitiated by: (a) the shortage of good quality animals; (b) artificial increase in prices of animals; and (c) absence of linkages and support structures for feed, health cover and marketing. On the other hand, the predominance of this activity can be explained by factors such as the familiarity of the beneficiaries and block functionaries alike, and absence of expertise in projectisation with respect to secondary and tertiary activities.

(v) While the Programme guidelines stipulated that 33 per cent of the beneficiaries and tertiary sectors, the actual percentage in earlier years was much lower. Though there has been a distinct improvement in the later years, there has been a tendency even now to concentrate on petty business activities. While these can yield quick returns with relatively low project investment levels, the life of the investment is likely to be short, and in many cases they may not become self-sustaining.

(vi) A disturbing distinction between the so-called production programmes and beneficiary-oriented programmes has been noticed. Even the banks have sometimes referred to IRDP loaning as credit at the expense of priority production sectors, although most of the activities taken up under IRDP would fall within that category.

(vii) A major problem has been found to lie in the absence of backward and forward linkages. It appears that no real steps have been taken to provide institutional support for the supply of raw materials and, more particularly, for marketing, which was an important component of the total Sixth Plan Strategy for Rural Development.

(viii) Inadequacy of banking infrastructure in certain areas, particularly in the North-East, has affected credit flow adversely: shortages of staff, almost everywhere, have resulted insufficient scrutiny and delayed disposal of loan applications, and absence of supervision and follow-up; insistence on security in spite of instructions to the contrary, has resulted in the exclusion of the poorer among the target group; prescription of unrealistic loan repayment schedules has resulted in non-productive use of assistance; and non-availability of loan pass books with the beneficiaries has encouraged malpractice and adversely affected repayments.

(ix) Another weakness of the IRDP which has been discovered during the implementation is non-adoption of the cluster or group approach.

(x) An important bottleneck has also been found to lie in administrative weaknesses both in terms of the qualified staff required at the block and district levels and in respect of vertical and horizontal coordination and integration between different departments.

Although there have been many shortcomings in the Programme, there have been strong positive features also. The evaluation studies have brought out that it has resulted in substantial additional incomes to a large number of beneficiaries and the creation of assets which, in 70-80 per cent cases., were found to be intact. In some cases it has actually resulted in a change in occupational structure. There has been a define shift in the sectoral coverage pattern also, with the secondary and tertiary sector activities having increased from about 6.44 per cent in 1980-81 to about 46 per cent in 1984-85. The per household investment has gone up from Rs 1642 in 1980-81 to RS. 3399 in 1984-85 and there has also been an increase in the credit-subsidy ratio.

With the objective of providing technical skills to rural youths to enable them to take up self employment in the broad fields of agriculture and allied activities, industries, services, and business activities, the scheme of Training of Rural Youth for Self-Employment was started on 15th August, 1979. The Sixth Plan aimed to train 2 lakh rural youths every year at the rate of 40 youths per block per annum. The target group comprised rural youths between the ages of 18 and 35 from families living below the poverty line. It was also indicated that a minimum of 30 per cent of the trained youths should belong to Scheduled Caste and Scheduled Tribe communities and a minimum of 331/3 per cent of the rural youths trained should be women.

Against the target of 10.05 lakh youths to be trained during the Sixth Plan, 9.4 lakh youths were actually trained which accounts for 93.3 per cent of the target. Of the 9.4 lakh youths trained, 4.64 lakh youths were self-employed. Members of SC and ST accounted for 31.5 per cent of the persons trained, while women accounted for 34.8 per cent of the total number of persons trained.

It was noticed in the first three years of the Plan that the benefits under the IRDP were not flowing to women in adequate measure. Therefore, a programme for Development of Women and Children in Rural Areas was introduced in September, 1982 in 50 blocks on a pilot basis with a view to increasing their income and also to provide support services needed to enable them to take up income-generating activities. For this purpose, assistance could be given either to individual woman or to those organised into homogeneous groups to take up economically viable activities on a group basis together with the provision of support services and childcare facilities for the women so organised.

The sixth Plan outlay for the scheme was Rs. 15.60 crores which was to be shared equally by the Centre and the States. In addition, UNICF assistance was to be made available to the extent of Rs 5.40 crores. It was realised that Government effort would require to be supplemented by voluntary agencies also and a scheme of assistance to voluntary agencies under DWCRA was formulated. Besides, need was also felt for the construction of multipurpose community centres for the purpose of imparting training to workers to enable them to take up income generating activities, demonstration of appropriate technology and living quarters for gramsevikas of the area. In all 3308, Groups covering

52,170 Women beneficiaries were actually organized under the Programme in the Sixth Plan.

Many of the shortcomings of the Integrated Rural Development Programme outlined alone would appear to stem from the fact that a programme of massive dimensions, having a multiplicity of critical parameters and functioning in a highly diverse environment, was launched with what can be called very little preparation. The Sixth Plan period could thus be called a period of trial in which the Programme has gradually come to be known, understood and even stabilized. The gaps that have been revealed and the weaknesses that have been experienced in the process will be remedied in the Seventh Plan so as to make the IRDP an effective instrument of poverty alleviation.

The programme will continue to aim at the poorest among the poor who will be identified by an annual household income of Rs. 4800, which is substantially lower than the cut-off income of around Rs. 6400 at the poverty line level. Towards achieving this end, much greater care will be exercised in the process of selection of beneficiaries. Detailed household surveys, with maximum involvement of the local community, will be carried out with the dual objective of identifying those who, having already received assistance in the Sixth Plan, require supplementary assistance to achieve economic viability and those in the lowest strata of the poverty group, who have not been approached so far. The survey may have to be accompanied by a process of registration of poor families with the objective of identification of target-group households, not only for the IRDP but also for the delivery of an integrated package of benefits under the other programmes connected with poverty alleviation and raising the levels of living the poor as the NREP/RLEGP and MNP, etc.

Considering the low absorptive capacity of the poorest among the poor, apart from the emphasis on the group approach indicating earlier, the adoption of the total house hold approach will be emphasised as a major plank of the Programme. This would mean not only the provision of a total package of benefits and services under different programmes to the identified households but also the provision of assistance under the IRDP in the form of more than one scheme of assets over a period of time, if necessary to different members of the household, so as to gradually create a capacity for productive absorption of credit and generation of self-sustaining income.

It is important to ensure a balanced sectoral coverage under the Programme. To achieve this objective there would be a renewed emphasis on decentralised planning at the district level with the objective of drawing up project and sub-sectoral profiles based on the local potential and the on-going sectoral plans and programmes which could help to identify the major potential thrust areas in different regions. Such plans at the district level would have to be prepared within the first year of the Seventh Plan. In the process, on-going target group-oriented schemes being implemented by different departments will be rationalised and others capable of such orientation, the Special Rice Programme, Operation Flood II, Programmes for Handlooms and Seri-culture, etc. would be given a specific direction towards the target group of the IRDP with a view to achieving maximum integration between the individual beneficiary-oriented content of IRDP, on the one hand, and the infrastructure and service support made available through such programmes, on the other. For example, the benefits intended to be provided to 10 million families under the OF-II could be easily directed first to the IRDP beneficiaries who might have got milch cattle, rather than having an independent selection of farmers who in most cases would be better off more easily able to fend for themselves.

Within the above broad framework, due emphasis would be given to augmenting productivity through IRDP by taking up land-based activities like minor irrigation, dry farming, horticulture and even farm forestry. With the emphasis of IRDP on the poorest of the poor, this would imply large scale conjunctive activity with land reforms, i.e., land distribution and grant of ownership rights to share-croppers and tenants and with programmes like NREP and RLEGP i.e, development of distributed/ distributable lands etc.

Concrete steps will be taken to step up activity in the industries, Services and Business sector. Realistic project profiles will be worked out for household enterprises, and wherever possible larger group enterprises, in areas of traditional skills. These will take into account the need to provide balancing equipment and improvement of existing capital stock along with the provision of working capital to maintain continued income flows and assets development and renewal. In a number of other sectors of the economy like water supply and sanitation and improved agricultural implements, there is considerable scope for developing productive ventures for production fabrication and service repair of new technology-based equipments, which will be exploited and developed to the maximum extent as part of secondary and tertiary sector activity under the IRDP. A major area of weakness under the Programme, i.e., the absence of infrastructural support and backward and forward linkages, will be given special attention. For the most part this will have to come from the sectoral departments in the form of development of appropriate technology, production and supply of good-quality assets and provision of other inputs and services.

In order to ensure this an attempt would be made to spell out the provision of such support specifically in the sectoral plans. In addition, to meet the requirements of programme-specific and balancing infrastructure at the local level, funds will be provided separately, over and above subsidy funds, as a part of the overall outlays under IRDP. These funds, among other things, would be utilised for developing institutions such as District Supply and Marketing Societies at the district level to take care of raw material/input requirements and marketing.

It will be emphasised that an infrastructure sub-plan should be prepared as an integral part of the sub-sectoral district plans mentioned earlier. While doing this, the support likely to be available through the plans of sectoral departments as well as the planned use of the IRDP infrastructure funds would both have to be spelt out. The process of skill endowment to members of the target group would be considered as an integral part of the IRDP. The training of youths under TRYSEM would, therefore, be provided on the basis of actual need and requirement, and there will be no separate targets at a macro-level for TRYSEM. The costs of training in the form of stipends, etc, will be met out of the funds set out for infrastructure, etc. under the IRDP. The Sixth Plan scheme for strengthening of training infrastructure for TRYSEM will be reoriented and replaced by a new scheme to develop Composite Rural Training and Technology Centres in each district as nodal institutions within a large system of training and technology dissemination covering the district as a whole. Such centres will be developed around existing ITIs,

Polytechnics, etc. The technology component of these Centres would be developed by CART acting through State-Level Science and Technology Institutions. For purposes of technology development and dissemination, major thrust areas and areas with evident potential for application in the context of small ventures under IRDP and other special programmes of rural development will be identified, and techno-economic profiles based on such technology will be prepared together with appropriate training packages, wherever necessary.

The dual objective of this would be to ensure widespread dissemination of technology already developed and to bring home the economic advantages of the same in maximum measure to members of the target group. In identified thrust areas where the state of technology may be in a relatively nascent stage, experimental projects would be taken by CART through different governmental and non-governmental agencies. A major role in the programme would continue to be played by the banking sector. It is expected that credit to the tune of around Rs. 4000 crores would have to be mobilised from the banking structure.

The role of cooperative institutions which had not been up to the mark in the Sixth Plan, will have to be emphasised, and a reasonable percentage of the total credit would have to be mobilised from these institutions. This would call for strengthening of the cooperative institutions both through the sectoral Plan funds and infrastructure funds available under the IRDP. In certain regions, particularly the north-east, the bank infrastructure will be substantially expanded and strengthened with a view to extending credit in areas hitherto deprived of it. Strict measures will be taken to enforce the instructions by which IRDP loans are exempted from security.

Besides, steps will be taken to see that the terms of loan and repayment schedules are rationalised so that the poorest of the poor are able to improve their levels of living from increases in productivity and, if necessary, a moratorium on repayment in certain cases would be considered. Steps will also be taken to ensure the provision of working capital and even a cash credit limit, wherever necessary and feasible. Loan pass books would be issued to all beneficiaries to ensure proper accounting and follow-up. The ceilings of subsidy fixed for different categories of beneficiaries in the Sixth Plan would continue. Within these, the average subsidy per household would be stepped up from around Rs. 1000 in the Sixth Plan to around Rs. 1333 to allow for a higher per capita investment level so as to ensure adequate income returns.

The position regarding the average subsidy per households can be reviewed for the last three years of the Plan. The manner of administering the subsidy will be reviewed and rationalised with a view to ensuring that packages are minimised and the beneficiary, without adding any extra burden, is motivated towards productive utilisation of the loan. Due emphasis would continue to be given under the IRDP to direct the maximum quantum of benefits towards women, who admittedly constitute a substantially deprived section of the community. Efforts to be made to this direction through IRDP would be supplemented by continuing the Programme for the Development of Women and Children in the Rural Areas in the Seventh Plan. Considering that the Sixth Plan experience with this programme was still of a pilot and experimental nature, the programme would be implemented in 1000 blocks.

The objective would be mainly to organise women in socio-economic activity groups with the dual objective of providing self-employment opportunities and social strength to them. In the process voluntary agencies and people's action group would be involved to the maximum extent possible. Efforts will also be made to integrate with the DWCRA other programmes for the development of Women and Children, viz., the ICDS and other State programmes like SIAD, so as to provide a bigger and more comprehensive coverage of women and children and to reduce duplication and increase the cost-effectiveness of the total effort. The special Livestock Production Programmes which had continued in the Sixth Plan as a separate programme, although financed through IRDP outlays, will be merged with the IRDP under which substantial activity in the milch cattle sector has in any case been noticed.

The pattern of assistance under the SLPP will wherever feasible be provided under the main IRD Programme. With the merger of this programme with the IRDP and considering the normal emphasis on milch cattle that is likely to continue in the IRDP even otherwise, there is likely to be a substantial demand for good quality heifers and other milch animals. Keeping this in view a new breeding programme, the Special Livestock Breeding Programmes, will replace the SLPP in the Seventh Plan. This would enable the farmers selected for this purpose to contribute to the poverty alleviation programmes by producing good quality animals, and create alternative market channels for animal sales towards the programme requirements even for target-group cattle-owners. Keeping in view the objective of bringing down the poverty ratio to less than 10% by 1994-95, it would be aimed to provide assistance to around 20 million households under the IRDP in the Seventh Plan.

Considering that between 50 and 60 percent of the Sixth Plan beneficiaries may not have actually crossed the poverty line, it is expected that around 50 percent of the beneficiaries to be assisted in the Seventh Plan will be cases requiring supplementary assistance on an average, at the rate of Rs. 500 per household.

To enable these targets to be achieved, an outlay of Rs. 1328.88 crores has been provided for IRDP and allied programmes in the Seventh Plan in the Central sector to be matched by an equal amount by the States.

This outlay would include provision for subsidy for the main programme, funds for infrastructure, training stipends, etc., to the extent of 20 per cent of the subsidy funds; setting up of the CRTTC and the Special Livestock Breeding Programme and certain other programmes like strengthening of Block Administration, Computerised District Rural Information system, strengthening of Extension Training Centres, etc. Of the total outlay, Rs. 1888.65 crores would be available for subsidy and RS. 488.0 crores for infrastructure, etc, under the IRDP.

The remaining amount would be for other schemes mentioned above. The outlays under the Programme will be based upon the principle of selectivity geared to actual incidence of poverty in different States.

For the first two years, 50 percent of the allocations will be made on the basis of an equal allocations per block as in the Sixth Plan, and the remaining 50 per cent on basis of incidence of poverty determined by the NSSO survey. From the third year onwards, the allocations would be based entirely on the incidence of poverty.

National rural employment programme

The NREP was launched in October, 1980 and became a regular Plan programme from April 1981. The programme was expected to generate additional gainful employment in the rural areas, to the extent of 300-400 million mandays per annum, create durable community assets, and improve nutritional status and living standards of the poor.

An outlay of Rs. 1620 crores was provided under this Programme out of which the outlay from 1980-81 onwards was to be shared equally between the Centre and the States. The year -wise performance under the Programme is indicated.

A major step was taken in 1983-84 when it was decided to subsidise the cost of the foodgrains to be distributed under this programme. A subsidy to the extent of 37 Paise to 40 Paise per kg. was provided for wheat and rice to be distributed under the Programme. According to the guidelines, foodgrains were to be provided at the rate of 1 kg. per man-day. The total foodgrains made available each year during 1980-85 and the utilisation are indicated.

The creation of durable assets was an important objective of this Programme and, in fact, the real distinguishing feature between the Food for Work Programme and the NREP. With a view to ensuring the durability of assets created a provision had been made allowing for expenditure on materials to the extent of 40 per cent of the total project cost. Table 34 shows the different categories of assets created under this Programme during the Sixth Plan. It would be seen from the foregoing review that the employment generation target under the NREP has been consistently achieved. However, it is not known as to how much of this has been directed towards those who are landless and the poorest amongst the poor. To this extent the programme has apparently lacked a direct focus on the target-group population, for whom it was meant. It has, however, had a substantial impact in terms of stabilisation of wages in the rural areas, containing prices of foodgrains and the creation of a wide variety of community assets which could be expected to help in raising the levels of living of the rural population.

As regards asset creation under NREP, it would be seen from Table that productive works such as soil conservation, social forestry and irrigation had shown a decline between 1980-83 while there was a sharp increase in building works, and roads continued to have an important place in the programme.

As regards specific type of assets reported to have been constructed, the reviews have brought out certain features which would have to be considered for the future:

(i) The growing propensity to take up all kinds of building works in increasing measure suggests local pulls and pressures geared to a desire for a very wide and thin coverage and easier implementability of such works as compared, example, with watershed based land development works which require expertise among the field planners. In the process, material costs have tended to be high with subsequent higher maintenance requirements, durability of assets in some has been suspect and long-term income generation and employment effects have been limited.

(ii) In the case of social forestry which constituted an important component of the programme it was found that in addition to road-side plantation which has been generally popular, projects in some States included growing of nurseries for distribution of samplings to all farmers, big and small village lots without adherence to appropriate cost and physical norms.

(iii) Ten per cent of the outlays had been earmarked for works of direct benefit to members of Scheduled Castes and Scheduled Tribes who are among the poorest of the poor. Such works could include drinking water wells, housing, on-farm works, etc., Although the number of such works showed an increase over the years, many States were not able to spend the earnmaked outlays. Moreover, sufficient details of the types of works taken up in the category have also not been available.

(iv) Projects for roads which have accounted for a substantial percentage of funds under NREP in many cases have not been found to have a meaningful relationship with priorities arising from the Minimum Needs Programme.

Measures proposed in the seventh plan

The National Rural Employment Programme will be continued in the Seventh Plan as an important component of the anti-poverty strategy. As indicated earlier, this will have to be viewed as an integral part of the total package, which would empty that an effort would have to be made to direct and monitor the wage employment opportunities accruing through this Programme to members of the target group including those identified for assistance under the IRDP.

The same principle would apply in the choice of projects which would therefore, have to take account of labour-intensity of projects their capacity to provide reasonably long spells of employment during implementation, direction towards poor, long-term income and employment generation potential, capacity to create a base for productive asset endowment and capacity for filling gaps in vital infrastructure. Based on this, priority will be accorded to works for the development of waste lands and marginal lands allotted under land reform measures, renovation of derelict tanks for large scale development of fisheries with the target-group orientation, social forestry including fuel and energy plantations, fodder and pasture development and roadside plantations with maximum involvement of the community/target-groups in their management coupled with nursery development of target-group land-holders.

Development of composite homestead projects for the shelterless in the form of housing complexes-cum-production estates within a larger concept of habitat development, field works in irrigation command areas and micro watersheds, roads according to well-defined techno-economic norms and within planned priorities such as those arising out of the MNP, and need-based construction of buildings which apart from schools, *Panchayat ghars*, etc., would provide vital economic infrastructures like buildings for godowns, banks and workshops/shops for target-group beneficiaries would be chosen. The broad objectives of the programme, while remaining the same as in the Sixth Plan, would have to conform to the above priorities. The Sixth Plan experience has shows that the distribution of foodgrains has not kept up to the stipulated level of 1 kg. per manday for a variety of reasons relating to problems of storage and movement, quality of foodgrains and diversion to the public distribution system, and in some cases because of local preferences for coarse grains.

The importance of foodgrain distribution under the Programme cannot be over-emphasised in view of its effects both on stabilization of prices and the improvement of nutritional standards of workers. With the comfortable food stocks, an additional 1 million tonnes of foodgrains will be provided for the Programme over and above its normal requirements.

The quantum of food-grains distribution per worker per day would also be stepped up. The States will be asked to prepare detailed action plans to ensure that the process of foodgrain distribution is streamlined to achieve the Programme objectives. Wherever necessary, coarse grains would have to be purchased locally and made available for the Programme. Efforts have been made successfully in some States to distribute other commodities such as sarees as wage payment in kind. Such efforts would be encouraged in other areas also in such manner as to provide encouragement to decentralised production of handloom textiles, etc.

With a view to overcoming the problems of *ad hoc* section of projects and suspicious about the quality of work, detailed guidelines for important sub-sectors figuring under the Programme such as roads, social forestry and housing have already been issued. These will have to be supplemented by the preparation of detailed techno-economic norms at the State level and of technical training manuals for the implementation staff. The provision allowing for spending upto 50 per cent of the allocations on materials would be continued in the interest of ensuring the durability of the assets created. Since the relative costs of labour and materials for different projects would vary, the stipulated ratio would be maintained for the district as a whole which would allow substantial flexibility in the context of decentralised economic planning.

Rural land employment guarantee programme (RLEGP)

RLEGP was introduced from 15th August, 1983 with the objective of (a) improving and expanding employment opportunities for the rural landless with a view to providing guarantee of employment to at least one member of every landless household upto 100 days in a year and (b) creating durable assets for strengthening the infrastructure so as to meet the growing requirements of the rural economy. An outlay of Rs. 500 crores to be fully financed by the Central Government was provided under this programme in the Sixth Plan. The implementation of the programme was entrusted to the States/UTs, but they were required to prepare specific projects for approval by a Central Committee. During the Central Committee approved 320 projects with an estimated cost of Rs.. 906,59 crores. The target for employment generation in 1983-95 and 1984-85 was fixed at 360 million man-days against which 260.18 million man-days of employment was actually generated. This programme is expected to have resulted in the creation of a large number of durable community assets and economic infrastructure in the rural areas. However, a tendency to concentrate on assets creation on the basis of departmental plans rather than on the basis of the requirements determined locally and of the need to provide the requisite quantum of employment to the landless labourers, has been noticed.

Concentration on road projects was also initially observed which was later sought to be restricted to not more than 50 per cent of the total outlays and also confined to the priorities arising out of the Minimum Needs Programme.

Mid-way during the Sixth Plan, the RLEGP was started with the dual objective of expanding employment opportunities in the rural areas and providing sharper focus on the landless labour house-holds which constitute the hard-core of the people below the poverty line. Suggestions have been made that this should be merged with the NREP. However, considering that a substantial part of the RLEGP funds would be committed to the on-going projects and also since it has not been found feasible to introduce a full guarantee of employment even to a limited section, this programme would continue as a separate entity for the time being.

In the meanwhile efforts would also be made to implement a limited guarantee for providing 80 to 100 days employment to the landless labour households through this programme. The issue of merger and a wider guarantee could be considered at the midterm Plan review stage. As in the case of the NREP, wage material cost-ratio will be 50 : 50, which, however, will be maintained on a project by project basis. Experience in the Sixth Plan in certain States has shown that if integrated projects are developed, this stipulation would still allow substantial scope for productive works to be planned within a decentralised frame work at the district level. Under both these Programmes 20 per cent of the resources will be earmarked for social forestry in view of the importance of eco-restoration and providing the benefits in the form of usufruct to the members of the community, particularly the poor. In addition, 10 per cent of th funds would be earmarked for works of direct and, if necessary, individual benefit to the members of scheduled castes.

A separate provision within the RLEGP will be made for rural housing with the objective of constructing one million houses in the Seventh Plan. This will be closely integrated with the housing component of the MNP. Five per cent of the outlays to the provided for RLEGP and NREP would be available for strengthening the implementation agencies. Further, based on past experience regarding problems of maintenance of assets created under such programmes, the question of providing funds to the extent of 10 per cent of the overall outlays for these programmes for maintenance will be considered.

Maintenance under this provision would generally have to relate to sectors for which maintenance funds and systems are ordinary not available and actual maintenance will have to be carried out on the basis of detailed maintenance plans to be drawn up for each district. An outlay of Rs. 1250.81 crores has been provided for NREP in the Central Sector which will be matched equally by to States. The outlay of Rs. 1743.78 crores has been provided for RLEGP to be born be entirely by the Centre. Based on the average wage of Rs. 8.61 per day as in 1984-85 and a wage material cost-ratio of 50 : 50 a total employment of 1445 million man-days under NREP and 1013 million man-days under RELGP is likely to be generated during the Seventh Plan at an average rate of around 290 million man-days and 200 million ma-days per annum, respectively. The formula for allocation of resources among the States, which provided for 25 per cent weightage to the incidence of poverty and 75 per cent weightage to the population of agriculture labourers and marginal farmers in the Sixth Plan will be changed to provide equal weightage to those from 1986-87 onwards, because it has been noticed that the existing formula has tended to benefit, in some cases, States which are more agriculturally advanced.

Drought-prone area programme (DPAP)

In the Fourth Plan, after the mid-term appraisal, this programme was re0-designated as Drought Prone Area Programme (DPAP) and reoriented as an integrated area development programme with the objective of developing the land, water, livestock and human resources of these areas. The programme has been in operation in 511 blocks of 70 districts in 13 States. A Task Force was constituted in 1980 to review the ongoing special programmes and development schemes taken up under DPAP to study the existing coverage of the DPAP; to lay down objective criteria for inclusion/exclusion of areas under the programme, to spell out the main components of the broad strategy of development under the programme and also to identify the linkages between DPAP and other on-going rural development programmes.

The Task Force submitted its report in 1982 and made several recommendations for improving the impact and coverage of the DPAP. While implementing the recommendations of the Task Force, some of the States had not agreed to the exclusion of some areas, from 1982-83, from this programme, whereas a few States had even suggested the inclusion of new areas which they considered to be drought-prone. An Inter-Department

Group on DPAP/DDP was set up in 1984 by the Department of Rural Development to examine the representations received from these States for purposes of inclusion/re-inclusion of blocks under these programmes.

It is as a result of the recommendations of the Inter-Departmental Group that 120 blocks were added to DPAP, while 16 blocks were deleted from the programme. The net addition has, therefore, been 104 blocks to the existing coverage of 511 blocks. During the Sixth Plan, the financing pattern was on the basis of equal sharing between the Centre and the States. The funding norm under the DPAP has been at the rate of Rs. 15 lakhs per block per year. The Sixth Plan allocations for DPAP was Rs. 350 crores. As against this, the actual expenditure amounted to Rs. 310 crores. The physical achievements during the Sixth Five Year Plan are as follows :

1. Soil and moisture conservation 4265.59
2. Creation of irrigation potential -do- 3276.67
3. Afforestation and pasture -do- 3869.86
4. Milk societies established Nos. 3426
5. Sheep societies established Nos. 622
6. Employment generated '000 176996

The strategy adopted in the Sixth Plan for DPAP will continue during the Seventh Plan which would *inter-alia* include increased stress on activities which can contribute directly to the restoration of the ecological balance and increasing the per capita income through the effective development of land and other natural resources including efficient utilisation of scares water, conservation of scanty rainfall, and arresting its run-off in drought-prone areas. Accordingly, the Programme, as at present, would continue to be implemented as an integrated area development programme rather than as a programme merely for creating increased employment opportunities.

Integrated district plans, taking into account resources available under sectoral programmes and other special programmes like NREP, RLEGP, and IRDP, will be prepared to achieve the objective of restoration of ecological balance of the area by way of soil and moisture conservation, development and management of irrigation, afforestation, restructuring of cropping pattern, and development of livestock resources. For DPAP the existing pattern of assistance and the funding norm per block per year would be continued during the Seventh Plan for which an outlay of Rs. 237 crores as Central share has been provided.

Land reforms

Land Reforms have been recognised to constitute a vital element both in terms of a anti-poverty strategy and for modernisation and increased productivity in agriculture, Redistribution of land could provide a permanent asset base for a large number of rural landless poor for taking up land-based and other supplementary activities. Similarly, consolidation of holdings, tenancy regulation and updating to land records, would widen the access of small and marginal land-holders to improved technology and inputs and thereby directly lead to increase in agricultural production.

A land reforms policy with a five-fold objective was continued in the Sixth Plan. The objective envisaged (i) abolition to intermediary tenures; (ii) tenancy reforms aimed at security of tenure, regulation of rent and conferment of ownership rights on tenants; (iii) celling on land-holdings and distribution of surplus land; (iv) consolidation of holdings; and (v) compilation and updating of land records. It was expected that legislative measures to confer ownership rights on tenants would be introduced in all States by 1981-82, that the programme of taking over and distribution of surplus ceiling land would be completed by 1982-83, that compilation updating of land records would be completed in a phased manner by 1985 and that consolidation of holdings would be taken up in all States with the aim of completing it in 10 years with priority being assigned to command areas of irrigation projects.

Land Reforms Amendment Acts were to be brought within the Ninth Schedule, Ceiling Laws were to be automatically enforced in command areas of irrigation systems and the State Governments were expected to take more initiative in the development of Bhoodan lands. A scheme for providing financial assistance to assigners of ceiling-surplus land had also been started in 1975-76 for the landless poor, so as to enable them to take to profitable cultivation on the assigned land which is generally of poor quality. As the scheme now stands, financial assistance is provided up to Rs. 2500 per hectare to be given as a grant to the assignee, for various purposes like simple land development, provision of inputs as well as immediate consumption needs. Since the inception of the scheme, Rs. 25.07 crores have been released to the States under r this Programme.

An outlay of Rs. 30 crores was provided for this Scheme in the Central Sector for the period 1980-85 and an equal amount was to be provided as matching outlay by the States. Actual utilisation of funds has, however, been very low, largely because the States have not been providing their matching share, and due to the non-submission of utilisation certificate of allocated resources, the Central release could not be made. It was also found that there was little or no linkage between this Programme and the IRDP or the NREP/RLEGP, and it functioned in isolation, generally throught the Revenue Agencies rather than the DRDA add the block. Ceiling laws are prevalent all over the country except in the north eastern region—Nagaland, Meghalaya, Arunachal Pradesh—where land is generally held by the community, and in the Union Territories of Andaman and Nicobar Islands, and Goa Daman and Diu.

The ceiling was first imposed on Land-holdings in the fifties and sixties. Later, National Guidelines on the subject were framed in 1972. Under the two sets of ceiling laws 7.2 million aces of land have been declared surplus, 5.6 million acres have been taken possession of, and 4.4 million acres distributed. Thus, 2.8 million acres of land declared surplus have not been distributed so far. Of this, 1.6 million acres involved in irrigation and 0.89 million acres have been reserved by specific public purposes. It would be seen that a very large chunk of surplus distributable land is blocked due to litigation. Jurisdiction of civil courts has been carried in respect of land reforms cases. However, the writ jurisdiction of the High Court and Supreme Court remains. Article 32 and of the Constitution provides of setting up land tribunals after extinguishing the jurisdiction of High Courts. But concerted action in this regard still remain to be taken.

About 4.2 million acres of land were received in *Bhoodan*, but so far only about 1.3 million acres have been distributed. The State Governments have not taken any initiative for the development of these hands even where these are in compact blocks. This is an area where a conscious thrust would be necessary. Similarly, there is an area of 16.7 million hectares or culturable wasteland in the country, the development and utilisation of which is not being monitored.

Some States have been distributing wastelands, but the total picture is not clear. There is thus an urgent need to bring both these categories of land into a comprehensive redistributive land reforms policy with appropriate measures for enforcement and monitoring. Fifteen out of the 22 States in the country have enacted laws on consolidation of land-holdings. Up to the year 1979-80, the consolidated area in the country was 46.2 million hectares.

Consolidation has been completed in Punjab and Haryana and is nearing completion in Uttar Pradesh, Bihar, Gujarat, Himachal Pradesh, Jammu & Kashmir and Karnataka. Madhya Pradesh and Orissa have also started consolidation operation. The total area consolidated during the Sixth Plan was 5.6 million hectares. Thus, the total consolidated so far is 51.8 million bectares, which is only 32 per cent of to total cropped area in the country. It is evident that efforts in this direction would have to be considerably stepped up.

Land reforms in the Seventh Plan would be looked upon as an intrinsic part of the anti-proverty strategy. Wherever laws have both been enacted by the States for securing the rights of tenants and regulation of rent, the State Governments will take appropriate steps to enact such laws during the Seventh Plan. In order to expedite the process, attempts will also be made to organise quick surveys for recording registration of tenants with maximum involvement of the local community and people's institutions. Such action may be necessary even in those States where tenancy, although abolished, may have re-emerged informally for a variety of reasons. Tribals and scheduled castes will be protected from alienation of their lands not only to non-tribals, but to the big land-owners among them, through appropriate legislation.

The full potential of land redistribution has not been realised both in terms of covering the entire surplus that may be available and taking possession of and distribution of that already identified. Legal and administrative bottlenecks have led to large gaps between declaration of surplus land, taking actual possession of the land and its distribution. Appropriate measures will have to be taken to reduce the gap. Reassessment of ceiling surplus land will have to be done by the states, especially in the command areas and other newly irrigated areas.

To ensure the best use of surplus land that cannot be distributed because it is unfit for cultivation, the State Governments would have to take possession in order to avoid encroachment and to ensure their development in a planned manner.

The scheme for financial assistance to the assignees of ceiling surplus land would be continued during the Seventh Plan. Since land as an endowed asset is only the first stage of productive self-employment for a large section of the poverty group, close linkages will have to be forged with IRDP and other rural development programmes so that assignees o ceiling and other lands are given priority in identification and their performance monitored separately. Consolidation operations have not made much headway in many States. Consolidation of land-holdings is especially important in the States of the eastern region where the Special Programme for Rice Production would be taken up. Some of the factors working against consolidation are: (a) fear of displacement among tenants and share-croppers; (b) advantage of having land in fragmented parcels, (b) advantage of having land in fragmented parcels in the event of floods and other natural calamities, and (c) apprehensions that the bigger farmers would get a better deal.

These factors would have to be borne in mind while considering a policy for consolidation in the Seventh Plan. As far as possible, the holdings of small and marginal farmers need to be consolidated in such a way that they form contiguous blocks of lands so that the exploitation of groundwater for them as well as provision of various agricultural services and inputs becomes economical.

Land records form the base for all land reform measures and therefore regular periodical updating of land records is essential in all States. This will necessarily have to include scientific surveys of unmeasured lands and recording of the rights of tenants and sharecroppers which have remained unrecorded up till now. A Centrally Sponsored Scheme is proposed to be implemented during the Seventh Plan on the basis of matching contributions by the States and Centre, for updating of land records. The States would also be assisted in strengthening the revenue machinery at the grassroots level as well as at the supervisory levels. Training programmes for revenue functionaries and surveys and settlement staff would be conducted to improve their efficiency as well as to bring about attitudinal changes.

A sum of Rs. 36.71 crores has been provided in the Centre for the Centrally Sponsored Scheme of financial assistance to assignees of ceiling surplus land strengthening of revenue machinery and updating of land records. For the programmes in the States a sum of Rs. 353.88 crores and for the Union Territories Rs. 5.24 crores have been provided.

Community development and panchayat raj

The Community Development Programme had provided an elaborate delivery mechanism in the form of development Blocks and the village level extension agency. However, over the years, this mechanism had suffered considerable erosion and gradual disintegration. With the launching of the IRDP in the Sixth Plan efforts were made to restore, to a substantial extent, the mechanism provided under the Community Development Programme. As a result the position improved but the total delivery system has still not been able to attain its effectiveness as originally envisaged.

The position varies in different States, but an almost uniform feature is the gradual erosion of the control of BDO over the extension team at the block and village levels. Simultaneously, a multiplicity of functionaries has emerged at this level for implementation of functionaries has emerged at this level for implementation of a large number of programmes aimed at the same people for raising their standard of living. Similarly although Panchayati Raj institutions, in one form or another exist in most States, they have for a variety of reasons not been actively and effectively involved in the implementation of rural development programmes except in a few States. On the other hand it has been seen that wherever this has happened the quality of programme implementation has been decidedly better. In terms of instruments of planning Community Development and *Panchayat Raj* institutions have been reduced to an extremely peripheral status with the budget provision in many cases being limited to maintenance of staff while in other cases there is duplication and repetition of a large number of small schemes which are being simultaneously executed on a much larger scale through sectoral and special programmes, e.g. those relating to health, sanitation, road-building panchayat ghars, etc.

With the launching of large-scale multi-sectoral, country-wide programmes of rural development aiming both at individual households and at the creation of assets in the rural areas the original concept of Community Development could be said to have been substantially restored. This would be further strengthened by the measure already taken or proposed to be taken to strengthen and rationalise the administration and delivery mechanism.

For purposes of the Seventh Plan Community Development and *Panchayati Raj* would have to be viewed in this context and would have to break free from the conventional methodology of including a large number of small schemes through minimal budget provisions. What does by the name of Community Development in the documents would have to be viewed now more in the nature of a scheme for village development which would imply the planning and implementation of a number of residual activities at the village level which do not get covered in the normal sectoral plans and special programmes e.g. village paths, drainage and sanitation. This in turn would have to be done on the basis on local, decentralised planning at the village and block levels for which block funds, both in the nature of outright and incentive grants, would have to be placed at the disposal of *Panchayati Raj* and Community Development bodies rather than by forming sectoral plans for the village at the State and National levels. This would imply a considerable degree of rationalisation in the drawing up of plans for Community Development and *Panchayati Raj* and substantial autonomy in their implementation.

In addition, the States would be called upon to active *Panchayati Raj* institutions, particularly at the village and block levels, with a view to ensuring their active involvement in the planning and implementation of the special programmes of rural development, particularly those concerned with poverty alleviation and the provision of minimum needs.

Special employment programme

In addition to the Central programmes, some of the State Governments have introduced their own special employment programmes in the rural sector. These are Andhra Pradesh, Gujarat, Jammu and Kashmir, Karnataka, Madhya Pradesh, Maharashtra, Nagaland, Tamil Nadu and West Bengal. The Seventh Plan outlay for these schemes is Rs. 509 24 crores.

In the Sixth Plan, the Monitoring process had been confined, more or less, to watching the physical and financial progress in terms of money spent and physical coverage achieved, together with some analysis of per household investment levels, unit cost of wage employment, etc. Evaluation studies, on the other hand, were postfacto in nature and were not of much help in applying correctives on a continuous basis. The whole machinery and system for monitoring and concurrent evaluation will be strengthened in the Seventh Plan.

A Central Scheme will be started for the establishment of a Computerised District Rural Information System (DRIS) in each district with the ultimate objective or providing a data base for planning, selection of beneficiaries and schemes and monitoring their performance. In addition, steps will be taken to strengthen the data collection and monitoring machinery at the block and district levels. A system of concurrent evaluation covering 72 blocks in 36 district with the beneficiary sample of around 1500, per month will also be launched for continuous follow-up and application of correctives.

Strengthening of administration

As already indicated, a High Level Committee has been set up to review the administrative Arrangements for Rural Development and Poverty Alleviation Programmes with a view to developing appropriate structural mechanisms to ensure that they are planned and implemented in an effective and integrated manner. In the meanwhile, the scheme for strengthening of Block Level Machinery, the objective of which was to restore the full complement of the administrative staff according to the schematic pattern of the community development programme, will be continued. Within this, steps would be taken to strengthen and upgrade the position of the BDO, rationalise and increase the strength of the workers at the village level and provide facilities for the implementing the supervisory staff for ways movement so that their efficiency is increased.

Training

It has been observed over the years that the emphasis that had been given to the training of the administrative and extension staff during the community development days has been gradually reduced both because of the disintegration of the programme itself and due to paucity of resources with the State Governments. A scheme of European Economic Community (EEC) assistance for this purpose will be continue and will be further supplemented by a Central Scheme to provide 100 per cent assistance for non-recurring expenditure and 50 per cent assistance for recurring expenditure involved in the setting up and strengthening of institute for rural development and extension training centres in the States. The National Institute of Rural Development will also be strengthened and will be expected to play an active role in the coordination of training arrangements for different levels of rural Development functionaries in the States.

Communication strategy

A communication strategy involving Doordarshan, Akashvani, and DAVP will be developed for creating awareness among the beneficiaries and the people at large about the anti-poverty and the Minimum Needs Programmes, through the dissemination of relevant information and knowledge and through the educational programmes devised for this purpose.

Rural energy

The pattern of rural energy consumption is dominated by non-commercial energy source such as firewood, agricultural waste and cowdung which from 90 per cent of the total energy consumed in the rural areas. These non-commercial energy sources also comprise about half of the total energy consumed in the country.

4

Five Year Plans in Rural Education

The First Plan has said that the Central Research Institutes are the I.A.R.I. at Delhi the Potato Research Institute at Patna, and the Rice Research Institute at Cuttack. The I.A.R.I. carries out fundamental research but its research programme is not coordinated by the I.C.A.R. with the research programme of the rest of the country. Apart from this draw back, the I.A.R.I. provides the back group against which applied research is carried out over the rest of the country. The First Five year plan had observed that the urgent necessity of providing education to the rural areas was obvious. To meet this need, the University Education Commission had recom-mended a new pattern under the name of rural university.

The plan had observed, "The Central Government should help to establish, during the period of the plan, at least one such university where ever the earlier stages worked out. Apart from serving the villages, the experiences gained in the working of rural universities is likely to be useful in affecting certain necessary reforms in our existing universities, there by enabling them to serve the national needs more effectively. The Plan had rightly cautioned about the fact that the rural universities that may be set up will have to pass through a period of experimentation, during which it is essential that they should have free scope for development. In order not to place the products of these institutions at a disadvantage, the degree of the rural universities should have as much validity in the matter of public appointments as those of older universities.

In this way we see that a complete hierarchy of the rural education had been developed right in the beginning of the planning process in India. During the Second Five Year Plan a Council for Rural Higher Education was constituted to follow up the programme of establishment of Rural Institutes. There institutes were to be started for providing facilities for higher studies to students who complete their post basic or higher secondary courses and for providing certificate courses in subjects such as rural hygiene, agriculture and rural engineering and also shorter courses and for providing comprehensive teaching cum research cum extension programmes. It had been visualised that Rural Institutes would function as cultural and training areas.

The Ministry of Education and proposed to establish 10 Rural Institutes in the Second Five Year Plan and had a provision of Rs. 2 crores for this purpose. A National of Basic Education is was also established as a research centre. In a similar manner programmes for agriculture in the Second Five Year Plan included rural education. The Third Five Year Plan provided for research for agricultural production. All the programmes for agricultural production included research and rural education.

The work of Rural Institutes received proper attention in the Third Five Year Plan. The planners during the Fourth Five Year Plan had been able to evolve an agricultural strategy. During the Fourth Plan training for agricultural and veterinary graduates had been provided at a very high level. It will thus be seen that the programme of rural education including agricultural education had been followed on planned lines India. In this volume the work done during the four plans has been reviewed.

Training and research are discussed in the including sections of the chapter; but most of the problems dealt with earlier, whether it be the supply of better seed and fertilisers, the protection of crops from pests, the improvement of agricultural implements, or the devising of better methods for conserving the moisture of the soil, depend for their solution on the successful application of scientific knowledge to the every day operations of the ordinary cultivator.

A timely and adequate supply of water is absolutely essential for securing the maximum output from the land. In India nearly four-fifths of the cultivated area is dependent on rainfall which is seldom adequate and timely throughout the whole country. Annual failure of crops in different regions of India is, therefore, a common feature of Indian Agriculture. the most effective way of increasing crop production in India is to provide through irrigation an additional source of water supply to cultivated land.

Irrigation is usually classified under two heads, major and mincr. The area under major and minor irrigation works is 20.6 million and 26.4 million acres respectively. Another classification is based on the agency providing irrigation i.e. whether private or Government. While most of the canals are government owned, wells and tanks etc, are largely owned by private parties. The area under private and canal irrigation has varied as follows during the last 25 years in two of the principal States for which comparable figures are available: It will be seen there has been practically on increase in private irrigation while the area under canal irrigation has increased by 83.71 and 11.6 per cent in U.P. and Madras respectively.

The fact that during the last 25 years the area under private irrigation has remained more or less unchanged, indicates that future scope for individual investment in irrigation works is small; and this is likely to be still further diminished by reduction in the present size of holdings consequent on land reform legislation. Such works will in future have to be increasingly undertaken on a community basis with or without State assistance. We endorse, however, recommendation of G.M.F. Enquiry Committee that separate funds should be allotted for sinking of wells by small landholders. Small and medium irrigation works have an important part to play in developing irrigation in the country.

They have many obvious advantages. They provide a large amount of dispersed employment. They involve smaller outlay and can be executed in a comparatively period. Being spread over the country, they confer widespread benefit, and it is, therefore, easier to mobilise public cooperation in their construction. In view of these advantages and their contribution to increase production, a special provision of Rs. 30 crores has been made in the Plan for minor irrigation schemes. We recommend that every State should carry out a systematic survey of the possibilities of undertaking such schemes, and formulate a programme of execution in an order of priority, so that their construction can be effected in a planned manner. An administrative arrangement under which a trained crops is available to execute such projects on condition that certain contributions in labour and cash are provided by the local people would stimulate local competition for their execution such an arrangement is being adopted for the Community Projects and should be extended as and when the State can put in the field a suitable organisation for the purpose. The question of maintaining these works in a proper state of repair has assumed importance, because the traditional systems in vogue have fallen into disuse. While legislation has been passed for the abolition of Zamindari, alternatives arrangements have not been made for the repair of tanks which were under the zamindars' management.

Frequently the beneficiaries of these works do not pay any water rate or other dues, and repairs are postponed, as responsibility for recovery of their cost cannot be fixed. In view of the large area irrigated by these works and the capital invested in them, we consider that the responsibility for their maintenance and repair should be unambiguously fixed and that the beneficiaries should be required to pay water rate in proportion to the advantage derived by them.

The management of these works should vest in the irrigation department which should be made responsible for their annual maintenance and repair and should utilise village panchayats or cooperatives where they exist, as an agencies for carrying out these repairs. Since so much of the cultivated area depends entirely on rainfall, problems of dry farming should receive much more attention than they do at present. By preventing field run off and surface evaporation the moisture of the soil can be conserved and crops successfully raised under dry conditions. Research on this important matter has been conducted at Sholapur and Bijapur in Bombay, and at Rohtak in the Punjab.

The experiments indicate that fair crop yields can be assured in a bad year and increased yield obtained in a normal year by following improved methods which include construction of bunds and embankments, production of soil much, proper weeding and hoeing and the use of drought resistant varieties of seed. There is scope for wider adoption of these practices by the cultivators. The difficulties experienced therein have to be studied by the extension staff and their solution found with the help of research. The Meteorological Department has five Regional Forecasting Centres in India which issue weather bulletin daily for farmers.

The bulletin is ready by noon, but it is broadcast by the All-India Radio in the Villagers' Programmes in the evening, so that the villagers can listen to it. The Director of Agricultural Meteorology receives check reports from government farms comparing the forecasts with the weather actually experienced. A periodical assessment of these returns shows that the forecasts have a very high degree of accuracy. No steps have yet been taken to ascertain how these forecasts can be used to secure better timing of agriculture operations. The Agricultural Experimental Stations which verify the forecasts could be utilised for this purpose. This will involve some of them equipped with radio sets to enable them to take full advantage of forecasts. It is necessary that this should be done as it has yet to be established that the knowledge provided by weather forecasts can be utilised for the better timing of agricultural operations and so for obtaining increased production. It is only after this is established that the forecasts can bypassed on to the cultivators and they can be advised to use them to guide their agricultural operations. Simultaneously with this, each State might select and area where communications can be so arranged that it is possible for the weather forecast to reach the cultivator the same day that it is issued. Observations could then be made how this knowledge helps the farmer in timing his agricultural operations. Many States have community radio sets in blocks of villages and we suggest that a beginning should be made in any such area where this can be organised.

One of the most outstanding achievements of modern agriculture is the production of improved varieties of seed for different crops. The cultivator is generally well aware of the importance of using good seed. Good cultivators are known to preserve their own seed. Certain varieties of seed have spread by themselves without special departmental efforts; and if improved seed is not making such headway as it should, the cause must be sought in some defect in the seed or elsewhere than in the apathy of the cultivators.

The mechanism for the production and distribution of pure seed is generally the same in all the States. A variety is bred and nucleus seed in produced on government farms. It is them multiplied in two or three stages with two or three classes of cultivators, usually known as A, B & C. The seed from government farms is handed forest for multiplication to 'A' class cultivators. The seed multiplied is then made over for further multiplication to 'B' class cultivators after which it is distributed. In some States, however, there is a third stage of multiplication. It is noticed that the larger the number of intermediate stages, the less the purity of the seed available for distribution. Failure to rogue properly, mixture with other remains and bad storage are some of the causes of the loss of purity and viability. The scope for securing increased production from the use of improved seed is very considerable. We are not satisfied with the progress achieved so far, and feel convinced that there is much room for improvement in the system of multiplication and distribution.

Some States have adopted legislation making the use of improved seed obligatory. In the case of crops liable to cross-fertilization, such a course is essential, but where soils differ considerably and require to b planted with different varieties of the same crop, compulsion would be possible only if pure seed of each variety is available. A strong public opinion has necessarily to be built up before legislation can be made effective. In some States the collection and distribution of pure seed was handed over to co-operative, but the results have not been altogether satisfactory. In the Punjab, where pure seed is collected along with other grains in the course of monopoly procurement, there have been complaints of seed deterioration.

We consider that the multiplication and distribution of pure seed should be decentralized as far as possible, so that nucleus seed can be made to reach every single village or a group of villages. This will need a large number of seed farms operated by or under the close supervision of the Agricultural Department. Such farms, if large enough, can also be used for every group of about 100 villages. These farms can supply pure seed to the surrounding villages, and the duty of multiplying that seed and making it available for local distribution should be case on holders for large farms. Pedigree seed, issued for cultivation in a particular area, has to be renewed every four or five to keep up its quality. This is the present experience of the Agricultural Departments, but scientific explanation for it is lacking.

There is need to obtain accurate information as to what exactly happens under the cultivator's field conditions which leads to the deterioration of sound seed. Gradually the responsibility of the Agricultural Department for the supply of pure seed will devolve on registered seed supply agencies, and this information would be useful in arranging this transfer. Experience has shown that pure seed of commercial crops, like sugarcane, groundnut, cotton, etc., spreads much faster than the seed of food crops. This may be partly due to the greater attention paid to these crops in the past, and to the work of specialised agencies created for their development.

The supply of pure seed for food crops improved somewhat in the past few years, when considerable stress was laid on their propagation as part of the G.M.F. campaign. In spite of this, the progress has not been very great. It may be that there is special difficulty in maintaining the purity of the seed of crops which are widely consumed as food. The question requires further examination. The Agricultural Departments should guard against the tendency to issue new varieties of seed for adoption by cultivators without full and complete trails conclusively establishing their superiority over those in use. In such cases, carefully docketed information on the experience of various growers of the new variety should be available. Frequent changes of seed—particularly if it is not fully tried—may shake the confidence of the cultivators and add to the difficulties of extension workers.

Attention has often been drawn to the spacing which

can be effected by a reduction in seed-rate but no systematic attempt has been made in any compact area to introduce sowing with a low seed-rate. the practice of treating the seed with a suitable fungicide before sowing requires to be introduced. The advantages of this practice are not widely known and deserve to be demonstrated. We recommend the appointment by the Indian Council of Agricultural Research of a Standing Committee of Plant Breeders and Extension Workers to review every year the technical and administrative aspects of the multiplication and spread of improved varieties of seed and to make recommendations in the light of the review.

Manures and fertilisers

Manures and fertilisers play the same part in relation to the soil as food in relation to the body. Just as a well-nourished body is capable of the maximum effort, a well nourished soil will have the best fertility. The quality of the soil varies greatly in a country of the size of India. A systematic survey of the soils of India has not yet been carried out, thought it is generally known that Indian soils are deficient in organic matter, nitrogen and phosphates. Soil samples have been analysed in different areas, but their correlation into a soil-survey for the whole country has not been undertaken.

Field experiments have been conducted in various regions to determine the response of crops to various combinations of organic and inorganic manures, but in most cases crops responses and soil analysis have not been linked up. A very little work in connection with the effects of trace-elements in the soil has been done hitherto. It is not proposed to undertake a programme, designed to correlate soils, manurial trials and crop responses over the whole country. A beginning will be made with the Community Projects areas and other selected areas in each State. A systematic study of the effect of trace elements in soils is also being made. Assistance under the T.C.A. has greatly facilitated this work. Organic matter, nitrogen, phosphorus and potash are the chief constituents which must be supplied to the soil. Nitrogen is of the first importance in crop production.

The soil has a mechanism by which it absorbs nitrogen from the atmosphere and makes it available to living beings in the form of grain and fodder; men and cattle derive energy from the consumption of these and the nitrogen taken from the soil is returned to it in the form of organic manures like farmyard manure, green manure, oilcakes, composts of various kinds, bonemeal and various types of chemical fertilizers, thus completing the nitrogen cycle.

Next in importance is phosphate. Plants absorb phosphates from the soil which are returned to it through animal and human excreta and through decayed plants and their ashes and the bones of dead animals. Indian soils, while deficient in nitrogen and phosphates, are generally rich in potash. Lack of potash does not, therefore, present a serious problem at present but it is one that should be watched.

Manures may be classified into two categories—(a) organic manures and (b) inorganic manures. Organic manures may further be sub-divided into (i) bulky organic measures; (ii) concentrated organic manures. Bulky organic manures include farmyard manure, compost manure, nightsoil and green manure, while concentrated manures are oil cakes, bonemeal, dried blood, horns and hoofs, etc.

Tropical soils often lack humus. The addition of bulky organic manures like farmyard manure, which is a by-product in farming by bullocks, helps this soil by increasing its water holding capacity, improving soil aeration, and by changing the plant nutrients through slow decomposition into form readily available to plants. There are other advantages in the use of organic manures namely (a) steadiness in yield over a period of time (b) benefit to the succeeding crops by their residual effects, and (c) ability to withstand unfavourable weather conditions.

On the basis of the 1951 livestock census the total production of fresh dung is estimated at 800 million tons; however all this valuable manure does not go back to the land. A large part of it—which may amount to nearly 50 per cent—is used a fuel by cultivators. The dung which is now burnt can be saved for agriculture if suitable supplies of fuel are made available. We have recommended in the chapter on Forests the creation of village plantations and popularising the use of coke.

The above estimate do note relate to cattle urine which is rich in nitrogen but mostly goes to waste. Conversation of cattle urine should be an item of extension work in all States and increasing attention should be paid to the conservation of this useful source of manure.

Human exerta and urine are very important sources of nitrogen, phosphorous and organic matter. Their maximum utilisation occurs in China and Japan but in those countries they are applied in a raw uncomposted form, and harmful bacteria find their way to the crop and affect the health of those who consume it. This is avoided in India, where such manure is almost invariably applied after proper composting. In urban areas, where the night oil is removed by sweepers, it is usually composted with refuse, and the manure is sold to the cultivators. Most State Governments have passed legislation making it obligatory on Municipalities and Notified Area Committees to dispose of night soil in this way, and a steady improvement in the amount of urban compost is noticeable.

Out of about 3,000 towns where Municipalities and Notified Area Committees are functioning, composting is in progress in 1684 towns only, yielding annually about 17 lakh tons of compost. Provision has been made in the Plan for extension of composting to the remaining towns. At the end of the period of the Plan about 30 lakh tons of compost would be available.

The utilisation of urine, whether human or animal, for manure is of even greater importance than the utilisation of nightsoil or dung, as the former provides a much larger proportion of nitrogen. We have not yet developed any sufficient and popular system or appliances for utilising urine as manure. Its collection is easier in towns with underground sewage which have a scheme of sewage-utilisation. In other towns only the nightsoil is collected by municipal authorities. Urine collection is not practicable, unless community urinals have proper appliances for soaking and utilising the urine, and a suitable urinal is devised for family use where the urine can be collected and absorbed.

Preliminary work has been done on this subject at the Indian Agricultural Research Institute and the 'Agri-San' urinal is being evolved. In the Punjab, the 'utility' urinal is being recommended for collection and utilisation of urine. The installation of these urinals would help to conserve urine in areas without underground drainage. In order to introduce these urinals into the daily life of the people a beginning should be made with institutions like jails, hospitals, schools, boarding houses, cinema house and other public places. In the rural areas the nightsoil and urine are not generally being utilised as manure. Here it is necessary to distinguish between a mere return of urine or nightsoil to the soil and its utilisation as manure. When a field is utilised for defection, as frequently happens in a village, there is a return to the soil but the manurial value of it is small as most of the valuable constituents are lost by exposure to the air and sun. It is necessary to devise a suitable latrine, which villagers can use and which will be sanitary, convenient, and fly-proof and can be shifted.

The trench-type holds the field at present. It may be mentioned that the cost of construction and maintenance of these latrines with local materials, can be covered by the sale of the manure that will be made available. Public urinals should also be located at suitable places in the village area.

It has been recently found that cattle and human wastes yield fuel gas by appropriate termination without much loss of organic matter and of nitrogen compared to the ordinary composting process. If this process, which has successfully passed through laboratory and pilot plant stages, is developed, it will check the burning of dung as fuel and thus augment materially the supplies of organic manures.

The growing of leguminous corps and burying them under the soil is a well known method of soil building. The nodule bacteria fix the atmospheric nitrogen in the soil in a form readily available to plants and the turning under of the crop adds organic matter which is essential for keeping the soil in god heart. The value of green manuring has been recognised but it has not become a common practice even in the area where adequate rainfall or ample irrigation facilities are available.

The pressure of population in such areas is generally so great that the cultivator cannot afford to bury a crop which does not directly bring him any return. On the other hand, larger land holders have been observed to practice green manuring on a reasonable scale. In the case of small cultivators, the introduction of leguminous catch crops, especially pulses, in the ordinary rotations preferably with phosphate manuring would do much to help increase the nitrogen contents of the soil. They will not only add to the food reserve of the country but would also be valuable as a rich source of proteins.

They are important also from the point of view of animal nutrition to which they contribute indirectly in the form of hulls and straw. Where conditions are favourable the State should take steps to encourage growing of such crops by providing necessary facilities and inducements such as supply of seed and irrigation at the time of sowing, and by offering concessions such as remission of water rate or land revenue.

The principal oilcakes available in the country are ground nut, sesamum, rape, linseed, cotton seed, castor, *mahua* and *neem*. They contain about 3 to 6 per cent nitrogen and 1 to 2 per cent phosphoric acid. Used as manure, they serve as carriers of available nitrogen and have shown consistently good results on a variety of crops. Most of the edible oilcakes are valued as cattle-feed, but lately some of them particularly ground-nut, are also being extensively used as manure. We consider this practice undesirable especially as there is a shortage of cattle-feed in the country. Non-edible oilcakes alone should be used directly as manure. Better results are obtained if chemical fertilizers are used in combination with these oilcakes.

Blood meals, horns, hoofs, and meat meal are the byproducts of the slaughter houses which can be used for fertilizing the soil. Fresh blood in its natural state contains 2.5 to 5 per cent of nitrogen while in the dried form it contains from 8 to 14 per cent of nitrogen depending largely upon the method of manufacture. Dried blood in the form of cakes grinds easily and can be used alone or mixed with other manures. It is estimated that about 10,000 tons of dried blood could be produced from the slaughter houses in the country.

Other material available from the slaughter houses consists of pieces of skin and rejected meat etc., which, mixed together, are general known under the trade name of 'tankage'. Tankage varies greatly in its chemical composition depending upon the various constituents forming it. It may contain from 3 to 10 per cent of nitrogen and from 7 to 20 per cent of phosphoric acid. These products can be a source of income to the Municipalities, if proper methods of conserving blood and tankage are adopted. The material prepared will soon find a market as a good fertilizer for fruits and vegetables.

The hoofs and horns of dead animals are collected in this country alone with the bones. At the assembling centres they fetch higher prices than the raw bones and are, therefore, crushed separately. A considerable quantity is at present exported. The horn meal contains about 15 per cent nitrogen and can be utilised as a fertilizer with advantage.

Benemeal is a good form of phosphatic manure which contains organic matter and some nitrogen also. It is suitable as a manure for all types of soils, more particularly acidic soils, where superphosphates cannot be used. Apart from its phosphatic value, bonemeal helps to increase the phosphorus content of grain and thus enhances its nutritive value. Sterilise bonemeal is also a valuable cattle feed, and its used in this form has great scope. The average annual collection of bones amounts to about 1,50,000 tons. This is only one-fourth of the estimated quantity available judging from the number of cattle that die in a year. It is possible to crush bones completely as bone-meal, but crushing factories, interested in the more lucrative export trade of grist, do not produce the maximum amount of bonemeal.

The demand for bonemeal has also to be built up. At present 25 per cent of the bones is converted into bonemeal and the remaining 75 per cent is exported as grist for which there is a considerable demand in foreign countries as it is a source of glue and gelatine. The export of bonemeal is prohibited and the whole of it is used internally as manure. The high price fetched by the export of grist enables the crushers to make bonemeal available at comparatively low prices.

The export of bones from India has been going on for a long time. The earliest record is for the year 1884-85, when 18,000 tons were exported. Since then exports have steadily increased between 1884 and 1951, a total of about 4 million tons of bones have been exported. This export has been. criticised on the ground that it deprives the Indian soil of a valuable manurial constituent which should return to it. Indian soils are known to be deficient in phosphates. While girls, which could be converted into bonemeal, is exported, the phosphatic deficiency is sought to be met by importing rock phosphate and converting it into superphosphates. Grist certainly does fetch high prices and there is some saving to the country in the export of grist and its substitution by superphosphates as a source of phosphatic fertilisers. On the other hand, the supply of organic matter and nitrogen is a feature of bonemeal which is not present in superphosphates. In order that the export of bones should cease, steps must be taken to manufacture by-products, like glue and gelatine, in India, Increased crushing capacity should also be provided, particularly in areas far away from railheads, so as to stimulate better collection of bones.

Our attention has been drawn to a bone digester which has been lately imported from Japan. Bones are streamed under pressure, and facts and glue are extracted; thereafter the bones become so brittle that they can be crushed in any pounding machine. The bonemeal thus obtained can be used as manure, as well as cattle-feed. The collection of bones will increase only if crushing units or plants like the bones digester are located in areas where collection is not paying because of the long distances from railheads. If any State considers it necessary to impose a provincial ban to enable it to increase the crushing capacity in the rural areas, such a request from it should be favourably considered by the Centre.

Coming now to inorganic or synthetic fertilisers, the most important nitrogenous ones are ammonium sulphate, ammonium nitrate, calcium nitrate, ammonium phosphate and urea. The important phosphatic fertilizers are superphosphate, rock phosphate, and ammonium phosphate. In the past 50 years several types of nitrogenous and phosphatic fertilisers were introduced into this country and experimented with at the different experimental stations. Of these, ammonium sulphate and superphosphate are most in use today, and these are at present being manufactured in the country. Ammonium sulphate requires for its manufacture gypsum which has to be transported over long distances.

Superphosphate is manufactured mostly from imported rock phosphate and sulphur or sulphuric acid. In the Indian Union there are no rich deposits of sulphur and the supply position of sulphur in the world is difficult. It is, therefore, desirable that the possibilities of manufacturing ammonium phosphate, which supplies both nitrogen and phosphorus to the soil should be investigated. Deposits of rock phosphate are reported to exist in India and the fertilising value of anmonium phosphate has already been established by field experiments in different parts of the country.

There has been some criticism of the introduction of chemical fertilisers without full steps being taken to mobilise all the manurial resources of the organic type. This criticism, in so far as it stresses the necessity of mobilising these resources, is just, but the process is bound to take some time as it necessitates the disturbance of age-old habits. We do not consider that it is necessary to wait for such full mobilisation before introducing chemical fertilisers.

The two processes should and can go on simultaneously. Both these types of manure are necessary for maintaining and increasing soil fertility. It is well known that a continuous application of chemical fertilisers only, without the support of any bulky organic manure, leads in course of years to soil deterioration and progressively lower yields. It has, therefore, been a practice to recommend the use of chemical fertilisers more particularly ammonium sulphate in conjunction with bulky organic manures.

Phosphate is best applied to leguminous corps for this not only helps the growth of that crop but also thereby augments the quantity of nitrogen added to the soil which increases with the yield of the leguminous crop. This is, therefore, a useful method of supplying the soil with the nitrogen and phosphorous so much needed for cereal crops.

The fact that fertilisers are in demand today shows that their use is profitable to the cultivators. But their high prices in recent years have resulted in larger quantities being utilised for commerical crops in preference to food crops. Unless, therefore, the prices of fertilisers are substantially reduced so as to be within the reach of the grower of foodgrains, any expansion of the use of fertilisers for food crops will be difficult.

The problems relating to the conservation, production, distribution and utilisation of manures and fertilisers are sufficiently large and important to warrant their being kept under review by a competent body of experts. We recommend the appointment of a Committee of the ICAR charged with the following functions:

(a) to review annually and to obtain accurate information on the potential supply of manurial resources and the quantities actually developed and utilised;

(b) to estimate the country's manurial and fertiliser requirements, the potentialities for production in different parts of the country and the optimum conditions for their utilisation;

(c) to estimate the response obtained by the use of fertilisers and their economic cost t the cultivators; and

(d) to report on the development of the utilisation of manures, human and cattle wastes, green manures and fuel gas.

Agricultural implements and machinery

Though State and Central Governments have paid considerable attention during the last 20 years to agricultural research, comparatively little has been done to improve indigenous implements. The Governments of Madras, U.P., and the Punjab have achieved something in this direction and so have educational institutions and manufacturers, but no definite schemes were drawn up nor was the work systematically followed up until the Agricultural Engineering Section was added to the Indian Agricultural Research Institute in 1945.

Agricultural implements may be classified broadly into the following categories: implements (a) for preparing the seed bed; (b) for cultivation operations; (c) for harvesting and threshing work; (d) for processing and utilisation of agricultural produce; and (e) for lifting water. Attention has been hitherto devoted mostly to improvement of the implements used for processing the produce and lifting water. Improved sugarcane crushers, the Persian Wheel, and the Revolving Drum illustrate this tendency. There exists considerable scope for improving the efficiency of implements used for seed bed preparation, planting cultivation and harvesting operations.

While Dr. Stewart considered that as long as the land is kept free from weeds it makes little difference to crop yields whether 'desi' implements or improved implements are used, it is generally accepted that by using improved implements a larger area can be covered in the same time, and the timely performance of agricultural operations results in reduction of costs as well as better yields. For certain agricultural operations. *e.g.* turning under of green manure improved implements are essential.

The need for encouraging research in this field is thus obvious. For this purpose we recommend that every State should have in its agricultural engineering section a whole-time officer for conducting research on indigenous tools and implements. Many of the existing agricultural engineering sections deal mainly with power drawn machinery, and a special officer is required to devote exclusive attention to the important subject of indigenous implements. The engineering section at the Indian Agricultural Research Institute will have to be similarly strengthened with a special officer.

The section so established in the States and Centre should have adequate facilities for research and trails. Besides conducting research on indigenous implements the special officer at the Centre will try out imported implements. He will also co-ordinate the work done in various parts of the country and pass on the information regarding improved implements to executive agencies. It will be his responsibility to furnish the results of research to manufacture for commercial development.

As implements have to be adjusted to crop, soil and climatic conditions, the research problems have to be examined on a regional basis, i.e. for a group of States. Regional Committees consisting of technical experts, enlightened farmers, representatives of the States Governments, manufacturers and dealers should therefore be set up by the I.C.A.R. The Committees should indicate the lines on which research and development work should proceed. They would also approve the schemes drawn up by the State and review their progress regularly. The special implements officers at the Indian Agricultural Research Institute should act as a convener of the regional committees.

The Indian Council of Agricultural Research might also convene an annual conference on implements and machinery to which nominees of the regional committees, prominent research workers, and manufacturers should be invited. The programmes of research drawn up by the State and accepted by the regional committees should be accorded a high priority by the Council which should provide necessary financial assistance. It should also offer technical advice and follow a policy of sponsoring research on implements in all the important State. Along with research, the difficult task of popularising improved implements and arranging their supply has to be tackled. This would also be the responsibility of the special officer to be appointed in every State. He will have to do this work with the assistance of the extension staff. As research gets organised in the States and at the Centre, new designs will be evolved.

These designs and models will be supplied to the fabricators for manufacturing the implements on a commerical scale. It may be desirable to encourage the establishment of small fabricating until which will provide employment to rural artisans. These could be further developed into workshop where the manufacture of steel trunks, buckets and other utilities could also be undertaken. It would be advantageous to organise local fabricators and blacksmith into cooperatives for undertaking production of implements. The implements manufactured should be recommended to cultivators only after careful trial and test by the implements officer of the

State, who should be provided with the necessary equipment for carrying out tests. As regards arrangements for distribution the implements can be supplied direct by the dealer or from the government depots or through the cooperative societies. Taccavi loans or loan from cooperative societies may be provided to popularise new implements if their cost is high.

The facilities for the servicing and repair of implements and tools are not very satisfactory. The technique of the local blacksmiths and carpenters needs to be improved by organising a short training course at important centres. Cooperatives of fabricators besides undertaking production should also provide servicing and repair facilities at reasonable rates. In addition the machine tractor stations and workshops which are being established by the Central and the State Governments should also have a section for undertaking repairs of indigenous implements. Spare parts needed for implements should also be stocked by the machine tractor stations and the cooperatives.

During and since the second world war cultivators have begun to use power driven machinery to a greater extent than before. Increased financial assistance under the G.M.F. campaign for the purchase of tractors, diesel engineers, electronic motors, has accelerated the process. The rising cost of labour as its scarcity in certain area are other factors which have tended in the same direction. The rapid increase in the use of tractors in this country may be judged from the judge from the following table:

The use of tractors has distinct advantages in certain operations such as:

(a) reclamation of waste or weed infested lands;

(b) cultivation of lands in sparsely populated areas where there is a shorter labour;

(c) drainage and soil conservation operations such as contour bunding, terracing ridging, etc. The utility of tractors for reclamation operations has been demonstrated by the Central Tractor Organisation which has been working in terai areas of U.P. and the kans infested tract of Madhya Pradesh, Madhya Bharat, and Bhopal. The States have also acquired some experience of this work during the last five years. The precise extent to which waste and fallow lands can be brought under the plough can be ascertained only after a detailed survey, but it is believed that out of 98 million acres classified as cultivable, yet lying waste about 11 million acres can be reclaimed in the near future. The Plan provides for reclamation of 2.62 million ares. While the pressure of population is generally heavy in the country as a whole there are thinly settled areas, particularly in Vindhya Pradesh, Madhya Bharat, Rajasthan, etc. where labour shortage is an important limiting factor in the expansion of cultivation. Reclamation by tractors and mechanised cultivation in such tracts has obvious advantages. Large areas can thus be developed either as State farms or for settlement of landless labourers on a co-operative basis.

While tractors can safely be utilised for the above purposes, care will have to be taken to see that their use for general cultivation work in other areas does not cause unemployment. The small size of holdings, the absence of avenues of employment other than agriculture, the shortage of fuel-oils and iron and steel are factors which militate against the use of tractors in this country for cultivation on any substantial scale and, by and large, Indian agriculture will continue to depend upon animal power for a long time to come.

Even though tractors reduce labour costs and facilitate agricultural operations there is no conclusive evidence that they increase production, though they are a valuable aid when speed of operations is a relevant factor. It is reported that some of the bigger cultivators have acquired tractors recently because of a feeling that those who adopt the mechanical means of cultivation will be accorded special treatment and allowed to retain larger holdings for personal cultivation in case a ceiling is imposed on existing holdings. This has led to displacement of tenants. This trend is likely to be maintained and may even increase unless protected tenancy rights are conferred on those who occupy the land as tenants-as-will and as sub-tenants. Some of the States have initiated action on these lines.

During the year 1951-52 tractors worth about Rs. 6 crores were imported into the country. Imports are likely to continue in future at this level and the total value of imported tractors during the Plan period may be around Rs. 30 crores. The imports include machines of numerous makes and designs from various countries. It is understood that about ten to fifteen per cent of the tractors remain out of use as many of them are not suitable for Indian conditions. Import and sale of machines whose utility has not been fully established, not only causes loss to the cultivators but also retards the pace of technological progress as the unfavourable experience of a few farmers discourages many others from making purchases. To avoid the wastage and losses that thus take place it is essential that imports of undesirable types of machines should be reduced to the minimum. For this purpose it is necessary that every make of tractor received should be tested in regard to its utility under Indian conditions.

The test may be carried out at a testing station to be established by the Government of India and imports regulated on the basis of the findings of the test. It should be possible to set up such a station at a cost of Rs. 2 to 2 1/2 lakhs in addition to the recurring expenditure which may be in the neighborhood of about Rs. 75,000. In this connection it would be an advantage to study the organisation of similar institutions which are operating in U.S.A. and U.K. The cultivators also experience difficult in obtaining spare parts and the arrangements for servicing and repairs are not always satisfactory.

The Government have been trying to remove these difficulties but there is considerable scope for improvement. The Government should see that adequate facilities for supply of spares and repairs are provided either by the dealers or at the State workshop as this would reduce breakdowns, avoid dislocation and lead to better utilisation of the equipment. Though some data are available regarding the cost of reclamation by tractors, comparative and thorough study of the economics of mechanised and bullock-power cultivation has yet to be made. The I.C.A.R. might undertake such a study for various regions and crops.

Besides tractors, other power driven machines, electric motors, diesel engines, etc. are becoming increasingly popular in rural areas as water lifting appliances. The power available from these engines can also be used for other agricultural operations such as cane and oilseed crushing, grading, etc. It is estimated that about 60 thousand diesel engines are required annually for agricultural purposes. To encourage their use many of the State Governments are providing assistance in the form of loans which the farmers can repay over a period of years. The testing station suggested in paragraph 51 above should also carry out tests on diesel engines and pumping sets, etc. so that the cultivators may be able to ascertain the makes which are inefficient of undesirable.

Plant protection, quarantine and storage

No systematic quantitative studies have been conducted so far to determine the losses caused by insect pests and plant diseases in Indian. The International Conference, organised by the Food and Agriculture Organization in London in 1947, considered that in tropical and sub-tropical countries, where climatic conditions are conductive to a rapid multiplication of pests, the losses in storage alone might be estimated at about 10 per cent. The losses in the field, particularly in the case of epidemics, can be very severe.

The Plant Protection Organisation at the Centre consists of a Directorate, with the Plant Protection Adviser as its head, and three main divisions, (i) Entomology, (ii) Plant Diseases, and (iii) Quarantine. There is a Storage Entomologist and a Quarantine Entomologist and other staff to help the Adviser. The directorate advises on the control of various diseases and pests and helps them in setting up Plant Protection Organisations in their areas. The locust control work is also its responsibility.

The primary function of the Plant Protection Organisations at the Centre and in the States is to fight outbreaks in epidemic form, and they should be sufficiently equipped for this purpose. At the time of an epidemic, the extension and the plant protection staff together with the equipment and insecticides have to be moved to the affected place at short notice.

A secondary function of the organisations in the States is the investigation of plant diseases and pests and the prescription of measures for their destruction. Research and investigation must be directed towards evolving remedies and methods which can be adapted to the local practices of the cultivators and which will utilise local materials. Imported insecticides and pesticides should be recommended only after trials when local materials and methods have failed to achieve results.

The pests and diseases which occur during the various stages of growth of a plant are well known, and so are the methods of fighting them. In the cause of disease, preventive measures have to be taken, generally at the sowing stage. Both these measure assume a routine character and can be taken by the ordinary field staff with some previous training. No separate organisation for this work at the village level is necessary. Technical staff is, however, required to locate the focus of an onset, to devise special measures in the case of epidemics and to train the field staff. It is necessary to state these considerations as we notice considerable variation in the strength of the plant protection staff in different States.

The pests and diseases which occur during the various stages of growth of a plant are well known and so are the methods of fighting them. In the cause of diseases, preventive measures have to be taken, generally at the sowing stage. Both these measures assume a routine character and can be taken by the ordinary field staff with some previous training. No separate organisation for this work at the village level is necessary. Technical staff is, however, required to locate the focus of an onset, to devise special measures in the case of epidemics and to train the field staff. It is necessary to state these considerations as we notice considerable variation in the strength of the plant protection staff in different States.

It may be an advantage for each State to study over a period of years all outbreaks which have assumed an epidemic form and to trace the factors favourable for their growth and subsidence. If the results are shown on maps it would facilitate the location of centres of attack, the siting of plant-protection equipment and the determination of the strength of staff required. It may also help in forecasting epidemics.

The methods of control adopted for preventing damage to crops by insects and pests may be classified under four categories:

(1) Quarantine,

(2) Biological Control,

(3) Cultural methods, and

(4) Chemical treatment.

Quarantine is the prevention of entry of plant and animal pests and diseases from countries outside India. In the past, owing to lack of efficient quarantine arrangements, injurious insects entered the country and established themselves as pests. The requirements for efficient quarantine operations are that the plant material coming into this country should be fumigated. A fumigatorium with modern equipment was established at the port of Bombay a few months ago. The plan provides for setting up quarantine and fumigating stations at Madras and

Calcutta. Land frontiers and air ports have also to be guarded against both plant and animal pests and diseases. Biological control involves employment of an insect to check the development of another insect pest or wood. A well known example of such control is the use of the cohineal insect for the eradication of prickly pear.

A considerable amount of work has been done in the country during the past twenty years on the science and practice of biological control and methods have been in operation against sugarcane borers and nephanthes of coconut in the South. There are facilities for biological control work at the Indian Agricultural Research Institute.

Variation in cultural practice is another useful method of control. Introduction of resistant varieties of crops, changes in rotation, time of sowing or planting, deep and shallow cultivation, giving, or withholding of irrigation, are the usual methods tried. The system of control has the advantage that the results are obtained without any additional cost and do not depend on equipment which may not always be locally available. Change in the time of sowing wheat was a major factor in Hessian fly control, and a similar method has dealt effectively with the *Tirak* disease in cotton.

The limitations of this method are, that a variation of cultural practice which prevents the onset of the disease or pest has also an adverse effect on crop yields, and the cultivator prefers the former risk. Sufficient stress has not been laid on these methods and there is a tendency to try out insecticides without fully investigating the possibilities of variation in cultural practices or other methods based on resources available to the cultivator. During recent years the use of insecticides particularly D.D.T. B.H.C., and other similar chemicals has increased considerably and manufacture of D.D.T. and B.H.C., which are at present imported, has been visualised in the Plan. These chemicals are superior to those previously used because they act both as contact and stomach poisons.

A ideal insecticide, however, in one which kills the harmful insect pests without creating any hazards to the consumer—human beings and cattle of the plants to which it is applied. It should also not upset in the long run the biological balance in nature by destroying other beneficent forms of plant and insect life. More experience regarding the use of these insecticides and experimental evidence of their effect on human beings and cattle, who consume the straw and grain of the treated plant is required before their extended use can be recommended. There is a difference of opinion regarding their after-effects even in the most advanced countries.

Organised guidance regarding the use of pesticides is also necessary in this country as at present different firms market a variety of brands without authorised tests of the claims made for their products. It should be the function of the Plant Protection Organisations to conduct experiments with the different brands on sale in the market and advise the extension agencies, etc. on the best material available.

As regards the manufacture of insecticides and fungicides, the possibilities of utilising indigenous material for this purpose should be more thoroughly explored. For example, pyrethrum has active ingredients of high toxity to many common insects. Blank mustard oil also has been claimed to have fungicidal value. The scope in this regard has to be examined as systematic cultivation of such crops would raise the income of the farmers. It is difficult to calculate the loss due to pernicious weeds in terms of money, but in the case of severe infestation, the yield is considerably reduced. Weeds, such as *pohli* and *kandiari* in wheat, cause harvesting difficulties. Some tenacious weeds such as *baru* and *kans* get such a firm hold on the soil that the land goes out of cultivation.

In the case of annual and biennial eradication of weeds, the treatment usually is their removal before seed formation, while perennial weeds are eradicated by deep ploughing and exposure of their stems and roots to the severity of the climate. In the United States weeds are being controlled on a large scale by the use of flame throwers and selective herbicides. A research scheme has been sanctioned by the ICAR for the investigation of the control of weeds by means of selective herbicides. While research is in progress for securing definite information on weedicides, control of weeds by mechanical and cultural methods should be encouraged.

During the present century there have been five locust cycles during which Rajasthan, Punjab, Pepsu, Saurashtra, Kutch, and parts of Bombay State have witnessed large scale invasions which often resulted in considerable damage. The permanent homes of locusts lie in extensive belts of Africa and countries of the Middle East. Locusts not only attach agricultural crops, but also forests and in fact any green vegetation available. The Government of India have maintained a Central Locust Organisation to fight this menace. This organisation is responsible for control operations in desert areas, while the States are in charge of the work in their cultivated areas. A fresh locust cycle which started in the year 1940-50 is still in progress and the Government have adopted necessary control measure which include spraying and dusting of chemicals on a large scale in the breeding areas. The attacks on crops in cultivated areas are met by mechanical and chemical methods such as the destruction of eggs by exposure after ploughing, burying them in trenches, etc. To intensify the campaign aid in form of aeroplanes, helicopters and other equipment is being obtained under the Technical Assistance Programme.

The crops have also to be protected from stray cattle let loose either through carelessness or willfully by unsocial elements. Such cattle when caught are impounded in cattle pounds. The charges levied for their release are often so small that they do not act as a deterrent. To reduce this nuisance it is necessary that heavier penalties be imposed and exemplary punishment awarded to habitual offenders. The Cattle Tress Pass Act should be amended to secure this. Damage by wild animals to crops and cattle is another menace in certain areas. Organised action against them is necessary as individual action only shifts the burden on to other cultivators. Destruction through gun-clubs, trench pits and similar methods is the only solution.

Losses in storage are also quite high. At the village level most of the surplus produce is marketed by the farmer soon after the harvest. Village storage is not, therefore, a major problem and the traditional system of storage is fairly satisfactory. It requires, however, to be further studied.

Losses are greater in the godowns and storage space in the assembling markets as they are continuously occupied and are generally maintained in a poor condition. In their case preventive measure against stored gram pests such as fumigation, super-heating and use of insecticides should be adopted on a wider scale. With the introduction of controls and government imports, steps were taken by the States to construct and lease storage accommodation. It is understood that the Central and State Governments have at present a storage capacity of about 51 lakh tons of which nearly 15 lakh tons are Government owned.

The Directorate of Storage and Inspection are responsible for the disinfection and fumigation of the Central Government stocks, and also supervise the work in the case of the State civil supplies departments. The Civil Supply godowns are generally located at importance railheads and *mandis* where the trade also has its facilities. It would be an advantage if the Civil Supplies staff also actively assist in the periodical inspection and disinfecting of the godowns.

Agricultural education and training

The ability of the extension service to appreciate the difficulties of the farmers and to render effective assistance in resolving them are factors which will largely contribute to the success of the agricultural programme. The extension staff, particularly at the village and tehsil level, has to be properly trained and equipped for this work. Provision of adequate teaching and training facilities for this staff is an important aspect of agricultural education. Another equally important but broader aspect is the education of the cultivators, so that they may practice scientific agriculture.

The main defect of the extension work carried on hitherto has been its relatively great reliance on propaganda rather than on actual demonstration to the cultivator under his field conditions. This is largely due to insufficient stress being laid in agricultural institutions on practical work and on the correlation of practice with theory. The complaint that students from agricultural institutions prefer jobs to private agriculture largely arises from this drawback.

A trainee must be moulded physically and mentally into the practice of the 'dirty hands' method, before he can be expected to demonstrate it successfully in the field, or practice it himself in his own cultivation. We commend the Manjri pattern of two year schools in the Bombay State as the best for ensuring that this background is sufficiently emphasised. These are boarding schools, and every items of work on the farm where the school is located has to be done by the students; servants are allowed on the farm only during the vacation period.

The schools have the additional advantage of being less costly and of enabling the student to supplement his income, during the school period. They supply village-level workers, and also offer agricultural training to sons of cultivators. Their drawback is that a student passing out from such a school is not able to prosecute his studies further in an agricultural college. This handicap should be removed, by extending the course by one year for those who want to prosecute their studies further. This may necessitate a special admission examination for them by the agricultural college.

All village-level workers are trained either at agricultural schools, or in special training centres. The total number of schools in the country is 38, and ten more will be started during the Plan period. The training period in the schools generally extends from two to three years. We recommend that all existing schools should be converted into the Bombay type of school as early as possible. As the full requirements of the village-level staff cannot be met by the existing schools, and a large number of village level workers are immediately required for manning the

Community Projects 30 special centres have been organised through the help of the Ford Foundation.

The training period at these centres is only six months, as ordinarily the trainees have a previous training in an agricultural school or a knowledge of practical agriculture. There are 22 agricultural colleges turning out annually about 1000 graduates, a large proportion of whom are employed by the Agricultural Departments for extension, research and educational work. These colleges, even in a greater measure than the schools, suffer from the same complaint of insufficient stress on practical work. Recognizing this drawback the Indian Council of Agricultural Education, recently set up by the Indian Council of Agricultural Research, has suggested that the course should include supervised intensive practical training under rural conditions for a period of two months every year.

Another drawback of college education is the absence of facilities for specialization in extension and farm management. Post-graduate education in research only is available. The result is that the responsibility for extension work or management of farms on a person, who has only received a general education in agriculture. A person would be better qualified for service either in the extension or farm management branch, or in the research and teaching branch after he has intensively studied these subjects. If the agricultural college course after graduation is considered too long for these qualifications, facilities should be provided for a bias in the field of special interest in the final year. Short practical courses for farmers of a general nature in different fields of agriculture, such as compost making, resowing treatment of seed, crop protection, cattle feeding, etc., have proved to be of great value. They can be held on each Demonstration Farm at suitable intervals.

Agricultural research

Prior to the constitution of the I.C.A.R. in 1930, agricultural research was carried out in the Indian Agricultural Research Institute at Pusa and in the Research Institute attached to the Departments of Agriculture in the various States. The Royal Commission on Agriculture found that 'there was lack of sufficiently close touch not only between Pusa and the Provincial Departments but also among the provincial departments themselves'. The Indian Council of Agricultural Research was, therefore, constituted in 1930, with the object of promoting, guiding and coordinating agricultural research in India.

In the course of research work a vast amount of valuable information has been obtained and striking results have been achieved particularly in the field of plant breeding, utilisation of manures and fertilizers and plants protection. The use of improved varieties of seed, pre-sowing treatment of seed, preparation and utilisation of compost manures, utilisation of fertilisers, etc., are some of the results of research which have come to form a part of an enlightened cultivator's agricultural practice. But the lack of a properly trained extension service has retarded this process. The recommendation of the G.M.F. Enquiry Committee is that such a service should be available throughout the country within a period of ten years, and a beginning is being made in connection with the Community Projects. An extension service helps to connect the research centre with the farmer in the field—his problems being brought to the research centre and new discoveries being carried to him.

The absence of such a service has had its effect on research work also, in that the demands on research workers were not sufficiently insistent or pressing and tended to be unrelated to the practical needs of the cultivator. Now that the foundation of an extension service for Indian is being laid, it is of the utmost importance that for each soil climate and region a compendium should be prepared,for the use of the extension service, of the various research practices which have been sufficiently proved for immediate adoption by the cultivators of the region, and of those which require further proof by trials in the cultivators' fields.

The I.C.A.R. should actively help the States in the preparation of these compendiums by a financial grant, if necessary. It may be necessary to appoint a special officer in each State for this purpose who will work under the guidance of the Agricultural Commissioner. Agricultural research is of a continuing nature. New knowledge has to gained, and fresh problems tackled. With this object Dr. Stewart had recommended the location of research and experimental stations in carefully selected centres for each crop soil-region. Unless these are established, or existing research centres converted to the attainment of these objectives, extension work may soon came to a standstill. These stations have been of great significance in the agricultural development of Japan, and we consider that the establishment of such stations should be as important concern of the J.C.A.R. and the State Governments.

The functions of the I.C.A.R. in respect of promoting, guiding and coordinating research work were masked to some extent by the growth of research by organisations over whose research programmes it had imperfect control *i.e.* the States, the Commodity Committees and the Central Research Institute. Research work in the States may be divided into two categories:

(i) schemes sponsored by the I.C.A.R. by sharing a portion of the cost, and

(ii) schemes, the cost of which is borne entirely by the States.

The latter category of schemes were never formally examined or considered by the I.C.A.R. Its annual review only related to the schemes, the cost of which it shared. The same was the case with the programmes of the Commodity Committees which were only sent to the I.C.A.R. for information. The Central Research Institutes also drew up their own programmes and the I.C.A.R. had no voice either in their framing or their modification. The I.C.A.R was thus till lately largely confined to the research programmes the cost of which it shared with the State Government. No overall review or coordination of research under such conditions was possible.

The idea underlying the Commodity Committees, which between 1921 and 1949 were established for cotton, jute, tobacco, sugarcane, oilseeds and other commercial crop, was that quick results could be obtained if a Special Committee representing all interests concerned with the commodity, *e.g.*, growers, traders, processors, etc., was charged with the function of advancing research in that commodity. These expectations have been fulfilled, and some Committees have done good work. But this exclusive attention to the problems of one crop led inevitably to the disregard of the problems of other crops grown in the same region. This type of crop-wise compartmentalisation of research was discouraged by the Royal Commission on

Agriculture in 1929 and also later by Dr. Stewart in 1946.

His view was that the functions of Commodity committees should be confined to problems which arise after a crop is grown, *e.g.*, processing, marketing, etc. but so far as agricultural research is concerned, it must comprise all crops grown on a soil, in the interest of allround agricultural development. "We must start with the soil and consider it in relation to all the crops which it is asked to grow, rather than starting from the opposite direction involved in the widely accepted policy of sectionalisting research into a series of crop compartments."

Another drawback of the Commodity approach is that it involves earmarking of funds in respect of particular crops, and prevents a balanced allotment of finances, according to the needs of the different crops. And this has actually happened. Relatively much more work has been done on corps under Commodity Committees than on other crops like millets, wheat and rice, though their importance in the national life is equally great, if not greater.

A logical result of the acceptance of the commodity idea would be to have Commodity Committees for each important crop in India. But today they are confined only to the commerical crops, like cotton, Jute, sugarcane, oilseeds coconuts, arecanuts, tobacco and do not include important food crops, like wheat, rice, pulses, millets, potatoes, etc. At a later stage, it appeared that instead of Commodity Committees, All-India Institutes for research in respect of food crops should be started, and we have all-India Research Institutes for rice and potatoes. But, as already indicated, there is considerable doubt whether crop-wise organisation of agricultural research is the best form of organisation; and in some cases it is impossible.

This may be illustrated by the example of the crops grown in the south-west corner of India. This area grows valuable crops, like pepper, cashew nuts, cardamom, cloves, lemon-grass, etc. A single organisation for research and development of these crops would lead to expeditious and co-ordinated action. Such a regional body could well have delegated to itself the functions of the I.C.A.R. A commodity approach here is an impossibility.

The Central Research Institutes are the I.A.R.I. at Delhi, the Potato Research Institute at Patna, and the rice Research Institute at Cuttack. The I.A.R.I. caries out fundamental research but its research programme is not coordinated by the I.C.A.R. with the research programme of the rest of the country. Apart from this drawback, the I.A.R.I. provides the back ground against which applied research is carried out over the rest of the country.

The same cannot be said of the Potato and Rice Research Institutes. Ordinarily there are no fundamental problems with respect of individual crops which are unrelated to the ecological conditions in which they are grown, and which would, therefore, have an all-India application. Even special work like cross-breeding with foreign varieties can be done in Research Stations, all over the country, and Central Institutes for particular crops do no appear to have a special advantage. Their present usefulness lies in enabling research men of high standing to work in a well-equipped laboratory, a facility which a State might not be able to afford on its own.

The role of universities in promoting agricultural research is a question which needs attention. Although universities are eminently suited for such research, especially of the more fundamental type, they have not taken it up to any significant extent in the past, owing perhaps to lack of funds and other causes. It is a striking fact, for example, that there is not a single chair of genetics in any Indian university, although breeding of plants and animals, which rests on the foundation of this science, has been in progress in the country for several decades.

It is important that whatever limitations there may be in the way of the universities taking an appropriate part in agricultural research should be removed and the universities encouraged to make their contribution to research. This will benefit the universities also by bringing their scientific staffs into direct contact with real problems which are in urgent need of solution for the betterment of the vast majority of our people.

India is now embarking on a vast programme of agricultural development. It has before it the ambitious target of doubling agricultural production in the next fifteen years. An extension service, which will cover the whole country in a ten year period, has been proposed to be constituted. The pace of agricultural development largely depends on the speed with which solutions to the practical problems of the cultivators are found by research workers. The whole organisation of agricultural research in India will have to be geared to fulfil this task.

The ICAR was constituted in 1929, and its work was subsequently reviewed in 1937 by Sir John Russell and some aspects of its in 1946 by Dr. Stewart. We feel that the stage has now been reached when a high level committee should examine the whole question of the organisation of research in India, and, in particular, the changes that should be brought about in the existing Commodity Committees and Central Research Institutes and research in universities so that they can answer the increased demands for research that will be made upon them. As things stand today, the ICAR organisation has to examine a large number of schemes, and it may have to be considered whether some regional decentralisation could not be usefully introduced.

In the meantime, we suggest that the following measures should be immediately adopted to remove some of the drawbacks which affect the Commodity Committees and the organisation of the I.C.A.R.

(a) All schemes of the Commodity Committees should be subject to examination and scrutiny by the same body which examines the research schemes pertaining to other corps grown in that area. This would ordinarily be the Standing Scientific Committees of the I.C.A.R. It would be the function of this body to suggest what other schemes should be undertaken on crops grown in the same region to ensure ail-rcund agricultural development and a balanced growth of research in that area.

(b) Wherever any research station is working under any Commodity Committee, the same staff should also carry out the research in respect of other corps in the area.

(c) The I.C.A.R. should have authority to suggest to a Commodity Committee what coordinated research in respect of other crops grown in the region or rotational crops grown with the main commodity should be undertaken by it.

In order that the I.C.A.R. may be enabled to discharge its statutory duty of coordinating all agricultural research in the country, it should be in a position:

(a) to review all research work done in the country. All research programmes, whether of the Commodity Committees, State Governments, or Central Institutes, should be sent this body for scrutiny and approval. Appropriate dates could be specified for the receipt of these programmes, so that all programmes are received at a time and considered together;

(b) to undertake a detailed examination of all research programmes received. The I.C.A.R. today tries to discharge this duty through Scientific Committees, which meet for a few days just before the annual meeting of the Advisory Board and the Governing Body. Such a procedure does not permit a detailed and proper examination. We suggest that these bodies should meet more frequently, and at least twice a year, once for examining the schemes received by the I.C.A.R. and once for assessing their progress. These meetings should allow sufficient time for a proper examination of these scheme;

(c) to take an overall view of research in the country as a whole, assess the result of the past years' working and indicate the direction of future research.

The Research Board which has been recently constituted by the ICAR is expected to perform this function. It must consist of top-tanking agricultural scientists in the country on whom would fall the ultimate responsibility of guiding and coordinating research in the country;

(d) to initiate research into utilisation of agricultural products which today go to waste. Such utilisation has an important bearing on the agricultural economy and no work in this direction has so far been done.

A matter which we would like to emphasise, particularly in connection with the research programmes in the States, is the need to associate representatives of progressive cultivators, traders and processors with the drawing up of annual research programmes and their evaluation. Though many of the problems of cultivators will be brought up by the extension service, such association will provide a more direct opportunity for the inclusion in the research programmes of matters which directly interest them.

The conditions of employment of the research workers is an important factor in determining the quality and quantity of the work done. In this respect the research workers employed in the projects sponsored by all India organisations, such as the I.C.A.R. or Commodity Committees. Suffer from the handicap that their tenure is temporary as the schemes on which they work are sanctioned for limited periods. Although it may be argued that a research worker is actually seldom thrown out of employment, the feeling of insecurity is always there. This needs to be removed and the research services brought more in line with other permanent services under the Government. As far as the human element in research is concerned, the important pre-requisites for the production of satisfactory results are stability of service and congenial conditions of work and proper guidance and direction.

Building up of a new system—rural universities

The urgent necessity of providing higher education to the rural areas is obvious. To meet this need, the University Education Commission has recommended a new pattern under the name of rural university. The Central Government should help to establish, during the period of the Plan, at least one such university, wherever the earlier stages of basic education, out of which it has to grow, have been worked out. Apart from serving the villages, the experience gained in the working of rural universities is likely to be useful in affecting certain necessary reforms in our existing universities, thereby enabling them to serve the national need more effectively.

Rural universities

The rural universities that may be set up will have to pass through a period of experimentation, during which it is essential that they should have free scope for development. In order not to place the products of these institutions at a disadvantage, the degree of the rural universities should have as much validity in the matter of public appointments as those of older universities.

Social education

The concept of adult education, which was mostly confined to literacy, was found to be too narrow to be able to meet the various needs of the adults. It was, therefore, widened to include, in addition to literacy, the health, recreation and home life of the adults, their economic life and citizenship training; and to denote this new concept the term 'social education' was coined Social education implies an all-comprehensive programme of community action. External aid may be there but only to stimulate, and not to replace, community effort. The importance of such a programme is obvious. It should not only make our limited resources much more effective, but also build up a self-reliant nation. in a country, where nearly 00 per cent of the population are illiterate, democracy will not take root until a progressive programme of primary education trains up a generation fit to undertake its responsibilities. Even the programme of primary education is considerably handicapped without a corresponding programme of the education of adults.

The work in the field of social education has been mostly confined to literacy. As a result of the work in recent years, especially during 1937-39 and since 1949-50, the literacy percentage increased from 8.3 in 1931 to 17.2 per cent in 1951. Most of the post-literacy work is done through libraries though, due to the dearth of suitable literature, the library movement has not made much headway in the villages. Recently the importance of recreational and cultural activities in programmes of social education has been increasingly recognised.

Our cultural agencies like dance, drama, puppet show, fairs and festivals, bhajan, kirtan, etc., have been used but without any systematic attempt being made to gauge, develop and fully exploit their potentialities for mass education. Fairs and festivals had a meaning in olden times. they have however, to be reinterpreted and modified to fit into the modern context and become live and full of meaning to the people today. Modern means of mass communication like the film and the radio have attracted much greater attention but, on account of their heavy cost, their use has been very much limited. Attempts have also been made in a few institutions to improve the economic condition of the villagers by teaching them improved crafts and agriculture. Very good all-round social education work has been done by some of the basic institutions. Co-operatives have also been developed as an agency of social education.

The approach to the problem has to be determined

in the light of our resources and the magnitude of the task ahead. The total expenditure on social education in 1950-51 was Rs. 83.45 lakhs. The average annual expenditure visualized in the Plan is Rs. 3.02 crores. We would, however, require an average annual expenditure of Rs.27 crores for the next ten years to make everybody literate and give him in addition, a veneer of social education in the larger sense of the term.

The situation, therefore, calls for a most carefully planned approach. At the national level, priorities in the programme of social education should be determined by the overall national priorities, thereby not only winning for it the enthusiasm and support of the country at large but also making it directly productive, as it would enable the human factor to respond fully to the national plans of development. Organization of cooperatives, agencies of village development, cooperative farming, agricultural extension work, etc., are priority tasks in the Plan.

We would, therefore, recommend that social education should be based on them. That is to say, in handling these activities utmost attention should be paid to inculcating in the adults right individual and collective habits, and the knowledge of various subject should be correlated to every step involved in these activities, thereby broadening the horizon of the adults and enabling them to understand and effectively participate in the wider national life. For that it would be necessary to give re-orientation courses to the personnel engaged in these departments and to prepare literature to guide them in this work. Within the broad framework of national priorities the actual programmes in a locality should be determined by local needs. Planning at the local level is equally essential if the danger of frittering away our meagre resources in a number of uncoordinated activities is to be avoided.

The principles which should govern our approach in this regard may be stated as follows. Our resources should be used in the first instance, as far as possible, for that programme which not only meets some immediately felt need of the local community, in whose midst the programme is conducted, but also builds up resources for developing the programme with the expanding awareness of the community of its own needs. That is the only way by which, with our limited resources, we can make any impression on the problem.

Secondly, the social education approach must permeate all programmes of State aid to the people. That is to say that before any programme of State aid is launched the people should be so educated in regard to it that their instinct to help themselves is fully aroused and they are anxious to receive the programme and do their utmost in the execution of it. Thirdly, there should be the closest integration of the various activities conducted in a locality so that the forces of friendship and goodwill released by one activity, immediately recognised by the villagers as good or pleasant, can be utilised for winning their cooperation for activities requiring more strenuous effort or the usefulness of which is nor so immediately apparent to them.

Fourthly, it should be our endeavour to increase the effectiveness of private agencies doing social education work in an area by giving them proper help.

The programme

Besides the social education work which various agencies

entrusted primarily with other work—like agriculture, animal husbandry, etc.—may carry on in close connection with their work, the programme of social education will fall into two parts. One should consist of whatever items any agency wants to or is capable of taking up out of the vast field of social education. Such agencies should be encouraged and helped, depending upon the usefulness of the work performed and the extent to which State resources can be diverted for the purpose.

The other part should consist of a planned programme outlined below which should be undertaken wherever a properly trained worker is available. This is calculated to achieve maximum results. State resources should naturally be concentrated more on the latter part of the programme and in training workers for it. This programme will differ in rural and urban areas, in view of the different conditions prevailing in each. In rural areas the point at which the social education programme in a locality can begin will of course depend on the conditions prevailing in the given area.

Attempt should, however, be made at the earliest opportunity to organise an economic activity on cooperative basis. The precise nature of the activity and the degree and nature of cooperation will of course very according to local needs and the degree of maturity of the local people. The underlying object is that not only will provide education to the participants by organising community efforts and pooling their resources but it will also by the more effective use of local resources, ensure economic gain, which will generate sustained interest and create confidence. The cooperative activity will be the rallying point for the community and mark the beginning of the community centre, the nucleus of which will be provided by the trained community organiser. Where a cooperative society already exists, the task of the worker will be to further improve it and transform it into an agency of social education.

Similarly, programmes of health education and health services should also be organised on cooperative lines. The test of the proper time for any programme is that the community is psychologically prepared so that it can organise it with its own resources. The importance of providing healthy recreation cannot be too strongly stressed. In organising recreational programmes special attention should be given to the revival and proper utilisation of our cultural agencies.

Occasions provided by fairs and festivals should be utilised for purposes of education, recreation and community organisation. Literature should be prepared explaining the significance of the various fairs and festivals and their relevance today as well as how their full educational potentialities can be developed and made use of. The State should encourage writers to produce plays containing constructive ideas for such occasions. Film shows by mobile vans may also be provided to the extent that resources permit. It should be remembered, however, that unless integrated with the programme of development going on in an area their use is strictly limited.

Certain films which will be relevant to conditions all over India, such as those dealing with common diseases and those calculated to inculate right individual and collective habits, should be prepared by the Central Government and lent out to the various States. Well-regulated radio broadcasts should also be increasingly used for recreation and instruction. In organising literacy and post-literacy work the aim should be to put it on a self-financing basis, as far as possible, by normally starting it only when the ground has been prepared by some more obviously useful activity like the economic activity, mentioned earlier, and the interest in knowledge has been sufficiently stimulated.

A news-sheet, locally produced, and carrying suggestions for improving their lot—suggestions which they can immediately put into practice and in which they have developed faith as a result of the work in the first stage—should find ready customers among the villagers. At a later stage the State can help with libraries to the extent that its resources allow. If we have provided the above four programmes, correlating relevant knowledge at every step, we will not only have met the primary needs of the masses but also taught them through living, most of the things that are required for the citizen of a modern democratic State. There is, however, no end to activities that might be included in a programme of social education and, as the capacity of the masses to help themselves increases, more and mare activities can be added.

The above intensive programme should be spread in the surrounding villages through local leaders thrown up as a result of the working of small groups in youth clubs, women's clubs, children's clubs, farmers' clubs, etc., which it should be the aim of the community organiser to set up. Short and intensive camps should be organised for these leaders where the working of the social education programme is explained to them. Thereafter continual guidance is given to them from his headquarters by the community organiser.

In the case of urban areas, there are so many groups that the problems will have to be studied in relation to each group. The problem of healthy and cheap creation is also more acute in the towns than in the villages. The overall considerations will, however, be the same as in the rural areas. The programmes must begin with felt needs and must have the capacity to grow by the resources of the local community. But in view of the congestion in town, the high price of land and buildings and the business of the townsman, the State or philanthropic organisations may have to provide a building for each community centre, though even here the attempt should be to mobilise as much of the local effort as possible for the purpose. As in the villages so in the towns, the State or other organisations that may be doing the work of social education should provide a worker, highly trained in community organisation and in the mobilisation of its resources. In urban areas, especially in industrial areas, special attention should be paid to improving the skill of the workers.

Selection and training of workers

The selection and training of workers are perhaps the most important tasks. Two types of social education workers will be required: those who have specialised in community organisation, and others who, with proper reorientation of outlook, can work under their guidance. In the case of the former especially, as the qualities of personality—initiative, resourcefulness, leadership, spirit of sacrifice and service and mastery of cheap, simple and intelligent living—are more important than mere academic qualifications, a new system of selection will have to be evolved. The training of community organisers should be very thorough and should consist of improved methods of Agriculture, Animal Husbandry, one or two of the most important cottage industries of the area concerned, principles and organisation of cooperatives, organisation of simple recreational programmes, organisation of community centres, etc., and above all the handling of these activities in such a way as to lead to the development of the minds of men most effectively.

Training in literacy work should also be given. The training of community organisers should be arranged in conjunction with a training centre for basic teachers, a post-basic school or an agricultural school or college, which should preferably be at an extension headquarters. The greatest stress should be laid on the development of the maximum possible self-help and self-support, consistent with other interests, as these workers have primarily to infuse that spirit among the people. The other category of social education workers will include school teachers, village level workers, various Government officers working in the locality concerned and workers of private agencies.

Regarding pupil-teachers, training in social education work should be compulsory in all training colleges. The State should provide special grants for the departments of social education in training colleges for some years to come to give an impetus to the work. Short and intensive training in social education work should be organised in camps for teachers already on the job. The training of village level workers should also include initiation into the human side of their work: mass psychology, mass approach, community organisation, etc. Training facilities should also be offered for workers of private agencies. Higher officers should be given a reorientation course, so that they develop an integrated outlook, which will not only enable them to guide the worker with sympathy and understanding but also make for better inter-departmental cooperation, upon which the success of the rural development programme in an area depends.

Literacy methods and production of literature

Teachers' training colleges should take up research in methods of imparting literacy. Work in the experimental centres of social education, which should be associated in the case of rural areas with the group of model basic institutions mentioned earlier, should provide sufficient material for literature suitable for adults. There is also considerable room here for inter-departmental cooperation and for cooperation between the States sharing a common linguistic area. The Centre should provide model guide books for workers and prepare pamphlets on certain standard subjects like health, democratic citizenship, cooperatives, etc.

The present stage of social education in the country is essentially experimental and needs Central guidance. The work should be coordinated with similar work in basic education and a common committee of experts should advise the Centre in the matter of initiating and aiding financially experimental work in both these fields in the States, and guide it, assess the results and make them available to other States A common national platform, where the various agencies can meet the intervals for mutual discussion—so necessary for evolving a common outlook and securing co-ordination of different agencies—is already provided by the Indian Adult Education Association.

The director of social education in a State should be a man highly trained in community organisation and should be able to advise and help the State in the matter of public participation in its various development programmes. He should have a body representing important non-official agencies to advise him.

At the field level it is mostly a task of re-organising and co-ordinating existing agencies rather than of creating new ones. The problem is different in rural and urban areas. In rural areas the following measures should be taken:

(1) Educational institutions should become examples of self-help, democratic community living cooperative labour and intelligent handling of economic activity. Education should centre round agriculture and cottage industries and educational institutions should be well equipped with agricultural farms, craft work-shops, etc. Educational institutions would thereby become excellent centres for spreading idea for improving our social and economic life. Basic schools, which are already conceived on the above lines, have special significance in this regard. All facilities should, therefore, be provided at the basic training centres so that the teachers are trained as first class social education workers.

(2) The village level worker, wherever provided, should also be stationed in a school, as far as possible. Under his guidance even an ordinary school may begin to make some contribution, which will also prepare it for ultimate conversion into a basic school.

(3) Besides the above agencies the State should provide, wherever possible, community organisers, say one of 50 villages, to make use of, help, guide and co-ordinate the activities of all agencies working in their respective spheres. These also should be attached to educational institutions.

(4) The role of private agencies has already been discussed.

In urban areas quite a large number of agencies exist and the key problem is to co-ordinate their activities for a comprehensive programme of social education. For this purpose city or town social education councils should be instituted, where they do not exist already, each consisting of the representatives of the various agencies operating in the town concerned. This Council should distribute items of social education work among the various agencies according to their capacity and willingness to undertake it. Social education in industrial areas in towns has special importance in view of the dull and drab conditions. of life prevailing in urban areas. Here the employer and the labour unions should be able to cooperate.

The census of 1951 showed that only 16.6 per cent of the population were literate and even if children below 10 years are excluded the proportion rises to 20 per cent only. Apart from the low percentage of literacy there is serious disparity in literacy between men and women and between the urban population and the rural population. Rapid social and economic progress along democratic lines and widespread illiteracy are scarcely compatible with each other.

As essential reforms proposed in the system of education are carried out, facilities for condition classes and social education classes at various levels should be developed. Plans of States provide for the opening of literacy and social education centres, training of social education workers and organisers, libraries, publication of literature, audio-visual education and establishment of Janata colleges. The total allotment in the plan for social education is about Rs. 15 crores, including about Rs. 10

crores in the national extension and community development programme.

The Ministry of Education propose to establish a fundamental education centre for training social education organisers and for continuing study and research in problems relating to social and basic education. While literacy is undoubtedly important, it should be recognised that it is one element in a wider concept of social education. Social education embodies a comprehensive approach to the solution of the problems of the community, primarily through community action. Besides literacy, it includes health, recreation and home life, economic activities and citizenship training.

The entire national extension and community development programme, social welfare extension projects, rural programmes undertaken by Government agencies in cooperation with the people, programmes of voluntary organisations like the Sarva Seva Sangh, the Bharat Sevak Samaj and others, the cooperative movement, village panchayats etc. are all facets of the nation-wide effort towards social education and rural improvement which is now in progress in the country. From this aspects the range of social education work is not to be judged merely by the financial provisions made specifically under this description. However, as an organised and systematic activity directed to specific purposes, social education is a new field of work.

A large number of development agencies are engaged in some form or other of social education. Their work has to be supplemented by suitable specialised agencies. The beginning made in this direction in national extension and community project areas has, therefore, much significance. A period of careful evaluation will help to determine the nature of specialised agencies and methods and techniques needed in this field, both in rural and in urban areas.

Higher rural education

A number of far-reaching proposals for the development of rural education at the higher levels were made by the University Education Commission which reported a few years ago. The subject has been examined afresh recently by the Higher Rural Education Committee which recommended the establishment or Rural Institutes. These institutes are intended to perform a variety of functions for the rural community and, more especially to provide (a) facilities for higher studies who complete their post-basic or higher secondary courses, (b) certificate courses in subjects such as rural hygiene, agriculture and rural engineering and also shorter courses, and (c) comprehensive teaching - cum - research - cum extension programmes.

It is visualised that Rural Institutes will function as cultural and training centres and as centres for development planning in rural areas. The Ministry of Education propose to establish 10 Rural Institutes in the second five year plan and have made a provision of Rs. 2 crores for this purpose. For locating these Institutes leading centres already engaged in rural work have been selected. For following up the programme the Central Government have recently constituted a Council for Rural Higher Education.

Teachers

At all times the teacher is the pivot in the system of education. This is specially the case in a period of basic change and reorientation. There is general agreement that the teaching profession fails to attract a sufficient number of persons who adopt teaching as a vocation and that far too many persons work as teachers for short periods and then move on to other occupations.

Improvement in the conditions of teachers is therefore an important desideratum of progress in education. Measures which are necessary, whether by way of better training or better salaries and conditions of service, may he held back because of the large number of teachers involved in any reform. Thus, the number of teachers has risen from 7.3 lakhs before the first plan to 10.24 lakhs in 1955-56 and is expected to increase to 13.56 lakhs in 1960-61. Before the first five year plan 59 per cent of teachers in primary schools and 54 per cent of teachers in secondary schools were trained teachers.

These proportions have risen to 64 and 56 per cent respectively by the end of the first plan. In the second plan Rs. 17 crores have been provided for increasing training facilities for teachers and, besides expanding existing institutions, it is proposed to establish 231 training schools and 30 training colleges. As the end of the second plan it is expected that the proportion of trained teachers will increase to 79 and 68 per cent in primary schools and secondary schools respectively. The number of basic training colleges is to be increased from 33 to 71 and basic training schools from 449 to 729. A national Institute of Basic Education is also being established as a research centre.

The question of improving the salaries of teachers has been under consideration for some time past. It is generally recognised that the provision of satisfactory services for teachers is a measure essential for the effective reorganization of the system of education. In many states steps to improve teachers' salaries have been taken during the past few years. In the nature of things teachers' salaries have to be fixed at levels consistent with the local pay structure, at which suitably qualified persons can be attracted and retained in the teaching profession.

The problem in different States is, therefore, by no means identical. While recognizing the importance of the question of improving salary scales of teachers, the Central Government have taken the view that responsibility for meeting additional expenditure on this account belongs to State Governments. As a temporary measure, until the next Finance Commission makes its proposals, the Central Government have, however, agreed to assist States to the extent of 50 per cent of additional expenditure which may be involved in raising salary scales of primary teachers suitably consistent with local conditions.

They have further suggested that in order to meet the additional cost involved in raising the salary scales of primary teachers, States should explore the possibility of reducing expenditure as far as they can on the construction of school buildings. They have also proposed that a special education cess may be levied by States to enable them to meet expenditure on the improvement of salary scales.

As regards conditions of service, the fact that teachers are employed by various authorities, such as State Governments, Municipalities, District Boards and private bodies, is an important element in variations in salaries, standards, working conditions and prospects of teachers which may be found within the same State. It is recommended that each State may consider bringing elementary school teachers in the State into its own service in appropriate cadres. When the services of teachers are placed at the disposal of local bodies or of private institutions, according to the cadres to which they belong, their terms of appointment would be maintained. This would enable State Governments to extend to teachers adequate benefits of security, pension, provident fund contributions, promotion and opportunities to quality for higher grades and also provide them appropriate amenities.

Programme for agriculture

The first five year plan accorded pride of place to programmes for agriculture and community development. This was a natural priority in a plan seeking to raise the standard of living of the mass of the people, specially in rural areas, but it was also justified in the special circumstances of shortage and inflation which existed when the plan was formulated. More than any other factor, the increase in agricultural production which has taken place since 1952-53 has helped to end inflation, stabilize the economy and prepare the way for a higher rate of development during the second five year plan.

The index of agricultural production, with 1949-50 as base, stood at 96 in 1950-51. It stood at 114 in 1953-54, and is expected to be 115 in 1955-56. During the first plan, the national product increased by 18 per cent, and income in the agricultural sector increased in the same proportion. Increase in agricultural production also stimulated growth in other sectors of the economy.

Review of the first plan

The first five year plan envisaged the following increases in agricultural production: These targets of addition production, especially of foodgrains, were worked out in terms of the contribution anticipated from different programmes such as irrigation, use of larger quantities of fertilisers, supply of improved seeds and programmes of land reclamation and development.

In other words, it was reckoned that if the developmental measures which the plan provided for were taken the production potential would increase to the extent indicated. In given years the actual levels production for different commodities would necessarily vary with weather conditions and other factors such as the relative prices for different crops. The course of agricultural production during the first plan is shown in the following statement: It will be seen that during the period of the plan 1953-54 was the year of peak production for foodgrains and 1954-55 for oilseeds and cotton.

In the case both of sugarcane and jute 1951-52 was the year of the highest production and although, after a period of decline, production improved towards the end of the plan, the targets which were set were not realised. These trends emerge more clearly from the following statement with sets out the index numbers of agricultural production during the period of the plan for various groups of crops: It is significant that the overall index of agricultural production has been maintained at a fairly high level during the past three years. This has been accompanied by some decline in foodgrains which account for about 67 per cent of the total value of agricultural production. Trends have to be studied over a longer period before firm conclusions can be established. The fact that agriculture depends on several unpredictable factors and agricultural targets must necessarily be in the nature of a tentative approach is illustrated by the actual statistics of increase in the production of individual foodgrains: Of the increase of 7.6 million tons anticipated over the first five year plan it was though that roughly rice might account for 4 million tons, wheat for 2 million tons, gram and pulses for a million tons and other cereal for 0.5 million tons.

The largest increase has occurred in millets and other cereals and the target for wheat production has been realised. On the whole, the expectation in respect of rise has not been fulfilled except in one specially favourable year. Nevertheless, the increase in food production made possible a reduction in imports from the level of 4.73 million tons in tons in 1950 and 3.86 million tons in 1951 to less than a million tons during each of the past two years. This was a distinct advantage to the general economy of the country. With the data available it would not be correct to attempt to relate too closely the progress of production in individual agricultural commodities to the actual progress made from year to year in implementing the programmes of the first five year plan.

In the nature of things many factors operate at the same time. It is proposed that the data bearing on agricultural production, during the first five year plan, including the results of crop cutting surveys, should be investigated through a number of intensive and specially designed studies. Among the aspects on which more objective knowledge would be of considerable value in the making of policy and in assessing results, the following may be specially mentioned:

(1) production trends in different regions,

(2) effects of agricultural production and extension programmes,

(3) range of influence of favourable and unfavourable conditions,

(4) review of yardsticks of additional production at present in use,

(5) yield trends for the principal crops, and

(6) cost of various agricultural production and extension measures in relation to the benefits realised.

From the limited information available it appears that among programmes of development which have contributed to increase in agricultural production during the first plan, minor irrigation works, increased use of fertilisers, land reclamation and development and the extension of area under cultivation have been specially significant. Minor irrigation programmes were being undertaken for several years before the plan.

During the period 1943-44 to 1950-51 programmes of the value of about Rs. 62 crores were approved in pursuance of the grow-more-food campaign and a major portion of these were devoted to minor irrigation. During the first plan about 10 million acres of land are expected to have been brought under irrigation from minor works and about 6.3 million acres from large and medium irrigation schemes. More than half the increase in the area benefiting from minor irrigation occurred during the first two years of the plan Considerable progress has been made in several States, notably, in Bihar, Uttar Pradesh, West Bengal, Punjab, Assam, Bombay, Madras and Mysore. The benefits of irrigation are realised to a greater extent when combined with the use of fertilisers. During the plan period the consumption of ammonium sulphate has more than doubled, from 275,000 tons before the plan began to 610,000 tons four years later. Special attention has been devoted to spreading the use of the 'Japanese method' of rice cultivation, the area brought within its scope so far being about 1.6 million acres. During the first four years of the first five year plan more than one million acres of land were reclaimed through the Central Tractor Organisation and 1.4 million acres through State tractor organisations. Besides this, about 5 million acres have been developed by cultivators through programmes such as assistance for mechanised cultivation, budding and living reclamation of land by manual labour.

The extension of cultivation has been a larger contributory factor towards increase in production than had been anticipated when the plans was drawn up. Thus, the total cropped area has increased from 326 million acres before the plan to 352 million acres in 1954-55. The area under food crops has risen from 257 million to 272 million acres and under commercial crops from 49 million to about 60 million acres. The area under commercial crops has increased from 15 per cent of the total cropped area to 17 per cent, while the area under food crops has diminished from 79 to 77 per cent of the cropped area. The area under other crops has shown little change.

During the first five year plan it was of crucial importance that agricultural programmes must succeed, for no other consideration had equal significance for the stability of the economy as a whole. In the second five year plan agricultural programmes are intended to provide adequate food to support the increased population and the raw materials needed for a growing industrial economy and also to make available larger exportable surpluses of agricultural commodities. The second five year plan implies, therefore, even more than the first a close interdependence between agricultural and industrial development.

While formulating programmes to achieve these objects, it is necessary to take a long-term view so as to secure the best possible use of material and human resources, ensure balanced development between different branches of agriculture and create conditions for an appreciable increase in rural incomes and standards of living. In framing agricultural programmes it is essential, from the national point of view, to place before the villagers a goal which they should strive to attain.

In connection with the preparation of the second five year plan it was stated that this goal should be the doubling, within a period of about ten years, of agricultural production, including food crops, oilseeds, cotton, sugar cane, plantation and other crops, animal husbandry products, etc. In relation to the food problem the factors to be considered are: (1) increase in the total population, (2) increase in the urban population, (3) the need to improve per capital consumption, (4) the need to counter possibilities of inflationary pressures resulting from the implementation of the second five year plan, and (5) effects on food consumption of increase in national income and changes in its distribution.

The total food requirements in 1960-61 at the present rate of consumption will be 70 5 million tons. By the end of the second plan the cate of consumption is estimated to rise to 18.3 ounces per adult, so that the total food requirements will be 75 million tons. The plan provides for increase in food production of 10 million tons over the next five years. In terms of calories the per adult consumption of food per day, which at present amounts to 2000, is expected to increase by 1960-61 to 2450 as against the minimum of 3000 calories recommended by nutrition experts. Compared to many other countries the rate of cereal consumption in India is relatively high. This is because such energy producing foods as milk and milk products, fruit and vegetables, eggs, fish and meat are far from adequately represented in the common diet.

Apart from the question of correct food habits, which is undoubtedly a matter of extreme importance, the output of each of these supplementary foods is at present grossly insufficient. During the second five year plan the aim will be to diversify agricultural production and to shift somewhat the emphasis which has been hitherto placed in a dominant degree on the production of cereal crops. The second plan also provides for programmes for increasing the production of crops like arecanut, coconut, lac, black pepper, cashewnut etc. which did not receive sufficient attention during the first plan. The scope for increasing the area under cultivation is extremely limited. Such increase as may take place in the area under cultivation is likely to increase the production mainly of the coarser grains.

As national income increases, there may be a general tendency for demand to shift from the coarser to the superior grains, especially to rice, what and maize. In the circumstances, the main source of increase in agricultural production must be increase in yields from more intensive, more efficient and more profitable agricultural production. Although the available data are not always comparable, there is little doubt that the average yields of principal crops like wheat and rice in India are considerably smaller than those current in several other countries. The crop cutting experiments which have been conducted in recent years in different parts of the country show large variations in the average yields of crops between different regions and even within each region.

Crop competitions which have been carried on fro some time past also afford an indication of levels which can be attained in Indian conditions when the necessary effort and assistance are forthcoming. It is now within the bounds of practical action to bring about a rapid and fairly widespread increase in agricultural yields. This requires more detailed and systematic planning in terms of regions, states, districts and project areas such as has not yet been undertaken. Data derived from crop competitions should be widely publicised, so that each area can set its goals in the light of established facts. To the extent necessary, the scope competitions should be widened.

What is required is not merely the encouragement of high levels of achievement on the part of individual farmers, but a more comprehensive effort which would raise the general average in each area. Every part of the country should have targets of average production for different crops based on a broad classification of physical conditions of irrigation, rainfall, terrain, etc. In pursuance of these targets there should be programmes for raising levels of productivity which go down to individual villages and individual families. Despite the uncertainties to which agriculture is necessarily subject it is important that a more studied effort to introduce a planned approach to agricultural development should be made The main elements in agricultural planning are:

(1) planning of land use;

(2) determination of targets, both long-term and short-term;

(3) linking up of development programmes and Government assistance to production targets and the land use plan; including allocation of fertilisers etc. according to plan; and

(4) an appropriate price policy.

Each district and, in particular, each national extension and community development project area should have a carefully worked out agricultural plan. This should indicate for villages the targets to be aimed at the broad distribution of land between different uses and the programme of development. Within the framework of an overall price such as has been outlined in an earlier chapter, such local plans will be valuable steps leading to more careful planning for States and regions and for the country as a whole.

The crop pattern envisaged by these local plans has in the main to be influenced through such incentives as the provision of irrigation, credit and marketing facilities, provision of fertilisers, and intimate contact with the cultivator on the part of extension workers and especially the village level workers. The nature of first estimates derived from calculations of the production potential expected to be added as a result of various developmental programmes. In view of the considerations outlined in paragraph 10 and especially the need to provide adequate safeguards against possibilities of inflation, it is considered that it is both necessary and possible to achieve higher agricultural targets with relatively small adjustments in regard to resources. In particular, through the national extension service it must be the aim to reach every village and every family and to organise supplies and services and short, medium and long-term finance required foı achieving these targets. With a view to fixing higher targets and ensuring their realisation, the Planning Commission and the Ministry of Food and Agriculture purpose to undertake further study of agricultural programmes in each state and regions with reference to its crop pattern, land and water resources and programmes of development in irrigation, national extension and other fields.

Foodgrains—The target for foodgrains has already been referred to earlier. It is expected that the increase of 10 million tons in foodgrains, rice may account for 3 to 4 million tons, wheat for 2 to 3 million tons, other cereals for 2 to 3 million tons and pulses for about 1.5 to 2 million tons.

Cotton—To fulfil the textile targets for the second five year plan, the production of raw cotton has to be raised from 4.2 million bales in 1955-56 to 5.5, million bales in 1960.-61. Programmes for the cotton development will continue the measures undertaken during the first five year plan such as provision of hybrid seed, multiplication and distribution of improved seed, grant of loans to cultivators for the purchase of seed and fertiliser and extension and propaganda among the cotton cultivators. An important feature of development under the second plan will be the emphasis on increasing the production of long staple varieties particularly in the areas brought under major irrigation projects. The achievements made so far the increasing the production of long staple varieties have been significant and the proportion of these varieties had gone up from 17.5 per cent in 1948-49 to about 37 per cent in 1954-55.

Jute—Before Partition, India had a virtual monopoly in the production and supply of raw jute, jute being always one of India's principal foreign exchange earners. After Partition, only about 19 percent of the total production of raw jute of undivided India came to the share of the Indian Union. While there has been substantial improvement in the production of jute from 1.7 million bales in 1947-48 to about 4 million bales in 1955-56, much of the additional jute produced in the country during the last few years was grown on marginal lands and was of poor quality, which consequently fetched low prices. The emphasis in the programme for jute production has to be changed from quantity to quality and new jute cultivation has to be undertaken in areas suitable for growing high quality jute.

The requirements of the industry for raw jute may be placed at 7.2 million bales if all the mills were to work to full capacity. In addition about 150,000 bales may be treated as extra-factory consumption. It is therefore proposed to provide 5 million bales from internal production and to import the balance. It should be possible to produce the additional quantity of 1 million bales of jute largely through intensive cultivation measures with the ultimate objective of achieving an average yield of 3 bales per acre of good quality jute.

The measures proposed in the second plan include the continuation on an expanded basis of the existing jute extension schemes, setting up of seed farms, supply of improved seeds, distribution of seed drills, construction of retting tanks etc. The organization of an extension service for demonstration of improved cultural practices is an important item in the jute development programme.

Oilseeds—Oilseeds and vegetable oils besides

constituting a source of fat supply in the diet of the population are valuable export commodities. The production of the five major oilseeds-groundnut, sesamum, linseed, rape and mustard and castor seed is expected to go up from 5.1 million tons in 1950-51 to about 5.5 million tons in 1955-56 which was the target fixed under the first plan. Under the second five year plan, it is proposed to increase the production of the five major oilseeds to 7 million tons as shown below: Schemes for the production and distribution of good quality seeds sponsored by the Indian Central Oilseeds Committee during the first plan period have given promising results. It is proposed to popularise these improved seeds on an intensive scale during the second plan.

Other schemes included in the plans of states cover application of fertilisers and manures, control of pests and diseases and research for evolving better and new varieties. Arrangements will also be made for improved marketing of oilseeds. In considering the effect of the target of additional oilseeds production on increasing the supply of vegetable fats and vegetable oils, account has to be taken of the production of the other important edible oil, namely, coconut oil, the quantities proposed to be exported, industrial consumption etc.

The following table given the position in respect of the five principle oils as also in cotton seed and oils. This assumes an export target of 5 lakhs tons of groundnut and 2 lakh tons of other oils (in terms of seed). Emphasis will also be placed on stepping up the production and export of cotton seed oil and oils from solvent extraction process.

Sugarcane—The consumption of sugar and gur has increased steadily during recent years. In 1950-51 during conditions of control about 10.7 lakhs tons of sugar were consumed. The amount consumed in 1954-55 was about 17 lakh tons. Under the second plan, it is proposed to raise the production of crystal sugar to 22.5 lakh tons and the installed capacity to 25 lakhs tons at the end of 196-061. In order to make available to sugar factories increased quantities of cane and also to provide for higher gur consumption, additional production of 13 lakh tons of sugarcane in terms of gur, is aimed at.

This will raise the total production from 5.8 million tons expected in 1955-56 to 7.1 million tons in 1960-61, the amount available per adult being 1.72 ozs. per day. Schemes for the intensive cultivation of sugarcane include provision of irrigation facilities, establishment of seed nurseries, distribution of manures and fertilisers, control of pests and diseases, organisation of demonstrations and crop competitions. The main emphasis will be on increasing the sources content of the cane and ensuring maximum supplies of cane during the crushing season.

Coconuts—India is the second largest coconut growing country in the world, producing as she does about 3800 million nuts a year. Still the country is deficit is expected to go upto 80,000 tons in 1960-61 after allowing for the increased population and possible rise in consumption standards. By undertaking both short-term as well as long-term measures, it is proposed to increase the production of coconuts to 210,000 tons in terms of oil by 1960-61 as against 130,000 tons at present. The short-term programme includes the setting up of demonstration centres to propagate improved methods of coconut cultivation including protection of the crop against pests and diseases. Under the long-term programme the area under coconut will be increased by bringing suitable waste lands, development of nurseries for the distribution of superior varieties of plants etc. It is also planned to increase the yield of coconuts from 30 to 45 nuts per tree.

Arecanuts—As in the case of coconut, the country is also deficit in the supply of arecanuts, the existing production being 81,100 tons as compared to the requirements of 118,000 tons at present. After allowing for the increase in population and also a slightly higher rate of consumption at the end of 1960-61, the requirements may be placed at 129,000 tons. But as the arecanut tree takes eight to ten years to bear fruit, extension of area under the crop will yield results only during the third plan period. However, it is proposed to increase the production of arecanut by about 25 per cent through incentive methods of cultivation and by prevention of pests and diseases, supply of quality seedlings, introduction of improved cultural practices etc. Efforts will be directed towards increasing the yields per acre from an average of 658 lbs. top 820 lbs.

The target of production at the end of 1960-61 may be placed at 99,000 tons. The Indian Central Arecaunt Committee has already carried out a survey of waste lands suitable for growing arecanuts and its is intended to investigate and exploit these possibilities fully in the course of the second plan.

Lac—Lac is the raw material for shellac and seed lac which are important items of export trade. The production of lack during the last few years has varied between 37,000 to 48,000 tons, the expected production in 1955-56 being of the order of 44,000 tons. In formulating the target of additional production, the possibilities of export demand for the commodity as well as competition from lac and from artificial substitutes produced abroad has to be kept in view. The second five year plan aims at stepping up production to 59,000 tons. Emphasis will also be given to the improvement of quality. These objectives are to be attained mainly through the establishment or regional brood farms in different areas, survey of idle host plant and imparting technical knowledge on lac cultivation. It is proposed to organise a lac extension service in important lack growing areas. In addition, it is also proposed to establish air-conditioned and ordinary godowns for storage of stick lac at important marketing centres.

Tobacco—Next to U.S.A. and China, India is the largest tobacco producing country in the world. In 1954-55, 250,000 tons of tobacco were produced. The problem which faces tobacco cultivation is not so much of expansion of production as improvement in quantity. Due to unfavourable weather conditions, a large proportion of crop during recent years turned out to be of low grade varieties and it was found difficult to sell it. This resulted in the accumulation of stocks and consequent fall in prices. Improvement of quality will be given the highest priority in the programme for the second five year plan, and increase in production as such is not envisaged.

Black Pepper—Black pepper is an important dollar earner and has also considerable local importance in Travancore-Cochin, Malabar and South Kanara. In recent years, however, India has been facing increasing competition from other countries. The lines on which pepper development and research should be organized have been recommended by a special committee. The scheme was started in 1954-55 and is proposed to be intensified during the second five year plan. The objective under the plan is to raise the area under pepper cultivation by about 50,000 acres and to increase production from 26,000 tons to 32,000 tons.

Cashew-nut—Cashew-nut is another important dollar earner. The annual production about 60,000 tons, the main producing areas being Madras and Travancore-Cochin. Although cashew-nuts are collected on a commercial scale in a few other countries, notably East Africa, the processing of cashew is practically the monopoly of India. In view of the growing competition of for the processing of cashew-nuts there is great need for developing the production of cashew-nuts in this country.

The Spices Enquiry Committee suggested that the cultivation of cashew-nuts should be undertaken on a plantation basis in the east coast districts of Madras, coastal districts of Konkan and certain other areas on the west coast. Plantations should be encouraged around processing factories. There is also scope for extending cashew-nut cultivation in Madhya Bharat, Mysore, Coorg, Andhra, Orissa, West Bengal and Andamans. It is proposed to increase the production of cashew-nut from 60,000 tons to 80,000 tons by the end of 1960-61.

Tea, Coffee and Rubber—Production and other programmes, for tea, coffee and rubber are at present being considered by the Plantations Enquiry Commission. Between 1950 and 1954 tea production has varied from 613 to 644 million pounds and exports from 427 to 470 pounds. On the whole, it appears that it should be possible to achieve a production target of 700 million pounds and an export target about 470 to 500 million pounds by the end of the plan. The Coffee Board is engaged in examining a fifteen year development plan for increasing the production of coffee, from 25,000 tons to 48,000 tons. Of the increase about 10,000 tons are proposed to be secured from intensive cultivation and rehabilitation of existing estates and 13,000 tons from reclamation and fresh plantings. A scheme drawn up by Rubber Board for replanting 70,000 acres of area under rubber at the rate of 7,000 acres a year over a period of 10 years and for bringing 10,000 acres of new land under rubber at 2,000 acres for a year is under the consideration of the Ministry of Commerce and Industry. For tea, coffee and rubber, firm development programmes yet to be approved.

Development programmes

It has been explained earlier that it is difficult to establish any precise correlation between the level of agricultural production and the extent of implementation of development programmes which are initiated under a plan. Such trends can be seen in perspective only after a period. It is even more difficult to attempt to relate the production of one set of crops such as foodgrains to developmental programmes which may be undertaken or to distinguish separately the influence which these programmes may have on the production of various groups of crops.

Nevertheless, as in the first five year plan,an attempt has been made to examine the possible sources of increase in production potential,especially in the context of food-grains.The increase of 10 million tons mentioned earlier is broadly ascribed to the following development programmes: Although, over a series of years rough yardsticks for increase in food production arising from irrigation or the use of fertilisers or other factors have been evolved, these are no more than a rough approach. Elaborate studies are needed before the effects of different programmes can be isolated and such measures devised as will permit reasonably accurate calculations even under normal weather conditions of anticipated increases in production.Programmes such as irrigation, fertilisers and improved agricultural practices have necessarily an interacting character and are interdependent.

Moreover, as the farmer takes to improved agricultural practices and his knowledge of means available to him for influencing his environment increases and local communities become better organised for action the effects on production from areas already under irrigation are likely to be substantial. During the second five year plan 21 million acres of land are expected to receive irrigation, 12 million acres from large and medium irrigation, schemes and 9 million acres from minor irrigation works.

The provision for minor irrigation is made in part in the agricultural programmes of States and in almost equal part in the national extension and community development programmes. The former includes also provision for about a million acres of land to be irrigated from State tubewell schemes. Over 3500 production tubewells are expected to be constructed in the various States. So far tubewells have been concentrated in the states of Uttar Pradesh, Bihar, Punjab and Pepsu. During the second Plan, the tubewell programme will be extended to new areas which are already being investigated for availablity of underground water under and exploratory tubewell project.

For the successful implementation of the minor irrigation programme it is essential that there should be close coordination in the States between the agricultural department and district development staff incharge of national extension and community projects. In each State and district the programme of minor irrigation works and the irrigation targets to be achieved should be drawn up jointly between these two agencies. Systematic surveys are needed with a view to locating suitable minor irrigation works. During the past decade in each area many works which were long through to be necessary and feasibly have been taken up and fresh investigations are now required.

A survey of water resources in Madhya Pradesh, Hyderabad and the eastern parts of Bombay State which are liable to scarcity conditions has been recently initiated by the Ministry of Food and Agriculture. Another aspect which calls for renewed attention is that while new minor irrigation works are being constructed a proportion of old works are falling into disuse.It is suggested that State Governments should review existing arrangements for the maintenance of minor irrigation works and, where necessary, they should enact new legislation placing adequate responsibility on village communities so that,if there is failure in maintaining works, repairs can be undertaken and the cost recovered from the communities concerned.

Panchayat legislation in several States contains provisions for the levy of labour contributions. Such contributions should be utilised for the maintenance of local irrigation works. The consumption of nitrogenous fertilisers is proposed to be raised during the second plan from 6,10,000 tons in 1955 to over 1.8 million tons. The consumption of phosphatic fertilisers is also proposed to be stepped up. The utilisation of sewage and town composts has been provided for in the plan. In all areas special attention should also be given to green manuring and the use of oil cakes and other manures. The procurement and distribution of chemical fertilisers on a greatly expanded scale during the second five year plan raises the question of strengthening the existing administrative arrangements both at the Centre and in the States. Since 1944 the Central Government have operated a trading scheme known as the central fertiliser pool.

The work of the pool consists in ascertaining the requirements of States and of consumers such as tea and coffee plantations, procurement of the quantities needed, fixation of prices and making the necessary arrangement for the distribution of fertilisers. Distribution within States is undertaken by State Governments though Government sale depots, private distribution agencies and cooperative organisation, the detailed arrangements varying considerably in different States. As new chemical fertilisers are being brought into use and manurial trials are being carried out in the country it is of the greatest importance that information regarding the use of fertilisers should be made available on the widest possible scale and cultivators should receive adequate guidance and assistance.

The number of depots where fertilisers can be purchased needs to be considerably increased. It is also necessary that adequate buffer stocks should be maintained so that uninterrupted supplies are assumed. Finally, cooperative societies should be increasingly used as the main agency for distribution at the village level. Plans and States provide for about 3,000 seed multiplication farms with a total area of about 93,000 acres. In general every national extension service block will be served by a seed farm and a seed store. Seed produced at local farms will be issued to cultivators after passing through one or more stages of further multiplication at farms belonging to registered seed growers. The seed multiplication and distribution programme is to be developed so as to be able to meet the full requirements of national extension areas. Seed testing stations are also to be set up with a view to ensuring and enforcing quality standards for certain categories of seeds, especially for vegetable production. Programmes for setting up cooperative seed stores have also been drawn up by several States. The area under the Japanese method of paddy cultivation is to be increased during the plan period from 1.6 to 4 million acres.

During the second plan it is proposed to reclaim 1.5 million acres of land and to carry out land improvement measures over an area of 2 million acres through the Central and State tractor organizations and other agencies and though manual labour of individual cultivators. According to the provisional programme which has been drawn up, the Central Tractor Organisation will undertake during the next two years the reclamation of about 96,000 acres of fallow and jungle land and the ploughing up of about 149,000 acres of land which has been previously cultivated. A tractor training centre has already been established in Bhopal and it is proposed to establish one more centre in order to provide opportunities for training for tractor mechanics and drivers. The plan provides for the establishment of a tractor testing station with will examine the suitability of all types of tractor under Indian conditions and will also test diesel engines and pumping sets.

In extension work in the States the contribution of dry farming techniques has not yet received sufficient attention. Despite the scale on which irrigation programmes are being undertaken, a large proportion of lands will continue to be rainfed. The importance of the widespread adoption of the best dry farming methods cannot therefore be too much stressed. In particular, both for the conservation of water and of soil, in extension and community project areas contour bunding should be specially encouraged. While in certain parts of the country it is necessary to provide for mechanical equipment as a general rule, contour bunding can be undertaken by local labour with some assistance and guidance from trained agricultural personnel.

The States of Bombay, Saurashtra, Hyderabad, Madhya Pradesh, Vindhya Pradesh, Bhopal and Uttar Pradesh have large scale programmes for contour bunding. Among themselves they aim at carrying out contour bunding operations on more than 1.5 million acres during the plan period. In several States the value of consolidation of holdings in dry areas is not being fully appreciated. In areas where minor irrigation works such as wells can be undertaken, the benefits of consolidation of holdings are undoubtedly larger, but they are quite considerable even under dry farming conditions. In the filed of plant protection government agencies have done valuable work especially in locust control. Greater attention should however be given to the education of the farmer in protecting his crops from pests and diseases.

Similarly, agricultural departments in the States should devote more continuous study to the question of evolving suitable types of bullock-drawn agricultural implements. Under the plan plant protection activities both of the Central and State Governments are to be intensified. Plant quarantine stations will be set up at the principal sea ports and air ports. Four centres for plant protection equipment were established under the first five year plan. These are to be strengthened and ten new contres are to be set up. A field centre for locust investigations will also be established. Provision has been made by Ministry of

Food and Agriculture for a scheme for designing and introducing improved types of agricultural implements. Such work has been undertaken in the past at several centres in the country and needs to be developed more rapidly during the second five year plan. Provision has been made by several states for making improved agricultural implements available to farmers at reasonable rates. It western countries agricultural journals, pamphlets and other literature have made a considerable contribution to the developed of improved agricultural practices.

The Indian Council of Agricultural Research has taken steps in this direction and the plan of the Ministry of Food & Agricultural provides for further measures. This again is an activity to which agricultural and extension officials and other agencies in the States should give a high priority.

Horticulture

While programmes for animal husbandry, dairying and milk supply and forests and soil conservation are explained at some length in later chapters, a word may be said here regarding steps proposed for developing the cultivation of fruit and vegetables during the second five year plan. At present levels of production the availability of fruit and vegetables is reckoned respectively at about 1.5 and 1 ounce per head. Increase in the production of fruit and vegetables is essential both for increasing the supply of protective foods and for bringing about greater diversity in agricultural production. The plan provides Rs. 8 crores for horticultural development. Long-term loans are to be given to farmers for establishing new orchards and short-term credit is to be provided for rejuvenating existing orchards. new nurseries are also to be set up. Provision has also been made for the training of *malis* and for strengthening the horticultural staff in the States. The plans of States envisage rejuvenation of about 500,000 acres of existing orchards and about 200,000 acres of new orchard lands. Production of vegetables is to be encouraged, especially in the neighbourhood of towns by supplying seeds and seeds and seedlings of quality on credit and making technical guidance available to the vegetable growers.

State plans also provide for the multiplication of nucleus potato seeds. Special attention is to be given to the organisation of marketing cooperatives for fruit and vegetable growers. For developing fruit and vegetable preservation, assisting the canning industry and setting up cold storage plants, the Ministry of Food and Agriculture has provided a sum of Rs. 1.75 crores. It is proposed to increase the annual production of canned fruit and vegetable from 20,000 tons to 50,000 tons. Measures for encouraging the export of preserved fruit and vegetable products are also envisaged in the plan, and it is expected that exports will increase from 1,000 tons to 11,000 tons by the end of plan.

In the more advanced national extension and community project areas farmers have readily accepted the results of research which have been communicated to them and have asked for more. This demand for solutions to problems old and new is likely to develop more rapidly during the Second Five Year Plan and agricultural departments and institutions have to prepare themselves to meet it. For many years past the Indian Council of Agricultural Research and institutions associated with it have been engaged in investigations of individual problems. There has been a lag in the application of the result or research and research workers have not drawn their problems sufficiently from the daily experience and needs of the farmer.

During the Second Five Year Plan, it is proposed to give close attention to the complex of problems which links research with development and also to continue work on fundamental problem. These are tasks to be carried out in cooperation between the Central and State Governments and the Indian Council of Agricultural Research and Agricultural colleges and other institutions in the States. Some problems relating to the organisation of agricultural research and education have been recently reviewed by a joint team of Indian and American experts.

The plan provides about Rs. 14.15 crores for agricultural research, 4.65 crores through the Central Commodity Committees and Rs. 9.50 crores in the programme of the Ministry of Food and Agriculture. State plans have a large number of research schemes which will be assisted on a matching basis by the Indian council of Agricultural Research. The Council has sponsored a number of important investigations which will be continued during the second plan.

These include breeding of rust resisting wheat, manurial experiments on fields of cultivators with a view to preparing manurial schedules and trials on cultivators, fields with new kinds of fertiliser. Agronomic experiments which have been carried out at 18 centres according to a scheme sponsored under the Indo-US Technical Cooperation Programme will be extended to 16 more centres. A scheme for investigating the methods of control by hormonal weedicides, which was begun during the first Five Year Plan, will be extended. Four research-cum-testing centres for bullock drawn agricultural implements are to be established. To test the quality of improved seeds in regard to germination and extent of contamination by weed seeds, 11 testing centres are expected to be established.

State Governments are to be assisted in strengthening their existing research laboratories and farms. The Indian Agricultural Research Institute, the Central Potato Research Institute, the Central Rice Research Institute and the Sugarcane Breeding Institute have drawn up programmes of basic research for the second five year plan. During the first plan the Indian Agriculture Research Institute has carried out investigations on soil fertility fertiliser use and wheat resistant to rust. Its research organisation and programme have been recently reviewed by an expert committee which has recommended strengthening of various departments.

New lines of investigations such as soil mapping, rapid soil tests, teasing and certification of insecticides, storage pests, appraisal of losses due to plant disease, and use of atomic energy in solving agricultural research problems are proposed to be undertaken. A new horticultural division is to be set up. The Institute's programme also includes the establishment of regional stations for virus research, a seed testing laboratory, and bureau of plant introduction. The Institute has drawn up 68 research projects to be carried out during the Second Five Year Plan.

The Central Potato Research Institute, which undertook a coordinated scheme for applied research and development of potatoes during the first five year plan, proposes to give special attention to the production and maintenance of disease-free nucleus seed stock of breeding material and improved varieties and to carry out investigations on ruber crops other than potatoes. The Central Rice Research Institute, which has been engaged in fundamental research work on rice and has been a coordination centre of information, proposes to establish sub-stations for breeding work on rice. Problems of sugarcane research are being studied under the aegis of the Indian Central Sugarcane Committee.

The programme of research projects includes the study of varieties of sugarcane giving hightonnage and high sugar recovery, their response to fertilizers and manures with special reference to yield and quality of juice, time of harvesting of plant cane for keeping ratoons, cultural and rotational practices best suited to different regions, control of weeds and fungal diseases, inheritance of disease resistance, influence of climatic conditions on insect pests like stem-borer and pyrilla, and research on improvement in the manufacture and storage of gur and improved types of can crushers and juice boiling furnaces. A number of research projects are also being taken up at the India Institute of Sugarcane Research, the Indian Institute of Sugar Technology and Sugarcane Breeding Institute.

Each of the seven Central Commodity Committees set up by the Government of India has drawn up a programme of investigations in the crops with which it is concerned. Thus, the Indian Central Cotton Committee, which has at present 72 research schemes under investigation, proposes to set up four regional research stations, to remodel the technical laboratory in Bombay and to intensify research work on long-staple cotton. The jute technological laboratory in Calcutta, which functions under the Indian Central Jute Committee, is to be developed and strengthened. An institute of oil technology is to be established by the Indian Central Oilseeds Committee which has evolved a few improved varieties of oilseeds and has proposed farther work on the breeding of improved high yielding varieties.

Research work on tobacco is to be stepped up by the Indian Central Tobacco Committee in view of the fact that with decline in the production of high grade tobacco in recent years exports of tobacco have diminished. Special emphasis is to be laid on improving the quality of tobacco and systematic trials of new varieties evolved at Rajamundry are to be carried out.

The production of coconut being insufficient to meet the requirements of the country, the Indian Central Coconut Committee proposes to strengthen its two-existing research stations and to organize three regional research stations with the object of increasing the yield per tree by improving cultural practices, evolving high yielding varieties and reducing losses due to plant diseases and insect pests. Research on arecanut, which is also in short supply, has to be undertaken as a long-range task as this is a perennial crop and takes 8 to 10 years to bear fruit.

A central research station and three regional research stations have already been set up and under the auspices of the Indian Central Arecanut Committee it is proposed to establish a central technological laboratory and three more regional stations. The Lac Cess Committee will also intensify research work on the technology and utilisation of lac. Finally, in view of the programme for fruit and vegetable development during the second plan besides establishing a horticultural division at the Indian Agricultural Research Institute, it is proposed to set up horticultural research stations on a regional basis for the improvement of important fruit crops such as mango, cirus, grape, guava, pineapple and apple. In addition to technical research programmes described above the economic aspects of agriculture are now being studied at four agro-economic research centres which were set up in 1954-55 at Delhi, Santiniketan, Poona, and Madras. It is proposed to establish two more agro-economic centres during the plan period.

Under the auspices of the Research Programmes Committee of the Planning Commission farm management studies are being conducted in Bombay, Punjab, West Bengal, Uttar Pradesh, Madhya Pradesh and Madras. Valuable data on the institutional aspects of agricultural development is becoming available from the work of the Programme Evaluation Organisation of the Planning Commission. With the help of these and other studies such as those undertaken by the Reserve Bank of India in the Rural Credit Survey studies it is hoped to fill important gaps in information concerning Indian agriculture, especially those relating to farm costs, economics of farm size, input and output relationships in agriculture, economic aspects of mixed farming, measurement of under-employment, credit needs, indebtedness, capital formation, etc.

With the decision to introduce the national extension service over the entire country, proposals to expand the available facilities for agricultural education were also considered. Bihar, Rajasthan and Travancore-Cochin were assisted in establishing new agricultural colleges. In Assam, Hyderabad, Madreas, Madhya Pradesh. The number of agricultural colleges has now risen to 28 and these institutions will be able to meet the total requirements of agricultural graduates during the second five year plan which are estimated to amount to 6,500. For the training of village level workers, in addition to the existing 54 basic agricultural schools and 44 extension centres, it is proposed to establish 25 new basic agricultural wings attached to extension training centres.

The primary consideration for the development of agricultural marketing is so to reorganize the existing system as to secure for the farmer his due share of the price paid by the consumer and subserve the needs of planned development. To achieve these objects, malpractice associated with buying and selling of agricultural produce have to be eliminated, arrangements made for the efficient distribution of marketable surpluses from producing to consuming areas and cooperative marketing has to be developed to the maximum extent possible. Rural marketing and finance have to be integrated through the development of marketing and processing on cooperative lines.

Programmes for cooperative marketing and processing which have been drawn up so far for the second five year plan have been outlined in an earlier chapter. Here it is proposed to refer to other aspects of agricultural marketing. It is estimated that cooperative agencies may be able to handle about per cent of the marketable surplus by the end of the second plan. The rest of the surplus will continue to be sold through other marketing agencies. In the interest of the primary producer, therefore, the importance of regulating markets and market practices needs more emphasis. Moreover, the success of co-operative marketing itself depends on the efficiency with which regulated markets function. It has been observed that in States in which regulated markets have not been established to any extent, the cultivator is in a situation of much greater disadvantage than elsewhere. The past few years have not been a period of marked progress in the regulation of agricultural markets. It had been recommended in the First Five Year that the operation of the State Agricultural Produce (Markets) Act should be extended so as to cover all important markets before the end of the plan period. Before the plan seven States had this legislation in operation.

During the plan only three more States have enacted legislation. The number of regulated markets which stood at 265 in 1950-51 has increased to over 450. In some of the States which have the necessary legislation trade in a number of important commodities is now being regulated, as for instance, in foodgrains, fruit and vegetables, cattle, etc. The practice o sales in villages in not free from abuse, but it has not yet been regulated to any extent. Municipal markets in towns, where the produce is received on consignment basis and also brought directly by the producers have so far remained generally outside the scope of the State Agricultural Produce (Markets) Act.

Except in relation proposals for cooperative marketing, plans of several States for the next five years do not provide adequately for the regulation of agricultural markets. Some States have, however, framed targets for this purpose. Those who have not done so should reviewed the present position and draw up suitable programmes for regulating all important wholesale markets during the second plan. On the programmes so far drawn up it appears that the number of regulated markets will be doubled by the end of the second five year plan.

Agricultural production

Programmes of agricultural production lie at the base of the comprehensive approach to the reconstruction of the rural economy which is embodied in the Third Five Year Plan. Development of irrigation, from large as well as small works, soil conservation programmes and supplies of fertilizers, improved seed and credit, along with the provision of extension services reaching down to the village level are measures undertaken directly to increase production. In support of these programmes, through the community development movement, the energies of each village community as a whole as a whole are sought to be harnessed and its manpower and other resources effectively mobilised.

Land reform policies aim at removing impediments to greater production due to the agrarian structure inherited from the past and to prepare the way for the development of a progressive agriculture organised on a cooperative basis. The various programmes of cooperative development which have been undertaken and will be given still greater emphasis in the Third Plan are intended to build up the necessary institutional framework for rapid economic development in rural areas such as will be of special benefit to the weaker sections of the rural population.

Schemes for increasing agricultural production are closely bound up with the success of animal husbandry and dairying and the development of fisheries and of rural industry. From the aspect of long-term development, care of forest wealth, conservation of soil and moisture and the growing of village fuel plantations are of great importance. In some parts of the country rural electrification is already beginning to make a significant impact on rural life through extension or irrigation and speeding up of technological change; this impact will become progressively larger. These various aspects of agricultural development and, in particular, the specific programmes for increasing agricultural production for which the Plan provides, gain in significance when seen against the wider background of the largescale transformation in rural life which is being brought about through successive Five Year Plans.

By the end of the Second Plan, the index of agricultural production rose to 135, the index for foodgrains being 132 and that for other crops 142. In the First Plan, agricultural production rose by about 17 per cent. During the Second Plan, who years out of five—1957-58 and 1959-60—were unfavourable, and the overall increase in agricultural production amounted to about 16 per cent. Before the Second Plan took final shape, it was realised that the programme of economic development with special emphasis on heavy industries which the Plan embodied would demand a larger increase in agricultural production than had been at first envisaged.

Accordingly, in consultation with State Governments, in initial targets were reviewed, and in November, 1956, the following revised target were proposed: foodgrains, 80.5 million tons; oilseeds, 7.6 million tons; sugarcane, 7.8 million tons; cotton, 6.5 million bales; and jute, 5.5 million bales. The Second Plan targets for the production of sugarcane has been exceeded; on the other hand, there has been stagnation in cotton and jute. In oilseeds also, production has fallen below the target. In view of the production tends during the Second Plan, it is of the highest importance that in the Third Plan, besides achieving self-sufficiency in foodgrains, substantial increases should be secured in commercial crops, specially cotton, oilseeds and jute. With the growth of the economy and increase in domestic demands as well as the need to step up exports, success in increasing the production of commercial crops is as vital as increase in the production of foodgrains. In the Second Plan, out of a total anticipated outlay under agriculture and community development of Rs. 529 crores, agricultural production programmes accounted for about Rs. 290 crores.

In addition, there was a total outlay of Rs. 372 crores on major and medium irrigation schemes. In the course of the Plan additional resources were provided for minor irrigation.

Apart from the influence of unfavourable seasons, greater progress might have been achieved in agricultural during the Second Plan if the benefits of the substantial investments incurred, for instance, in the extension of irrigation, both from small and large irrigation works, and in the establishment of seed farms could have been realised more speedily. Programmes which require large-scale participation on the part of the people, such as, soil conservation, made only limited progress. The consumption of fertilisers, which has been recently stepped up to a considerable extent, increased very slowly during the first four years of the Second Plan.

This was due both to the storage of foreign exchange and to the inadequate progress made in establishing the new fertiliser plants. When the agricultural targets for the Second Plan were reviewed in 1956, it was specially emphasised that programmes for the multiplication of improved seeds, for the use of fertilisers and for irrigation, soil conservation, etc., would be implemented so as to yield the maximum benefits within the shortest time. It was envisaged that there would be carefully worked out programmes for covering every acre of land enjoying irrigation or assured rainfall with improved seeds and that the supply of fertilizers and organic and green manures would be ensured. Sufficient progress was not made in these directions. Consequently, a much larger task in agricultural remains to be accomplished during the Third Plan. More than any other factor, the success of the Third Plan will turn on the fulfillment of its agricultural targets.

Third plan

In formulating agricultural production programmes for the Third plan, the guiding consideration has been that the agricultural efforts should not be impeded in any manner for want of financial or other resources. Accordingly, finance is being provided on a scale which is considered adequate, and the further assurance is given that if, for achieving the targets of production, additional resources are found necessary, those will be provided as the Plan proceeds. Supplies of fertilisers are also to be made available on a large scale. Efforts are being made to strengthen agricultural administration in the States, and stress is being placed on the closet possible coordination between different agencies notably, those concerned with agriculture, cooperation, community development and irrigation. Supplies of credit through cooperative agencies are being expanded, and the need for linking credit with production and marketing is emphasised. It may be stressed, however, that whole these efforts should go a long way, they are not in themselves a sufficient guarantee that the agricultural objectives of the Third Plan can be realised.

The central task of the community development organisation and of extension workers at the block and village levels is to mobilise the rural community for intensive agricultural development, to impart a sense of urgency and direction to the work of all the agencies operating on behalf of the Government, and to ensure that the requisite supplies, services and technical assistance are available at the right time and place and in the most effective manner possible.

At the same time, the Agriculture Departments must place at the disposal of the community development organisation at the block level the supplies, trained personnel and other resources needed. This means that all families in the village, specially those engaged in cultivation, must be involved in the agricultural effort through the village cooperative and the panchayat, and enabled to achieve larger results through village production plans. In view of the experience in the Second Plan, these essential conditions cannot be too greatly stressed. As the country enters upon the larger tasks of the Third Plan, there is urgent need to improve the organisation of agricultural programmes at the local level as well as at higher levels in the States and at the Centre.

The Third Plan provides for an outlay on production programmes in agriculture, including large and small irrigation schemes, soil conservation and cooperation of about Rs. 128 crores, the comparable outlay ion the Second Plan being of the order of about Rs. 667 crores.

Besides resources provided for the Third Plan, finance from cooperative agencies will also increase substantially. Short-term and medium-term loans are expected to go up from about Rs. 200 crores and the amount outstanding on account of long-term loans from about Rs. 34 crores in the last year of the Second Plan to about Rs. 530 crores and Rs. 150 crores respectively by the end of the Third Plan.

Programmes and targets for agriculture embodied in the Draft Outline of the Third Plan were based on preliminary studies undertaken by State Governments and the Central Ministries concerned. These were intended to provide a basis for detailed agricultural programmes to be prepared in the light of local conditions and possibilities in district, blocks and villages. It was suggested that with a view to securing the largest measure of local participation and in the fullest particular, utilusation of the local man-power resources, programmes relating to agriculture, minor irrigation, soil conservation and the devclopment of cooperation should be formulated through district and block plans.

At attempt has been made in several States to draw up local plants on these lines. It has been observed, however, that plans at the local level are easier to formulate after the broad dimension and objectives of the State plans have been established. Although in proposing targets and in evolving programmes. State Government have taken advantage of their experience in preparing district and block agricultural plans, on the whole, the programmes and the estimates of production which now form part of the plans of States have been arrived at through studies by the Departments concerned at the State level. Their proposals have been considered in two series of discussions between the States, the Planning Commission and the Central Ministries and care has been taken to prepare them in some detail.

Nevertheless, the limitation persists that they are not yet as firmly based on area plans as had been earlier hoped for. For realising the programmes and targets accepted by

States there must, therefore, be continuing emphasis on the drawing up of annual district and block agricultural plans within the general scheme of the five year programme. Without district, block and village agricultural production plans, it will be difficult to ensure the widespread cooperation and local initiative and understanding of the tasks to be accomplished which are the fundamental conditions for success in agricultural development.

Increasing agricultural production

The principal technical programmes for increasing agricultural production, around which intensive work is to be organised, are: (1) irrigation, (2) soil conservation, dry farming and land reclamation, (3) supply of fertilisers and manures, (4) seed multiplication and distribution, (5) plant protection, (6) better ploughs and improved agricultural implements, and adoption of scientific agricultural practices. In all areas, and specially in the development blocks taken up under the community development programme, these programmes will need to be implemented with the largest measures of participation on the part of local communities and to reach as many families as possible through the village production plans.

In addition, in fifteen districts, in which conditions are specially favourable on account of the availability of irrigation and assured rainfall, and the cooperative movement is fairly established, it is proposed to undertake agricultural programmes on a more intensive scale then may be generally feasible. In all areas, and more especially in these, a concentrated effort will be made to reach all farmers and to promote the adoption by them of a minimum combination of improved practices. The targets of agricultural development agreed to in consultation with individual States are set out in Annexure I to this chapter.

Minor irrigation

The gross area irrigated during the Third Plan from irrigation schemes is estimated at 25.6 million acres—12.8 million acres each from major and medium irrigation works. Of the latter, schemes financed from provisions under the community development programme are expected to irrigate about 3.3 million acres, the rest of the irrigation being secured from schemes within the agricultural programme. Statistics relating to land utilisation are not yet available beyond 1957-58, and it is difficult to ascertain the actual increase in net irrigated area during the first two plans as a result of the irrigation programmes which have been carried out.

Minor irrigation works include a variety of schemes, some of which stabilise exiting irrigation or, as in the case of drainage schemes and embankments, improve the existing irrigation without necessarily increasing the area irrigated. Allowance has also to be made for minor irrigation schemes go out of use on account of 'depreciation' or are replaced by irrigation from major and medium irrigation schemes. In the Draft Outline it was reckoned that at the end of the Second Plan the net irrigated area might be the order of 70 million acres, increasing to about 90 million acres by end of the Third Plan.

Recent estimates appear to suggest lower figures, but the available data are far from satisfactory. There is considerable discrepancy between statistics of progress reported in respect of both large and small irrigation schemes, and those relating to land utilisation which become available after a lag of about three years. It is proposed to undertake a specially investigation into these differences. In the Third Plan the total outlay on minor irrigation from provisions under agriculture and community development is likely to be about Rs.250 crores, in addition to such finance as cooperative agencies may provide. Thus, minor irrigation is one of the larger investment programmes in the Third Plan.

The principal advantages of minor irrigation works are that they can be executed quickly, entail small outlays and there is only a short lag between their completion and the realisation of benefits. Moreover, they can be undertaken at the initiative of individuals and small groups and offer scope for participation by the community. Yet, it has been observed that minor irrigation programmes are tending increasingly to develop as programmes for small-scale irrigation works executed by Government agencies with little voluntary labour or participation by the people. It is of the utmost importance that for the greater part minor irrigation should be developed in all States as essentially a community programme in which local contributions is money and labour are specially stressed.

When the scale of the minor irrigation programme becomes large, it involves problems of organisation, investigation and utilisation which may in some ways be even more difficult than those which arise in the case of larger irrigation works. In the early phases of the minor irrigation programme the simpler categories of works can be taken up and the need for extended surveys is not always felt. Preliminary studies suggest that the possibilities of minor irrigation development could extend eventually to a gross area of about 75 million acres. To realise this potential, surveys and investigations should be undertaken in every State in a systematic manner for various river basins, and there should be adequately staffed investigation units working in different areas. At present few areas have minor irrigation projects which are worked out sufficiently in advance for implementation without delay. Experience during the First and Second Plans sugggests certain directions in which the implementation of the minor irrigation programme needs to be improved if full benefits by way of increase in agricultural production as well as adequate financial returns are to be realised.

These relate to better maintenance, adoption of appropriate crop patterns, better utilisation and water management, and efficiency in execution. Investigations undertaken by the Committee on Plan Projects and other studies have pointed to the need for strengthening the present arrangements for the maintenance of minor irrigation works on the part of the State Governments as well as local communities, thereby reducing losses due to 'depreciation' which appear to occur at present at an alarmingly high rate. An increasing proportion of minor irrigation works now under construction are such that State Governments should undertake responsibility for their maintenance.

The technical and administrative organisation for minor irrigation works must therefore be strengthened and regular inspection and supervision assured. It is also essential that certain obligations should be placed by law on local communities and beneficiaries. In most parts of India obligations relating to the maintenance of field channels were long in existence and were entered in revenue records. These customary obligations have, however, tended to fall into disuse, and greater definiteness has now to be given to them through legislation.

Some States have already enacted such legislation. The main obligations to be undertaken relate to construction and maintenance of field channels, maintenance of bunds and tanks, and desilting of the beds of tanks where the works are not of such magnitude that they must be taken up by Government. It is envisaged that statutory powers should be conferred on village panchayats for enforcing these obligations on the part of beneficiaries. If the latter fail to carry out works in time, the panchayats should carry them out and realise the cost. In the event of village panchayats failing to carry out the works,the Government or, on its behalf, the Panchayat Samiti of the development block may arrange for their execution, the cost being recovered eventually from beneficiaries.

The problem of reducing time lags between the completion of works and realisation of their benefits arises not only for large schemes but also for a large proportion of small irrigation schemes. Being widely dispersed, minor irrigation works demand in fact greater attention from the extension agencies. A recent field study of the problems of minor irrigation by the Programme Evaluation Organisation suggests that non-utilisation of facilities is a factor of quite serious dimensions even in the case of minor irrigation, and calls for close study in each area with reference to different types of works. Irrigation in any area calls for a series of agricultural measures, including adoption of new crop patterns, land development, soil and water conservation and other improved agricultural practices. It is important that agricultural extension personnel should concentrate on these measures, so that irrigation yields the expected benefits. The methods to be adopted are well-known and the question is primarily one of advance planning and of giving continuous attention to the tasks mentioned above. Execution of the minor irrigation programme has suffered to some extent because experienced personnel able to adapt their technical knowledge to different kinds of construction works have not been available in sufficient numbers.

The situation has improved to some extent. However, in view of the large size of the programme to be carried out in the Third Plan, it is necessary that suitable technical cadres should now be built up in the States. This will become all the more important if a large-scale rural works programme devoted specially to agricultural development, as has been visualised, is to be successfully organised. Moreover, in several parts of the country the scope of the minor irrigation programme is itself being enlarged through the development of rural electrification.

During the Second Plan, minor irrigation programmes suffered to some extent from difficulties in acquiring land, inadequate delegation of financial and administrative powers to personnel in charge of works, and failure to sanction works in advance of the construction season. There are other problems of an administrative nature to which attention should be drawn. There has been a tendency for overlapping financial provision for minor irrigation schemes under agriculture and under community development. It is necessary that the financial provisions for minor irrigation schemes, whether under agriculture or community development, are pooled together at the block level and utilised for the maximum benefit of area. It is considered that for individuals assistance for minor irrigation works should come, as far as possible, from cooperative agencies and taccavi loans and from the Agricultural Departments. Provisions available under the community development block budget should give preference to schemes benefiting large numbers of persons jointly. They may be undertaken either by village panchayats or by cooperative groups.

In recently years, in irrigation as in other fields of agricultural development, different kinds of subsidies have been used as a method of stimulating new activity. The general policy should be to reduce these subsidies progressively and, where possible, to eliminate them. There might be some justification for a subside which is intended to benefit the poorer sections of the community or to support for a limited period innovations or improved practices which have not yet been accepted. The existing schemes of subsidies should be reviewed critically and, after examining other ways of achieving the objects, phased programmes should be drawn up for reducing and, to the extent feasible, terminating the subsidies.

For the Third Plan the Central Government have sponsored two new schemes in the field of minor irrigation. A programme of applied research is to be taken up for the study of problems which arise in the execution of minor irrigation works with a view to effecting economy in construction costs, efficient operation of irrigation works and economic use of water reaching the fields. A scheme for training agricultural graduates in irrigation water use has also been formulated. These schemes will be undertaken through the agency of both Central and State institutions.

In some parts of the country, specially the Punjab and Uttar Pradesh, the problem of water-logging has become serious. With a view to reclaiming water-logged areas and checking deterioration, agricultural programme provide for schemes for improving surface drainage and installing shallow tubewells.

For Several areas an extensive programme of exploratory tubewells has been in operation. Out of 379 drillings which have been attempted, as many as 195 have proved successful upto March, 1961. The successful tubewells are being taken over by the State Governments concerned. If the data are made available more widely, the construction of private and cooperative tubewells could be encouraged in the more favourable areas.

Soil conservation, dry farming and land reclamation- Considerable emphasis is being given in the Third Plan to soil conservation and dry farming. These programmes are dealt with in the Chapter on Soil Conservation. A word may, however, be said here on land reclamation. A technical committee is at present engaged, in cooperation with States, in surveying and locating large blocks of waste lands. The committee has already completed its surveys of land classified as "other uncultivated lands excluding fallow lands" and "fallow lands other than current fallows" in seven States.In these, a total area of nearly one million acres comprising blocks of land of 250 acres or more which may be available for reclamation and resettlement has been located. Schemes for reclaiming these blocks will have to be drawn up. The area of 3.6 million acres shown as the target for land reclamation includes about 2 million acres in Rajasthan and also some other lands recommended by the technical committee. The programme for mechanised land reclamation operations will require personnel trained in the operation, maintenance and repair of tractors. In addition to the existing Tractor Training Centre at Budni the Third Plan provides for the establishment of a second centre. The centre at Budni in also being developed.

Fertilisers and manures-Supplies of fertilisers are proposed to be increased during the Third Plan in accordance with the following provisional schedule: Programmes for indigenous production and for imports both of fertilisers and of the raw materials needed, are based on the above estimates. Although there has been rapid growth in the demand for fertilisers and in recent years it has not been possible to meet the full requirements of cultivators, it will be a considerable administrative task to ensure the efficient distribution and use of increased supplies contemplated for the Third Plan.

In this connection, reference may be made to the recommendations made by the Fertiliser Distribution Enquiry committee, in particular, to the emphasis on the use of fertilisers in the form of mixtures with a view to promoting balanced fertilisers and making the best use of supplies of nitrogenous fertilisers, improved arrangements for distribution and attention to quality, and reduction in costs of distribution. As suggested by the Committee, for dealing effectively with problems arising out of increased distribution of chemical fertilisers, their storage and sales promotion, etc., a Central fertilisers Marketing Corporation is proposed to be set up during the Third Plan period. The U.N. Fertiliser Mission which has recently studied the fertiliser problem has stressed the need for educational work with the small farmer for extensive soil tests to determine the kinds and quantities of fertilisers needed under different conditions, and for continuous research into the use of fertilisers. The availability of credit for enabling small cultivators to use fertilisers is also of the greatest importance. These considerations should be kept in view in implementing the programmes formulated by the States. Despite progress in some directions, on the whole, sufficient stress is still not being laid extension work on the development of local manurial resources, specially organic manures. Among the target adopted by States for the Third Plan are above 5 million tons of urban compost, about 150 million tons of rural compost, and green manuring of about 41 million acres of land comparing to about 12 million acres at the and of the Second Plan Except for the urban compost programme, which is organised through municipal committees and the larger village panchayats, fulfilment of the other target is difficult to measure. It is hoped that through intensive work at the block and village levels the targets for green manuring and rural compost will be further improved upon. Increasing emphasis is also proposed to be laid on utllisation of sewage.

A direction in which there is need for intensive work is the production of nightsoil compost. This has been taken up on a pilot basis in several places, and it is suggested that the experience gained should now be studied with a view to formulating a larger and a more extended programme of development. Some progress has been made in developing cowdung gas and manure plants suitable for use in villages. The Indian Agricultural Research Institute has designed a model of the gas plant which is being used in some villages near Delhi and elsewhere. The gas plant costs about Rs.400 to Rs. 450, and this is a factor inhibiting its adoption on a wider scale. The more extended use of the gas plant will help increase soil fertility and crop yields contributing to the solution of the fuel problem.

Soil testing has an important contribution to make in

determining the right use of fertilisers for increasing crop yields and maintaining soil fertility. In recent years a number of laboratories have been established and their studies are coordinated by the Indian Agricultural Research Institute. With the object of compiling data on soils, providing training in soil science and soil mechanics and undertaking both fundamental and applied soil research, it is proposed to set up a Central Institute of Pedology and soil Mechanics.

Seed multiplication and distribution - Establishment of seed in all development blocks to meet the requirements of foundation seed of improved varieties was one of the principal programmes undertaken in the Second Plan. In all, about 4000 seed farms are reported to have been set up and about 800 more are expected to be established in the early years of the Third Plan. At the end of the Second Plan, a large proportion of the farms established have begun to provide seed for multiplication by registered growers, and it may take two or three years before the benefits of the programme begin to be realised on a significant scale. Although, on an average, an area of 25 acres for a seed farm was first indicated, a fair proportion of seed farms are of larger size. At the larger farms it is easier to provide technical personnel of the requisite quality and to undertake production on a more economic basis. These considerations should be kept in view, especially in respect of seed farms which have still to be set up, and of those which, as a temporary measure, were started on leased lands. Each seed farm provides for a seed store. To ensure better distribution, in the Third Plan States have generally provided for the setting up additional seed store in every development block. At the end of the second Plan, the area under crops covered by improved seed is estimated at 55 million acres. This is expected to increase by 148 million acres in the course of the Third Plan. While registered growers have a valuable role to playing the multiplication of improved varieties of seed, in formulating block and village agricultural plans, the aim should be to ensure that every village produces its own requirements of improved seed, undertaking as large a share of this task on a cooperative basis, but also making use of the better farmers.

A field study of the multiplication and distribution programme for improved seed undertaken by the Programme Evolution Organisation has revealed a number of weaknesses in the existing situation and in the working of seed farms. It is suggested that State Governments may review their proposals for the Third Plan in the light of these findings.

Considerable research has been undertaken in recent years for evolving high-hybrids of maize, and it has been found that with moderate amounts of nitrogenous fertilisers the yield of maize hybrids increases more than twice that of the local varieties. It is therefore proposed to take up the cultivation of hybrid maize on a countrywide scale, the first stage being to bring about 25 per cent of the maize area under hybrid varieties during the Third Plan. It is also intended to make a start with the production of hybrid jowar seed.

The Ministry of Food and Agriculture propose shortly to establish a Seed Corporation with object of ensuring production at selected farms under conditions of efficient management and maintaining purity and the maximum yield. An organisation is to be set up for the production of nucleus seed, and it is envisaged that cooperatives and other suitable organisations and, where necessary, individuals should function as certified seed agencies.

Legislation for controling the quality of seeds and regulating their production, marketing and movement is also under consideration.

Plant protection- over the past decade, plant protection measures have lagged behind several other aspects of the agricultural programme. In the Second Plan, the programme covered about 16 million acres of land. For the Third Plan, States have indicated a target of 50 million acres. The precise damage to crops from insects, rodent and other animal pests and on account of diseases, weeds and parasitic flowering Plans, is difficult to assess, but there can be no doubt of its serious dimensions.

Similarly, considerable losses are caused by deterioration of foodgrains and other agricultural commodities during storage through insects, rats, mice, etc. Much of the damage can be prevented if plant protection measures are adopted on an adequate scale as an integral part of the agricultural programme. Plant protection organisations in several States need to be strengthened at various levels. In addition to special units which might function over larger areas, it is necessary that with a view to securing the maximum extension effect, manually operated dusters and sprayers should be supplied extensively to farmers and to village panchayats. With these it is essential to ensure the timely supply to pesticides.

Improved agricultural implements—A serious gap in the agricultural programmes undertaken during the First and Second Plans has been in the field of improved agricultural implements. There is general recognition of the importance for scientific agriculture of improved village and harvesting practices, but specific action has been slow and insufficient. As has been pointed out, progress in the introduction of improved agricultural implements calls for steps at the same time in a number of directions.

The broad features of the programme for the adoption of improved agricultural implements proposed for the Third Plan may be briefly set out as follows:

(1) Adequate supplies of iron and steel of the categories required for agricultural implements should be made available. Precise estimates of requirements should be prepared each year in advance based on the actual programme of production which it is proposed to carry out. Requirements for manufacture of implements should be estimated separately from those for repairs and maintenance. It will be an advantage to place the supplies of iron and steel for agricultural purposes at the disposal of the Agricultural Departments in the States.

(2) The principal implements which should be recommended in each State for popularisation have been selected provisionally by groups of experts. The suggestions should be considered by States and a final selection should be made with a view to arranging for production, distribution, etc.

(3) Four regional research, testing and training centres for improved agricultural implements have been set up by the Indian Council of Agricultural Research as part of its programme in the Second Plan, and are to be transferred to she States in which they are situated. It is proposed to establish one research, testing and training centre in improved agricultural implements in every State. Research, testing and training centres should be free to undertake manufacture on a commercial scale but, in the main, they should concentrate on the production of

improved proto-types and of implements which are not in the market and of components of special quality which may be used by other fabricators. As part of the intensive agricultural district programme, workshops are also being established in a number of districts. For improved implements to spread out rapidly, their production should be taken up as a development programme at the district and block level, and industrial cooperatives for the manufacture of agricultural implements should be actively supported.

(4) According to their conditions suitable extension arrangements should be made by State Government at the district and block levels for demonstrating and popularising improved agricultural implements. It would not be possible to set up such units at the block level in all the development blocks in the country. It would, therefore, be an advantage to consider the possibility of setting up a small number of units, say four, at the district level and attach them to the district agricultural officer. These units could move between development blocks, working in each block under the direction and guidance of the Agricultural Extension Officer and the Block Development Officer. The units could provide the necessary orientation to village level workers and village artisans and could demonstrate improved implements to the cultivators.At the block headquarters there should be a stock of implements readily available for demonstration and hire. These implements could be purchased from within the block budget and additional implements could be provided by the State Agricultural Department.

(5) Steps be taken to strengthen the agricultural

engineering section of State Agricultural Departments. The financial assistance extended to States for implementing the recommendations of the Report of the Agricultural Administration Committee will also be available for strengthening agricultural engineering personnel of the State Agricultural Departments at the State level and at the district level.

(6) With due regard to the size of the programme to be undertaken each year, assured arrangements for credit for supplying improved implements should be made. Credit should be provided both through cooperative agencies and way of taccavi loans Plans for cooperative development drawn up so far do not provide sufficiently for credit for agricultural implements, and this aspect should receive special attention.

(7) Agricultural workshops have been established at 25 extension training centre. It is proposed that all extension training centres should now be equipped with agricultural workshops for providing training facilities for village level workers, mechanics and artisans.

(8) At the State level, there may be a Committee or a Board, including representatives from amongst farmers and manufacturers and others, for assisting in drawing up production programmes and devising suitable arrangements for distribution and ensuring supplies of raw materials.

With expansion in the agricultural implements programme there will be need for considerably larger numbers agricultural engineers than existing training facilities are likely to make available. This aspect has been taken into account in formulating the programme of technical education. The total provision in the Third Plan for the programme of agricultural implements is about Rs.8 crores.

Intensive agricultural district programme—In recommending the selection of certain areas for more intensive efforts, the Agricultural Production Team sponsored by the ford Foundation observed that there were no inherent soil, climatic or other physical reasons for the present low yields. The Team, therefore, suggested that those selected crops and those selected areas in each State should be chosen which have the greatest increase potentialities. In pursuance of this proposal, the intensive agricultural district programme has been taken up to begin with, in one district in each State.

The programme is intended to contribute both to rapid increase in agricultural production in the selected areas and to suggest new innovations and combinations of practices which may be of special value elsewhere. In the selected districts an attempt will be made to provide all the essential elements for increasing production to the extent needed, such as, supplies of fertilisers, pesticides and improved seeds and improved implements, and composite scientific demonstrations will be laid out on a large scale. An effort will be made to provide credit on a scale sufficient to reach all farmers, including those previously considered uncreditworthy and credit and marketing will be linked. Extension personnel, specially in agriculture and cooperation, are being made available on a somewhat larger scale than in other areas so that they can work intensively which Panchayat Samitis and village Panchayats and with cooperative organisations. Through benchmark surveys and systematic evaluation,high standards of performance will be insisted upon in these districts. The districts chosen for intensive development should give to the agricultural and other services in each State special opportunities for developing improved methods for extension and for planning of agricultural production at the block and village levels as well as in relation to the individual farmer.

The development programmes which have been described above constitute the essential targets of the Third Plan. However, for various purposes, it is useful to estimate additions to production likely to be achieved on the assumption that the various development programmes are carried out and, along with these, improved agricultural practices are adopted on the scale contemplated. Although efforts have been made in recent years to base 'yardsticks' of additional production on precise experimental data, the measures adopted must be regarded at best as rough guides rather than as a satisfactory basis for firm targets. Moreover, in agriculture weather conditions are always dominant element. These limitations should be kept in view in comparing the following estimates of production which may be realised by the end of the Third Plan.

According to the estimates of increased production the index of agricultural production should rise from 135 in 1960-61 to 176 in 1965-66, the total increase being about 30 per cent over the five year period. Increased production of the order envisaged above can take place only on the assumption that the various development programmes will be carried out effectively and with widespread public participation and use of local manpower and other resources and that intensive effort will be made in every block to adopt improved agricultural practices. The greater part of increase in yields will necessarily have to be secured in areas under irrigation and assured rainfall, but even in other areas through soil conservation and dry farming there should be some improvement in yields. The estimates of production for the Third Plan given in table 5 represent an appreciable increase in per capita availability. In foodgrains, the availability per capita is expected to increase from 16oz in 1960-61 to 17.5 oz per day in 1965-66 and consumption of cloth from about 15.5 yards to 17.2 yards per year. Consumption of edible oil is expected to go up from 0.4 oz to 0.5 oz per day over the Third Plan period.

A preliminary assessment of the likely changes in the Third Plan in the pattern of land utilisation suggests that the net area sown may increase from about 327 to 335 million acres area sown more than once from about 52 to 67 million ares. The area of culturable waste is expected to diminish from about 47 to 51 million acres.

Commercial crops—Except for sugarcane, the targets set for commercial crops in the Second Plan have fallen short to a considerable extent. Therefore, in the Third Plan it is essential to intensify for increasing the production of these crops, specially,cotton, jute and oilseeds. Over and above the provision for programmes like minor irrigation, seed farms and plant protection which will benefit all crops, outlays to the extent of about Rs.26 crores have been provided for special development schemes relating to different commercial crops. As the Plan proceeds, it might be necessary to make larger resources available for development schemes of commercial crops. Special care will be taken to ensure adequate supplies of fertilisers for these crops. It might also be necessary to facilitate diversion of areas from millets to commercial crops. The aim is not only to attain higher levels of production, but also to secure larger supplies of varieties which have considerable export demand or which will save on imports.

Detailed programmes relating to different commercial crops have been worked out by various commodity committees. In the main, these involve expansion and intensification of programmes already adopted during the Second Plan. Some features of these programmes, on which special stress is being laid in the Third Plan, may be briefly mentioned. It is proposed to provide necessary support for increasing the production of cotton and specially of long-staple varieties of cotton,such as, sea-island cotton in Mysore and Kerala and hybrid cotton in Gujarat and Maharashtra. The cultivation of sea-island cotton is to be extended from about 20,000 acres at present to about 300,000 acres at the end of the Third Plan.

Programmes for just development are directed, in particular, towards improvement in quality through the provision of retting tanks and of high quality seeds. Greater attention will be given to the development of supplementary fibres, such as, mesta, sisal, ramie, etc.

Increase in the production of oilseeds is one of the critical targets in the Third Plan both to meet higher domestic demand and to provide surpluses for export. To increase the availability of vegetable oils for exports, it is proposed that in the course of the Third Plan at least about one-half of the cotton seed available should be utilised for extracting, oil, and solvent extraction of expeller oilcakes should be substantially increased. Greater attention will also be given to problems connected with the development of non-edible oilseeds like *mahuva* and neem as also rice bran, etc. The Ministry of Food and Agriculture propose to set up a Spices and Cashewnut Committee for undertaking research and guiding development in these crops. The programme for cashewnut development involves bringing under cultivation an additional area of about 300,000 acres.

In tobacco the main problem is to produce varieties for which there is demand. Greater attention will, there fore, be given to the improvement of Virginia and other types of tobacco by ensuring supply of pure seed, provision of the types of fertiliser required, careful handling of leaves and better arrangements for curing. The increase in production during the Third Plan from 300,000 to 325,000 tons is intended almost entirely for the production of Virginia tobacco.

Tea, coffee and rubber—Plantation crops, specially tea, coffee and rubber, have been assigned high priority in the Third Plan. The Plan envisages increase in the export of tea from 465 to 550 million lbs. and more than twofold increase in exports of coffee from the present level of 340,000 cwt. The consumption of rubber has increased rapidly in recent years and is now estimated at 50,000 tons. Requirements by the end of the Third Plan are estimated at about 100,000 tons. In the course of the Third Plan it is proposed to increase the production of natural rubber from about 26,000 to 45,000 tons and also to produce about 15,000 tons of reclaimed rubber and 50,000 tons of synthetic rubber. Supplies of fertilisers on an adequate scale will be provided for all plantation crops. To facilitate replanting programmes arrangements are also being made to provide the necessary finance.

Horticulture—A number of new schemes were introduced during the Second Plan for the development of fruit production. These include provision of financial assistance for planting new orchards and rejuvenating old ones, as well as facilities for training gardeners. During the Second Plan about 166,000 acres of new orchards were planted and about 132,000 acres of old orchards were rejuvenated, and 4,000 gardeners were trained.

The total area at present under fruits and vegetables is estimated to be about 6 million acres, of which nearly one half is under fruit cultivation. In the Third Plan, the total area under fruits and vegetables is expected to increase to about 7 million acres. It is proposed to bring 235,000 acres under new orchards and to rejuvenate 250.000 acres under old orchards. Besides continuing schemes already in operation, the plans of States provide for the establishment of progeny orchards with nurseries and garden colonies.

The nurseries will help in the supply of planting material of reliable parentage and guaranteed performance. For the development of vegetable production, the plans of States provide for supply of improved varieties of seeds, plant protection measures and technical advice. Arrangements are also being made for certification of vegetable seeds.

Development of fruit and vegetable preservation has been assisted for some years past through subsidy on tinplate for fruit and vegetable products, rebate of excise duty on sugar used for exported products, and provision of training facilities, technical advice and development loans. The output of fruit and vegetable products increased from about 20,000 tons at the end of the First Plan about 40,000 tons in 1960-61 and is expected to rise to about 100,000 tons by the end of the Third Plan.

Subsidiary foods—Subsidiary foods include primarily potatoes, sweet potatoes and tapioca and other vegetables and fruits and certain processed and derived fruits. The Third Plan includes programmes for the increased production of these articles. Their greater use is intended to help diversify the pattern of food consumption and promote balanced nutrition.

The Plan also includes development schemes for the conservation and effective utilisation of perishable foodstuffs through refrigerated transport, establishment of dehydration units, cold storage and development of protein rich foods.

Agricultural marketing—The total number of markets in the country is about 2500. The number of regulated market increased from about 470 at the end of the First Plan to 725 at the end of the Second Plan. In the course of the Third Plan it is proposed to bring the remaining markets within the scheme of regulation. The programme for grading commodities under the Agricultural produce Act is also being expanded.

The market intelligence service now covers about 500 markets. In the Third Plan it is proposed to extend further the number of reporting centres so as to provide adequate coverage for all areas in the country and strengthen the dissemination of market news. An increasingly aspect of agricultural marketing is the development of co-operative marketing organisations at various levels. Programmes for the expansion of cooperative marketing have been described in an earlier chapter.

Storage—Programmes for the expansion of storage capacity with the Government, warehousing corporations and various cooperative organisations were initiated during the Second Plan. The Central Government has at present a total storage capacity of about 2.5 million tons, of about a third owned by Government. It is proposed to increase this to about 5 million tons, of which about 3.5 million tons will be owned by Government. The warehouses of the Central and State warehousing corporations have a storage capacity of about 350,000 tons; this is to be increased to over 1.6 million tons.

In addition, the capacity of the godowns of cooperative marketing societies and primary societies is expected to go up from about 800,000 tons to about 2 million tons. The Plan has allotted Rs.25 crores for the construction of additional godowns by the Government for the storage of foodgrains and Rs. 8 crores for warehousing programmes. The provision of storage capacity is a vital step in the implementation of price policies number the such further resources as may be needed will be made available.

Agricultural education- proposals in the Third Plan relating to the expansion of agricultural education and research are discussed in the Chapters on Technical Education and Scientific and Technological Research. In the course of the Third Plan, the number of agricultural colleges will increase from 53 to 57and the annual intake go up from 5600 to 6200. The total requirements of agricultural graduates for the plan period are estimated at about 20,000 and these are expected to be met.

During the Second Plan, an agricultural university was established at Pantnagar in Uttar Pradesh. Further proposals for setting up agricultural universities are under examination. The view that agricultural universities have a special contribution to make towards the development of agriculture has been urged in a series of expert reports on agricultural education. It is pointed out that if India's agriculture is to be raised to levels comparable with those of advanced countries, agriculture education of the traditional type, which is not sufficiently linked with research and extension will not be adequate in relation to the complex and changing problems of the vast body of cultivators, most of them operating very small holdings.

The agricultural university seeks to bring together a number of related fields of study, such as, agriculture, animal husbandry, veterinary science, dairying, basic sciences and humanities. The underlying concept is that the responsibility of the agricultural university extends beyond teaching to applied as well as fundamental research in agriculture and involves special obligations towards cultivators in the area served by the university, in particular, to discuss their problems by working with them, transmit the results of research, and bring teaching, research and extension into an integrated view of agriculture and agricultural education.

Agricultural research—The Plan provides for an outlay of about Rs. 28 crores for agricultural research—about Rs. 11 crores at the Centre Rs. 17 crores in the States. In the past, agricultural research tended to be confined mainly to government farms and research stations and its results did not reach cultivators to any great extent. Extension activities have brought research workers into closer contact with farmers and presented them with new problems. Research organisations in the States are being strengthened for dealing with these problems. For crops like wheat, rice, millets, cotton and oilseeds, it is proposed to develop research facilities on a regional basis in addition to work undertaken in the States. The plan provides for intensive study of irrigation practices in river valley projects and for working out the water requirements of crops, new rotations, and problems connected with the use of fertilisers in irrigated areas. Among the new centres research to be established in the Third Plan are an institute for soil science and pedology, a forage and grasslands research institute and virus research institute.

Agricultural administration—In view of the large programmes of agricultural development, the need for strengthening Agricultural Departments in the States has been felt for several years. To this end a series of proposals were made three years ago by the Agricultural Administration Committee. These include strengthening of staff at various levels, revision of terms and conditions, and expansion of facilities for training, education and research. To a considerable extent, the plans of States incorporate schemes for strengthening Agricultural Departments which have been worked out in the light of the recommendations made by the Committee. However, there has been some delay in implementing proposals for strengthening State agricultural administration. It is, therefore, suggested that these should be given effect to as a matter of first priority.

State farms—A Central mechanised farm with an area of about 30,00 0acres was established in 1956 at Suratgarh in Rajasthan. The possibility of establishing more State farms on similar lines has been studied and it is proposed to set up one and possibly two more farms during the Third Plan.

Agricultural price policy—For achieving the high targets of agricultural production set for the Third Plan, it is important that growers should have full confidence that the additional effort and investment which are called for will yield adequate return. Changes in the prices and Production of fibres during the few years show that wide fluctuations in prices affect the growers' capacity to make sustained efforts for increasing production.The fall in prices of jute in 1958 affected production in subsequent years. The assurance of minimum remunerative prices and cash crops like cotton, oilseeds and jute over the period of the Plan will provide the necessary incentives for increasing production, thus adding to the effectiveness of the various development programmes provided for in the Third Plan.

5

Necessity of Adult Education in Rural Areas

This chapter reviews some of the connections which have been made between rural development and adult education. The second part focuses on evaluating the adequacy of existing theory and research in this area. A question commonly posed by those with an interest in adult learning is 'What are the implications of adult development for adult and continuing education practitioners?' Knox outlines three possible implications:

1 To predict and explain success in education: 'Practitioners are typically interested in developmental generalizations regarding performance or personality in order to predict and explain successful participation in educative activity'.

2 To help people adapt to changing adult roles: 'Adult life cycle trends in performance in family, occupational and community roles suggest ways in which continuing education participation might facilitate adaptation and growth related to each role area'.

3 To improve the effectiveness of marketing and instructional activities: 'From time to time, the stability of adulthood is punctuated by role change events such as the birth of the first child, a move to another community or retirement... Such change events typically produce heightened readiness to learn which, if recognized, can contribute to the effectiveness of marketing and instructional activities'.

The whole tenor of the above implications indicates a view about adult development and an attitude to adult education. That is, that the various 'roles' of adult life are inevitable and people must learn to cope with them as they arise; and that adult education agencies, if they wish to be successful, should gear their marketing and instructional activities to cater for the different needs of adults at different life-stages. There is no sense in which adult roles are portrayed as arbitrary or even oppressive, or that alternative roles and options are possible for a given life period. In this sense adult education contributes towards the maintenance of social norms and structures. One need not look very far to find other instances of this type of approach.

A significant example can be found in McCoy's tabulation of 'Adult life cycle tasks and educational program responses' which is reproduced in Chickering's influential volume The Modern American College. McCoy identifies seven developmental stages, each of which is characterized by a set of common tasks. For example, the 'leaving home' stage has the associated tasks of 'break psychological ties','choose career','enter work', 'manage time' and so on. Each stage is then related to an appropriate range of programme responses, with a final column indicating the outcomes sought from the educational re-programme. The table is too lengthy to reproduce here but a cross-section of one stage only will be sufficient to illustrate the general strategy. Table shows the 'tasks' and 'program responses' appropriate for the developmental stage 'becoming adult'.

Educational responses to life-cycle tasks

Task	*Programme responses*
1 Select mate	Marriage workshops
2 Settle in work, begin career ladder	Management, advancement training
3 Parent	Parenting workshops
4 Become involved in community	Civic education; volunteer training
5 Consume wisely	Consumer education; financial management training
6 Homo-own	Homo-owning, maintenance workshops
7 Socially interact	Human relations groups, translation analysis
8 Achieve autonomy	Living alone, divorce workshops
9 Problem-solve	Creative problem-solving workshops
10 Manage stress accompanying change	Stress management, biofeedback, relaxation, workshops

A casual glance at the list of tasks and how each of them relates to specified programmes confirms my general point about adult education supporting the status quo. Even a non-specific 'task' such as 'achieving autonomy', is interpreted in the most narrow sense possible - that is, as the capacity to 'live alone successfully'. It is unnecessary to elaborate further, the tabulation speaks for itself. What is surprising, and disappointing, is that anyone in adult education would take such an analysis seriously as anything other than a narrow descriptive exercise. Yet there is a strongly held view among adult educators that the everyday reality of learners should be acknowledged, no matter how culturally specific that reality may be. The reader may remonstrate that McCoy is simply following this precept—what, then, is so objectionable? As I see it, there are two objections.

The first of these is that there is no acknowledgement of the narrow culturally specific 'tasks' which are identified. Quite the opposite, the 'tasks' are presented as a generalizable framework to be used by adult education agencies in formulating their programmes. There is no sense in which McCoy is using her analysis as a case study of a process for others to emulate in a different cultural context. The second objection, already mentioned in relation to Knox, is that the response of adult education is depicted as solely adaptive. There is no scope for questioning and challenging the tasks - they constitute the taken for granted reality of the learners and the adult educators. There are many adult educators who, being dismissive of the above approach, nevertheless subscribe to the view that adult development is a central concept in adult education.

An interest in adult development stems quite naturally from a commitment to the notion of lifelong learning and the associated concepts of 'lifelong education', 'recurrent education' and *'education permanente'*. The policy and research documents of UNESCO, the OECD and the

Council of Europe, which are the major sponsoring bodies of these concepts, frequently cite adult development as a central concern of any lifelong learning strategy. However, they do not understand adult development to be an immutable sequence of stages through which people pass at more or less predictable ages. Indeed, they challenge the concept of the 'typical' life cycle and support their view with an analysis of contemporary social and economic change. This is particularly apparent in the literature on recurrent education, and the following extract, taken from an article by one of its chief proponents, Jarl Bengtsson, typifies this approach: Significant changes are taking place in the relationship between work and non-work time seen over the individual's whole life cycle in terms of increased education, earlier retirement, longer holidays, etc. It has also been made clear that these changes affect social groups according to their hierarchical position in working life, as well as the way their work is being scheduled, i.e. full-time, part-time, shift-work, long spells of employment, etc. The claim is not that more non-work time is or will be used for education, although that certainly remains a strong possibility. Rather it is that to look at recurrent education from this perspective provides a very useful point of departure for placing it in the broader context of emerging new life-styles and life cycles. Most likely, the crucial factors behind changes in the individual's life-cycle pattern will be the economic and employment conditions that the industrialized countries will face during coming years.

Recurrent education, and its closely related concepts, accepts the diversity of life-cycle patterns and the need for educational institutions to respond to and foster this diversity through a diversity of provision. It supports the notion that individual options should be extended, especially the way in which paid work, education and leisure are combined. The principles espoused can be seen as a response to the effects of social, economic and technological change. Changes in demographic patterns, the sexual division of labour, the length of working life, hours spent at work, retirement age and so on, are all seen as relevant to the proposition that educational opportunities should be distributed, in a recurring way, across the life-span. Recurrent education also embodies the notion of social justice, and its evolution as a concept from the late 1960s has been linked with a host of terms implying broad social reforms: industrial democracy, participation in planning, social equity, decentralization, links between education and work and between younger and older generations, and concern with the disadvantaged. An underlying value in all this is a humanistic concern for the individual.

The idea of self-development, which is based on notions of individuality and growth, is contrasted with the opposing notions of enslavement, alienation and stagnation—which are the psychological consequences of clinging to an outmoded conception of the 'normal' life cycle. There are two persistent problems which are a feature of adult developmental psychology. The first is that there are insurmountable methodological difficulties in establishing 'phases' or 'stages' of adult life. The second is that much of the literature is historically and socially rooted and lacks any worthwhile generalizability.

Methodological difficulties

Not all adult development studies adopt a stage-sequence approach; nevertheless, they usually have a stake in making comparisons between different 'ages', 'phases' or 'stages' of life. Leaving aside the problem of deciding what type of data to gather, the common methodological problem is to construct a research design which generates comparative data. Many of the most influential studies in adult development use research design which fail to do this. Three basic research designs are the 'cross-sectional', 'longitudinal' and 'time-lag' designs. Perhaps the best known example of this technique is to be found in the research of Gould. In an initial study Gould observed and recorded the concerns expressed by a number of psychiatric outpatients. He hypothesized that these concerns differed among different age groups.

He then used these expressed concerns to construct a questionnaire which contained 160 questions divided into ten areas of life. This questionnaire was then administered, in a later study, to a sample of 524 non-patients, who were white middle-class men and women aged 16-50 years. The difficulty with a research design such as this is that the observed differences in 'concerns' may be due to the different life experiences of the different age cohorts. For example, the life history of a 5-year-old in 1972 would necessarily include the 'great depression' of the 1930s and the experience of the Second World War.

This would be quite different from the life history of 22-year-old in 1972 who would have experienced the economic boom of the post-Second World War years and the social changes of the 1960s. It seems reasonable to assume that such historical events and trends affect people's 'concerns'. Indeed they may be more significant in explaining the different concerns of different age cohorts than any hypothesized notion of the life cycle.

One way to avoid making comparisons between different cohorts is to investigate a single age cohort over a number of years. Ninety-four college graduates from the early 1940s were followed through until 1969. They were part of an initial study of 268 male undergraduates who were given extensive physiological and psychological examinations early in their college years.

After graduation the sample of 94 graduates completed annual questionnaires untitled 1955, and every two years after that date. They were interviewed in their homes twice, between 1950 and 1952 and in 1969. Vaillant reports the results in detail, but his thesis is simple: that ego defence mechanisms mature through the life cycle and that healthy adults progress through a hierarchy of adaptive mechanisms as shown in Table.

Hierarchy of adaptive mechanisms

Level I:	Psychotic mechanisms (common in psychosis, dreams, childhood)
	Denial (of external reality)
	Distortion
	Delusional projection
Level II:	Immature mechanisms (common in severe depression, personality disorders and adolescence)
	Fantasy (schizoid withdrawal, dental through fantasy)
	Projection
	Hypochondriasis
	Passive-aggressive behavior (masochism, turning against the self)
	Acting out (compulsive delinquency, perversion)

Lvel III:	Neurotic mechanisms (common in everyone) Intellectualization (isolation, obsessive behavior, undoing, rationalization) Repression Reaction formation Displacement (conversion, phobias, wit) Dissociation (neurotic denial)
Level IV:	Mature mechanisms (common in 'healthy' adults) Sublimation Altruism Suppression Anticipation Humor

There are some well-documented problems with long and practice effects and time-of-measurement effects. A significant problem, and one often overlooked, is that over, say, a 30 year period, there are bound to be shifts in the theoretical perspective of the theory upon which the research is based. This often means that the initial questions and modes of analysis become obsolescent and are replaced by more contemporary techniques. This certainly happened in Vaillant's study:

Unfortunately, the work of four other innovative students of personality in the 1930s was ignored. I say unfortunately because the work of these four men and women has affected my interpretation of the results of the Study. Erik Erikson, Anna Freud, Harry Stack Sullivan and Heinz Hartmen all significantly influenced modern understanding of personality; but in 1937-1942 their work was still too novel to shape the early design of the Grant Study.

By 1940 Harry Stack Sullivan had begun to revolutionize the psychodynamic theory of personality. Slowly, Sullivan and his British counterpart, Melanie Klein, led psychiatrists to realize that interpersonal, relations played as important a role in shaping personality as did the intrapersonal relations between ego, conscience and instinct, but not before the Grant Study was well under way. For example, although in college the psychiatric interviews had included a careful history of adolescent sexual development, the Study psychiatrists did not inquire into the boys' friendship patterns, or their efforts at heterosexual intimacy. Not until 1950, really, did the Grant Study begin to pay close attention to the men's relationships with older men and women.

In 1937 Anna Freud first published in English 'The Ego and The Mechanisms of Defense' and Heinz Hartmann had presented German 'Ego Psychology and the Problem of Adaptation'. Not until 1967 did the Grant Study focus on these men's styles of psychological adaptation.

In the late 1930s at the University of California Erikson had begun the work that in 1950 was to culminate in 'Childhood and Society'-providing convincing evidence that adults mature as well as children. During the same period, the Grant Study staff, like their colleagues elsewhere, saw psychodynamic maturation as being largely completed by adolescence.

Even though longitudinal studies overcome the problems of comparing different cohorts, they nevertheless remain historically bound. This means that generalizations to different cohort groups can only be made on the assumption that historical variation is unimportant.

Is it possible to avoid the influence of historical variation? The answer to this question rests heavily on one's analysis of how history and culture influence the psychological make-up of individuals. From a research design of view it is certainly possible to control for historical effects by using some combination of longitudinal and cross-sectional designs.

Vertical columns in Figure would represent a cross-sectional sequence where all four cohort groups are investigated twice, once in 1970 and again in 1980. Similarly, combining the bottom two rows would represent a longitudinal sequence, where two cohort groups are investigated simultaneously over a number of years. Though such techniques it is possible to obtain data about the effects of cohort differences, time-of-easurement differences and age differences.

For example, the differences between 20-year-olds can be compared with the differences between 30-year-olds in order to gauge the effect of cohort membership on the general difference between 20-and 30-year-olds. This, in effect, is a way of 'controlling' for historical variation. But the control gained through such a practice is very limited. First, it depends on whether the changes being monitored are easily quantifiable. In fact, most of the studies of this kind have been developed by those with an interest in measuring the development of human abilities, especially intellectual development.

The research designs employed were initially intended to partial out the historical effects of improvements in educational provision during or between the lifetimes of the subjects being studied. This is easy to do when it is simply a matter of comparing test scores, but it is a dubious task to take such comparisons with qualitative data of the king found in adult personality development. Second, there is an assumption that the impact of histories linear and cumulative. But this is an untenable assumption. Another way of minimizing the impact of historical variation on developmental research is to gather 'data' of a high level of generality. For example, Lowenthal et al. used a cross-sectional technique to investigate the adaptive processes of men and women across the life-span.

In their study they documented such general psychological qualities as complexity, self-image, expressiveness and perceptions in continuity of value structure. The biographical interview technique of Levinson was primarily aimed at elucidating changes in the relationship between self and world throughout the life course. Loevinger was also concerned with the rather abstract notion of ego as a central frame of reference for understanding self and others. However, a closer look at this research will still reveal its social and historical specificity.

Social and historical bias

In the immediately preceding section on methodological difficulties I outlined some of the research design problems when comparing different people of different ages at a given time or when comparing the same people at different ages. Unfortunately, research in adult development, especially the genre concerned with life 'stages' or 'phases', seems prone and historical bias. This is evident in four ways; the existence of purely descriptive inventories of life 'tasks', the selection of subjects for research, the data gathering techniques, and the way in which the concept of the 'healthy' personality is constructed.

Descriptive inventories

This approach, whereby an inventory of life tasks is constructed, has its origins in Havighurst's Developmental Tasks and Education which was written in the early 1940s. It is similar to the inventory of McCoy and the same objections apply here. It is worthwhile noting, however, Havighurst's comments on his original inventory. The tasks the individual must learn—the developmental task of life-are those things that constitute healthy and satisfactory growth in our society.

They are the things a person must learn if he is to be judged and to judge himself to be a reasonably happy and successful person. A developmental task is a task which arises at or about a certain period in the life of the individual, successful achievement of which leads to his happiness and to success with later tasks, while failure leads to unhappiness in the individual, disapproval by the society, and difficulty with later tasks.

Thus the developmental tasks of life amount to a socially approved timetable for individual growth and development. In a pluralistic society this timetable will differ between social groups. While it may be useful to identify the developmental tasks of particular social or community groups, as Tucker and Huerta have done in their study of Mexican-American females, it is dangerous to generalize about the developmental tasks of society as such.

Data gathering techniques

Table sets out the sample, method and developmental processes identified by each of six well-known adult developmental psychologists. Five of these gathered data prior to formulating their views about adult development. An impressionistic description of the samples used is that they consisted of North American, white, middle class, better educated, predominantly male subjects. The techniques for gathering data were the structured interview, questionnaire, self-rating checklist, standard psychological test and observer rating. But one should be wary of accepting reported results without a detailed knowledge of how these techniques were applied in each case.

Healthy personality

Development implies growth and progress, not merely change. But growth and progress towards what end? The answer to this question is often the starting point for theories of adult development, and it is the conception of the end point of development, the 'mature' or 'healthy' personality which frequently governs how progress and growth is monitored and explained within a given theory. Many developmental psychologists construe the end point of development with terms like 'individuality', 'autonomy' and the 'integrated self'.

But do such descriptions represent a particular way of looking at the world which excludes certain cultures or sections of the population? A closer look may help to resolve this issue. Levinson, for example, makes the following remarks about the 'individuation' prices:

Throughout the life cycle, but especially in the key transition periods such as infancy, pubescence and the Mid-life Transition, the developmental process of individuation is going on. This term refers to the changes in a person's relationship to himself and to the external world. These changes are part of the individuation process. In successive periods of development, as this process goes on, the person forms a clearer boundary between self and world.

He forms a stronger sense of who he is and what he wants, and a more realistic, sophisticated view of the world: what it is like, what it offers him and demands from him. Greater individuation allows him to be more separate from the world, to be more independent and self-generating. But it also gives him the confidence and understanding to have more intense attachments in the world and to feel more fully a part of it. This emphasis on 'separateness', 'independence' and 'self-generation' is the language of the ethic of individualism, it is worthwhile noting the claims of at least one commentator, Gilligan, that the emphasis on the development of individual identity among developmental theories is an aspect of gender bias which pervades the literature.

She begins her analysis by referring to the work of Chodorow, who observes that, in general, girls are parented by a person of the same gender while boys are parented by a person if the opposite gender. The significance of this is that the identity of boys is built on the perception of contrast and separateness from their primary caregiver, while the identity of girls is built upon the perception of sameness and attachment to their primary caregiver. Consequently, relationships, and particularly issues of dependency, are experienced differently by women and men. For boys and men, separation and individuation are critically tied to gender identity since separation from the mother is essential for the development for masculinity. For girls and women, issues of feminity or feminine identity do not depend on the achievement of separation from the mother or on the progress of individuation. Since masculinity is defined through separation while femininity is defined through attachment, male gender identity is threatened by intimacy while female gender identity is threatened by separation.

Thus males tend to have difficulty with relationships, while females tend to have problems with individuation. The quality of embeddedness in social interaction and personal relationships that characterizes women's lives in contrast to men's, however, becomes not only a descriptive difference but also a developmental liability when the milestones of childhood and adolescent development in the psychological literature are markets of increasing separation. Women's failure to separate then becomes by definition a failure to develop.

Gilligan then proceeds to cite evidence of the undervaluing of female characteristics—the concern with relationships and responsibilities, empathy and attachment-among developmental theories. For example, Freud considered the persistence of women's pre-Oedipal attachment to their mother to be linked with their failure to resolve completely their Oedipal feelings and their consequent failure to develop a strong superego. This developmental failure in women results in their having little sense of justice:

> The fact that women must be regarded as having little sense of justice is no doubt related to the predominance of envy in their mental life...

Another example comes from Jean Piaget, who observed sex differences in the way children engage in games. Girls, because of their more flexible attitude towards rules and their enforcement were considered to have a less developed legal sense than boys—which is the cornertone of corstone o moral development.

The rule is no longer an imperative coming from an adult and accepted without discussion, it is a means of agreement resulting from co-operation itself. But girls are less explicit about this agreement and this is our reason for suspecting them of being less concerned with legal elaborations. A rule is good so long as the game repay it.

Kohlberg too is open to the same criticism. Gilligan observes that his empirical work, which led to the formulation of moral development stages, was based on a sample of boys only. According to Gilligan, this is because the higher stages of kohlberg's scale are constructed from what are traditionally 'male' qualities—the concern with justice and rights rather than with responsibilities and relationships.

The thrust of Gilligan's argument is that womanhood is rarely equated with mature healthy adulthood in much of the adult developmental literature. This is because the healthy personality is too often portrayed from a male perspective, with an emphasis on individuation and autonomy.

The elusive mystery of women's development lies in its recognition of the continuing importance of attachment in the human life cycle. Woman's place in man's life cycle is to protect this recognition while the developmental litany intones the celebration of separation, autonomy, individuation, and natural rights.

An alternative to documenting the 'stages' and 'phases' of adult life is to understand development as an ongoing dialectical process. The basic notion here is that there is a constant 'dialectic' between the changing or developing person and the changing or evolving society. That is, the person creates, and is created by the society in which he/she lives. Accompanying this notion is the rejection of those psychological approaches which search for stability, equilibrium and balance in the life course.

The person is construed as a changing person in a changing world, and the dialectical approach is very much concerned with the dynamics of change: The preference for an equilibrium model in the behavioral science has been as firmly established as has the preference for abstract traits or competencies. Without any debate it has been taken for granted that a state of balance, stability, and rest is more desirable than a state of upheaval, conflict and change. Thus we have always aimed for a psychology of satisfaction but not of excitement.

This preference has found expression in balance theory, equilibrium theory, steady state theory, and indirectly in the theory of cognitive dissonance. With the possible exception for the latter, these interpretations fail to explore the fact that every change has to be explained by the process of imbalance which forms the basis for any movement. Once this pre-requisite is recognized, stability appears as a transitory condition in the stream of ceaseless changes.

One source of such change is the historical change in one's culture, the other source is the change associated with one's age-related social category. Such changes are primarily mediated through people interacting in everyday life -thus an investigation of developmental change will entail an analysis of common, everyday interactions and the dialogues contained in them.

Rriegel's position has much in common with Berger and Luckmann's exposition for how personal identity is shaped, maintained and transmitted within a given social order. Their analysis offers a powerful account of how personal identity is a social construction which, especially in a modern pluralistic society, is constantly open to change and transformation. What is meant by the proposition that personal identity is a social construction? Put simply, the idea is as follows:

1 We do not have biologically determined identities;

2 We are all born into a particular social world which has been constructed by humans;

3 We develop a notion of who we are from the way 'significant' others;

4 These 'significant' ohters represent the social world and mediate it to us.

5 We take on the roles and attitudes of significant others, internalize them and make them our own;

6 We extend our identification with significant others to an identification with society as whole: 'Only by virtue of this generalized identification does his own self-identification attain stability and continuity. He now has not only an identity vis-a vis this or that significant other, but an identity in general...'

Identity, as a social construction, needs to be maintained through social interaction. The routines of everyday life serve to confirm the reality of the world and our place in it. In particular, the language used in everyday conversations confirms for us the silent, taken-for-granted world that forms the foundation of our personal identity. In modern pluralistic society, however, there is a multiplicity of world views or realities. Because there is no common social reality there is no socially produced stable structure of personal identity. This means that achieving a stable personal identity in modern society becomes an individual, private enterprise. Moreover, the possibility of transforming one's identity is always present. Indeed, one could argue that many life events require a change or re-orientation of identity.

Berger and Luckmann maintain that any transformation of identity requires a process of re-socialization. In extreme cases, such as with religious conversion, there may be a complete dismantling of one's former identity. This would require the following:

1 Affiliation with the new community;

2 Segregation for the individual from the inhabitants of other 'worlds', especially those from the 'world' being left behind;

3 A reinterpretation of the old 'reality ' in terms of the new 'reality'

Each of these steps can be recognized as extreme versions of what happens to many adults as they develop new personal, family, work and leisure pursuits. The difference between this analysis and the life-span development literature is that transformation does not imply a move towards some state of maturity—it simply means change, not improvement. Also, there are no propositions about the regularity and predictability of change—only that personal identity is open to change, subject to the existence of a community of others who maintain the change through discourse in everyday life.

The idea of the malleability of personal identity is both a source of hope and an occasion for despair. Hope, because it means that change is always possible' despair, because it implies that a belief in the real, true, authentic self is a fanciful indulgence. The studies cited in this chapter represent only a sampling of a rich and diverse field of enquiry. They were chosen to reveal some of the pitfalls in theory and research in adult development.

Adult development is, in principle germane to anyone with an interest in adult education. Too often, however, people with an applied intent will latch on to an easily assimilated theory, one which clearly differentiates and orders the 'phases' or 'stages' of life and which advances an unambiguous account of the process and end point of development. Adult educators may find such theories useful but they need to be wary of the methodological and conceptual difficulties.

6

Future of Adult Education in Rural Areas

Learning activities and learning styles vary so much with physiology, culture, and personality that generalized statements about the nature of adult learning have very low predictive power. The most that Dubin and Okun will say in their review of eight school of learning theory is that different elements of the theories of these schools can help to explain certain limited phenomena. It is all the more surprising, therefore to hear confident generalizations regarding the characteristics of adult learning pour forth from the lips of graduate students and those presenting research papers. According to Simpson, the two distinguishing characteristics of adult learning most frequently advanced by theorists are the adult's autonomy of direction in the act of learning and the use of personal experience as a learning resource. It is important to recognize, however, that self-direction in learning is not an empirically verifiable concomitant of adulthood. There are many individuals who are chronologically adult but who show a marked disinclination to behave in anything approaching a self-directed manner in many areas of their lives. Self-directedness is rather being advanced as a prescriptively defining characteristic of adulthood. Hence, for an act of learning to be characteristically adult, it will have to exhibit some aspect of self-directedness. But before examining further the nature and form of self-directedness, let us consider the range of theoretical perspectives that have been elaborated with regard to adult learning.

To specify generic principles of learning is an activity full of intellectual pitfalls. Even if we leave aside the variables of physiology, personality, and cultural background, we still have to consider the implication of those developmental theories that hold that adults function in very different ways when responding to the societal and personal imperatives required of them in young adulthood, midlife, and old age.

This suggests that the generic concept of adulthood is so broad and oversimplified as to be of limited use as a research construct. Nonetheless, in the last twenty-five years a number of respected theorists have made an attempt to identify generalizable principles of adult learning in their quest to build a theory of adult learning that would aid practice. The earliest of these attempts was that of Gibb, who presented the following principles of adult learning as the basis for a "functional" theory: Learning must be problem centered, learning must be experience centered, experience must be meaningful to the learner, the learner must be free to look at experience, goals must be set and pursued by the learner, and the learner must have feedback about progress toward goals. As with other specifications of principles of adult learning, however, what Gibb actually offers is a mix of pedagogic procedures and learning theory.

Following on from Gibb, Miller identified six crucial conditions for learning premised on the belief that at the higher levels of human development in adulthood cognitive models of learning, rather than behaviorist ones, were necessary.

Thus, Miller argued that students must be adequately motivated to change behavior, they must be aware of the inadequacy of present behaviors, they must have a clear picture of the behavior required, they must have the opportunity to practice required behaviours, they must obtain reinforcement of correct behaviour, and they must have a sequence of appropriate materials. Despite Miller's emphasis on cognition, however, the conditions he specifies actually appear to fit the behaviorist paradigm. In this review of theories of learning and their applicability to adulthood, Kidd identified the concepts that he felt informed the efforts of researchers into adult learning.

These concepts were derived from the changing conditions of the adult's life-span, role changes required by changing societal imperatives, the egalitarian nature of adult student-teacher relationship, the greater differentiation of the organs and functions of adults, the self-directing nature of the adult, the physical, cultural, and emotional meaning of time, and attitudes surrounding aging and the prospect of death.

Gibb, Miller, and Kidd all based their arguments concerning the nature of adult learning on speculative grounds. Knox, however, produced a widely referenced study of adult development and learning in which he offered a number of broad observations concerning adult learning. In Knox's view, for example, adilts learn continually and informally as they adults to role changes and other adaptations. Adults' learning achievements are, however, thought to be modified by individual characteristics. The learning context of the physical, social, and personal characteristics sorrounding the learning act, as well as the content and pace of learning, also affect the learning achievement. Knox also concludes that adults tend to underestimate their abilities and by over emphasizing school experience and interests, often perform below their capacity. Longitudinal studies show a retention of, and sometimes increases in learning abilities during adulthood, though cross-sectional studies tend to contradict this finding.

Fluid intelligence decreases and crystallized intelligence increases in adulthood, and adults are able to learn as well in their forties and fifties as in their twenties and thirties, when and if they can control the pace of learning. Knox found the level of formal education to be associated much more with learning ability than with age, and recency of participation in formal education to be correlated with more effective learning. This finding, incidentally,was supported by earlier studies of Knox and Sjorgen and Knox, Grotelueschen, and Sjorgen.

Other findings from Knox's survey were that effective learning entailed an active search for meaning in which new tasks were somehow related to earlier activities. Knox found that short-term memory held stable until late adulthood and that long-term memory apparently improved with age. In terms of the mechanics of learning, practice was deemed to be initially important for the reinforcement of learning. Prior learning experiences had the potential to enhance or interfere with new learning. Older adults were able to learn most effectively when they set their own pace, when they took periodic breaks, and when learning episodes were distributed according to a rationale dictated by content. Knox found learning transfer to decrease with age, though his findings on problem-solving abilities were ambiguous, with a decline according to cross-sectional studies and a holding steady with longitudinal studies. The same difference was evident in studies undertaken of critical thinking.

Task complexity and creativity were found to reflect individual differences and to be related only marginally to age. Knox concluded his summary in an optimistic vein, declaring that individual differences in learning were mostly unrelated to age and that "almost any adult can learn anything they want to, given time, persistence, and assistance." One of the most ambitious attempts to identify the cardinal principles of adult learning and to put these to practical use is that of Brundage and Mackeracher. These writers identify thirty-six learning principles and draw from each principle facilitating and planning implications.

For example, Brundage and Mackeracher believe that adults are able to learn throughout their lifetimes. Their past experience can be a help or hindrance to learning. It is through such experience, however, that individuals construct the meanings and value frameworks that in turn determine how they code new stimuli and information. Brundage and Mackeracher declare that past experience needs to be respected by teachers and that it can be directly applied to current situation for good educative effect. Those adults with positive self-concepts are thought to be more responsive to learning.

Environments that reinforce the self-concepts of adults, that are supportive of change, and that value the status of learner will produce the greatest amount of learning. These writers judge adults to be strongly motivated to learn in areas relevant to their current developmental tasks, social roles, life crises, and transition periods. The development of skills requires adults to have a clear perception of desired behaviors. Reinterpreting past experience is time consuming and requires a redefinition of values and meanings. In Brundage and the Mackeracher's view, voluntary participation in education and training is likely to create a nonthreatening climate of instruction that will result in a greater amount of learning.

Learning will be further enhanced by regular feedback on progress, and positive feedback will act as a reinforcer for the pursuit of more learning. They think that a certain degree of arousal is necessary for learning to occur, whereas stress acts as a major block to learning. Brundage and Mackeracher also think adults learn best when they can control the pace of their learning and when they enjoy good health. However, because each individual will have an idiosyncratic learning style, it is dangerous to prescribe one mode of learning for all adults.

Typical points of personally significant transition occur at the ages of twenty, forty, and sixty, and adults are said to be most responsive to learning programs that are related to these transition. Collaborative modes of teaching and learning will enhance the self-concepts of those involved and result in more meaningful and effective learning. A blend of learning for autonomous mastery of life with participation in groups is said to provide the greatest satisfaction for the learner.

As a result of a career-long exploration of the development of adults' learning-to-learn capacities, Smith has identified six general observation concerning the nature of learning: It is lifelong, it is personal, it involves change, it is partially a function of human development, it pertains to experience, and it is partially intuitive. Adult learners, however, also exhibit four essential characteristics. First, they have multiple roles and responsibilities, and this results in a different orientation to learning from that of children and adolescents. For example, they wish to make good educational use of the finite time they invest in education, they often take responsibility for identifying what they wish to learn, and they have a partially or fully formed self-concept Second, adults have accumulated many life experiences, and these result in distinct preferences for modes of learning and learning environments, such modes and environments comprising the essentials of individual learning styles.

Third, adults pass through a number of developmental phases in the physical, psychological, and social spheres, and the transitions from one phase to another provide for the reinterpretation and rearrangement of past experience. Finally, Smith argues, adult experience anxiety and ambivalence in their orientation to learning. In particular, attempts to become more autonomous and self-directed are likely to involve threatening elements. Anxiety and stress may also be the result of job pressure, relational problems with significant others or of the adult's recalling the anxiety produced by earlier schooling experiences.

These four characteristics of adult learners-their special orientation to learning, their experiential base, their particular developmental changes and tasks, and their anxiety regarding learning generate, according to Smith, certain conditions for learning. Adults learn best when they feel the need to learn and when they have a sense of responsibility for what, why, and how they learn. Adults use experience as a resource in learning so the learning content and process must bear a perceived and meaningful relationship to past experience What is to be learned should be related to the individual's developmental changes and life tasks.

The learning method used wil foster, to different degrees, the adult's exercise of autonomy. Adults will, however, generally learn best in an atmosphere that is nonhreatening and supportive of experimentation and in which different learning styles are recognized. Darkenwald and Merriam present a list of eight principles of learning derived from learning process research that they believe can serve as guidelines for effective facilitation. They surmise that adults' readiness to learn depends on the amount of their previous learning, that intrinsic motivation produces more pervasive and permanent learning, that positive reinforcement is effective, that the material to be learned should be presented in some organized fashion, that learning is enhanced by repetition, that meaningful tasks and material are more fully and easily learned, that active participation in learning improves retention, and that environmental factors affect learning. The specification of principles of adult learning undertaken by Gibb, Miller, Kidd, Knox, Brundage and Mackeracher, Smith, and Darkenwald and Merriam can be summarized as follows: Adults learn throughour their lives, with the negotiations of the transitional stages in the life-span being the immediate causes and motives for much of this learning.

They exhibit diverse learning styles-strategies for coding information, cognitive procedures, mental sets and learn in different ways, at different times, for different purposes. As a rules, however, they like their learning activities to be problem centered and to be meaningful to their life situation, and they want the learning outcomes to have some immediacy of application. The past experiences of adults affect their current learning, sometimes serving as an enhancement, sometimes as a hindrance. Effective learning is also linked to the adult's subscription to a self-concept of himself or herself as a learner. Finally, adults exhibit a tendency toward self-directedness in their learning. Such conclusions constitute a catechism familiar to educators and trainers of adults, as well as to learning theorists. They support Simpson's contention referred to at the outset of this chapter that adult learning theorists most commonly emphasize the experiential dimension of adult learning and stress the self-directedness of adults.

Self-directedness is seen both as an empirically observable trait and as a propensity that should be encouraged. We should note, however, that the samples for the studies on which these generalizations concerning the nature of adult learning are based are culturally specific. To this extent, the research on adult learning is no different from that on its childhood equivalent, where, as a massive comparative study of primary school quality recently acknowledged, "With less than 5 per cent of the world's school population, the United States accounts for the majority of the world's empirical research on education".

In research into adult learning, moreover, the adults who form the sampling frames are for the most part ethnically homogeneous; that is, they are Causasian Americans. They are also drawn chiefly from middle-class or upwardly mobile working-class families, since this is the foremost clientele of continuing education programs. To base a comprehensive theory of adult learning on observations of white, middle-class Americans in continuing or extension education classes in the post-Second World War era is conceptually and empirically naive. It is, admittedly, cumbersome to preface every comment regarding adult learning theory with a caveat concerning the cultural and class specificity of one's sample and, hence, the limited generalizability of one's conclusions. Nonetheless, we fall far too frequently into the mistake of declaring that research reveals that adults, in a generic sense, learn in a certain way. The eagerness to construct an empirically verifiable theory of adult learning is inextricably bound up with the quest for professional identity on the part of adult educators. As much as we would like to believe that the conduct and dissemination of research are motivated by an intellectually altruistic search for truth, it must be recognized that the definition of research "problems" and the selection of appropriate topics for investigation often reflect wider societal or professional imperatives.

In this case, the reality is that the discovery of a set of learning behaviors that are unmistakably adult would be a cause for substantial professional celebration. If we could discover certain empirically verifiable differences in learning styles between children and adults then we could lay claim to a substantive area for research that would be unchallengeably the property of educators and trainers of adults. Such a claim would provide us with a professional identity. It would ease the sense of insecurity and defensiveness that frequently assails educators and trainers of adults in all settings when faced with the accusation that they are practicing a nondiscipline. The discovery of an empirically discrete domain of adult learning would grant to us an intellectual and professional raison d'etrae.

Such a revelation is unlikely to transpire for some considerable time, and it may be that the most empirically attestable claim that can be made on behalf of adult learning style concerns their range and diversity. Certainly we should be wary of claiming too high a level of generalizability for theories and concepts of adult learning derived from studies of white Americans in the lower-middle, amiddle and upper classes.

How can we write confidently of adult learning style in any generic sense when we know little of the cognitive operations of, for example, Asian peasants, African tribespeople or Chinese cooperative labourers? Even within North American culture the empirical accuracy of generalizations about adult learning principles is highly questionanble in that we have few studies of the learning styles of Native Americans, while working-class adults, Hispanics, blacks, or orientals.

The body of research literature discussed in the preceding section is one characterized by a mixture of speculation and empirically observed features of adult learning. The studies cited use a variety of methodological approaches and survey different samples, with the result that baseline comparisons are extremely hard to make. In recent years a number of researchers and practitioners have sought to synthesize the findings of this body of research into some framework of central adult learning principles.

These central principles have then been converted into various research instruments that their designers believe can be applied to examining the extent to which principles of adult learning are being exemplified in any given practice setting. Two of these instruments the Principles of Adult Learning Scale (PALS) and the Andragogy in Practice Inventory (API)-were designed to test the presence of effective facilitation in practice rather than to provide empirical measures of forms of adult learning. In other words, both these instruments can be used to determine whether or not teachers or programmers are behaving as effective facilitators. The PALS was devised by Conti to measure the extent to which practitioners supported the collaborative mode of teaching-learning that is usually cited by writers in the field as an exemplification of good practice. Conti surveyed a number of highly regarded theorists, including Freire, Lindeman, Houle, Knox, Kidd, Knowles, and Bergevin, to discover what they held to be the basic assumptions of adult learning.

Not surprisingly, his findings are similar to those identified by the theorists revieed in the present chapter and to the central principles of effective facilitation. Hence, Conti found these writers to argue that "the curriculum should be learner centered, that learning episodes should capitalize on the learner's experience, that adults are self-directed, that the learner should participate in needs diagnosis, goals formation, and outcomes evaluation, that adults are problem centered, and that the teacher should serve as a facilitator rather than as a repository of facts". For his doctoral dissertation, Conti determined "to develop and validate an instrument capable of measuring the degree to which adult education practitioners accept and adhere to the adult learning principles that are congruent with the collaborative teaching-learning mode".

Drawing on Flanders's Interaction Analysis Categories that were established to assess student initiating actions, Conti constructed a five-point Likert scale to record practitioner responses on a number of items that were based on collaborative principles but "reworded in behavioral terms compatible with realistic experiences of practitioners". For each of the items said to describe actions congruent with the collaborative mode, a separate item was included to describe mode. The PALS instrument was tested for construct, content, and criterion-related validity by two juries of adult education professors and fifty-seven practitioners in six separate programs.

Testing for reliability was undertaken in phase two of the field testing by twice administering the scale to twenty-three adult basic education practitioners in chicago and comparing the congruence of the scores. The outcome of the study was a forty-four-item rating scale that Conti believes can be used to assess the effectiveness of collaborative modes in producing significant learning gains or to identify themes and topics around which in-service training activities could be designed for staff development. Since its initial framing, Conti reports that the PALS has been used in numerous training workshops and that it has formed the basis for three research studies.

Dinges used the instrument to study 265 Illinois ABE teachers in a staff development needs assessment, Pearson administered PALS to 99 midwestern training directors to investigate the relationship between managerial style and the adoption of collaborative modes of facilitation, and Douglass used it to examine the relationship of professional training in educating adults to the degree of support granted to the collaborative mode by 204 hospital educators and cooperative extension educators in the state of Washington.

In addition, scores have been collected from 153 Texas practitioners in adult basic and allied health education. Not surprisingly, perhaps, the research of Pearson and kouglass indicates that the chief variable positively correlated with the adoption of a collaborative approach in management training, hospital education, and cooperative extension is the amount of previous formal education undertaken by these practitioners. It seems, from these studies at least, that those who are trained as educators of adults do indeed incorporate collaborative principles into their subsequent professional activities.

After Conti's presentation of the PALS research at a recent conference of university adult educators in Britain, we can expect some cross-cultural validation of this instrument through comparative analyses of educators' use of the collaborative mode in Britain and North America. Turning to the API, which was devised by Suanmali on the basis of Mezirow's interpretation of andragogy and his specification of a charter for andragogy, we find that it is a ten item inventory of educator practices. To help adults enhance their capability to function as self- directed learners, the education must:

1. progressively decrease the learner's dependency on the educators;
2. help the learner to understand how to use learning resources-especially the experiences of others, including the educator, and how to engage others in reciprocal learning relations;
3. assist the learner to define his/her learning needs—both in terms of immediate awareness and of understanding the cultural and psychological assumptions influencing his/her perceptions of needs;
4. assist learners to assume increasing responsibility for defining their learning objectives, planning their own learning programs and evaluating their progress;
5. organize what is to be learned in relationship to his/her current personal problems, concerns and levels of understanding;

6. foster learner decision-making-select learner-relevant learning experiences which require choosing, expand the learner's range of options, facilitate taking the perspectives of others who have alternative ways of understanding;
7. encourage the use of criteria for judging which are increasingly inclusive and differentiating in awareness, self-reflexive and integrative of experience;
8. facilitate problem-posing and problem-solving, including problems associated with the implementation of individual and collective action; rocognition of relationship between personal problems and public issues;
9. reinforce the self concept of the learner as a learner and doer by providing for progressive mastery; supportive climate with feedback to encourage provisional efforts to change and to take risks; avoidance of competitive judgment of performance; appropriate use of mutual support groups;
10. emphasize experiential, participative and projective instructional methods; appropriate use of modelling and learning contracts;

This instrument was examined by 147 members of the American Commission of Professors of Adult Education. The professors interviewed displayed a remarkable degree of agreement concerning the extent to which the practices identified above were indicative of good andragogical practice. Finally, James and Manley have conducted small-scale Delphi investigations of what practitioners and professors of adult education regard as exemplary principles of practice that facilitate adult learning. Manley's review of the literature and her survey of eighteen members of the American Commission of Professors of Adult Education yield a familiar cluster of categories.

The professors surveyed agree that adult learning is best facilitated when learners are engaged as participants in the design of learning, when they are encouraged to be self-directed, when the educator functions as a facilitator rather than didactic instructor, when individual learner needs and learning styles are taken into account, when a climate conducive to learning is established, when learners' past experiences are utilized in the classroom, and when learning activities are deemed to have some direct relevance or utility to the learners' circumstances. In a more ambitious study, similar to Conti's researches, James devised the following set of basic principles of adult learning after a team of researchers had undertaken a search of articles, research reports, dissertations, and textbooks on adult learning.

1. Adults maintain the ability to learn.
2. Adults are a highly diversified group of individuals with widely differing preferences, needs, backgrounds, and skills.
3. Adults experience a gradual decline in physical/sensory capabilities.
4. Experience of the learner is a major resource in learning situations.
5. Self-concept moves from dependency to independency as individuals grow in responsibilities, experience and cconfidence.
6. Adults tend to be life-centered in their orientation to learning.

7. Adults are motivated to learn by a variety of factors.
8. Active learner participation in the learning process contributes to learning.
9. A comfortable supportive environment is a key to successful learning.

All nine principles were validated by a jury of national adult education leaders, and from these principles a questionnaire was constructed comprisig forty-five statements. The questionnaire was then administered to educators in five settings: hospital patient education, university extension programs, community colleges, business and industry, and agricultural extension. Some interesting differentials emerged in the study.

Hospital patient educators, university extension instructors, community college instructors, and agricultural extension instructors all perceived themselves as implementing all the principles identified "frequently," while business and industry personnel perceived themselves as implementing principles one, two, and eight "sometimes" but the others "frequently." An interesting difference was also revealed regarding the principle ranked highest by these practitioners.

In hospitals, universities, community colleges, and agricultural extension, principle nine "a comfortable, supportive environment is a key to successful learning"-was ranked as the most important. In business and industry, however, principle three "adults experience a gradual decline in physical/sensory capabilities"-was ranked highest. In contrast to the findings of Conti's PALS research, the principle referring most explicitly to collaborative modes of teaching and learning was ranked relatively low by instructors in all five settings. In particular, a number of studies of how practitioners do or do not conform to principles of good practice in real life program development settings will be examined.

Developing in adults a sense of their personal power and self-worth is seen as a fundamental purpose of all education and training efforts. Only if such a sense of individual empowerment is realized will adults possess the emotional strength to challenge behaviours, values, and beliefs accepted uncritically by a majority. Both causally antecedent to, and concurrent with, this developing sense of self-worth in the individual comes an awareness of the contextuality of knowledge and beliefs. The task of the educator, then, becomes that of encouraging adults to perceive the relative, contextual nature of previously unquestioned givens.

Additionally, the educator should assist the adult to reflect on the manner in which values, beliefs, and bahaviours previously deemed unchallengable can be critically analyzed. Through presenting alternative ways of interpreting and creating the world to adults, the educator fosters a willingness to consider alternative ways of living. These criteria are offered for consideration by educators as fundamental indicators by which they may judge the worth of a formal or informal effort to facilitate learning. In real life, of course, all adult will not develop a sense of self-worth, an awareness of the contextuality of knowledge, a willingness to speculate on alternatives, and a capacity to re-create their personal and social worlds, according to the neatly sequenced stages described in the previous paragraph. Some adults will come to appreciate the contextuality of knowledge or learn to speculate on alternatives, without having the sense of self-worth and personal power needed to realize those alternatives. Others will have the internal strength to alter certain peripheral features of their lives but will be unable to change the patterns that govern their significant personal relationships. Still others may consider social alternatives and even imagine new political forms, but lack the techniques, skills, or collective support needed to effect change. This does not mean, however, that we should abandon attempts to specify as clearly as possible the criteria we are adopting to determine the success of our efforts.

Such criteria will inevitably, take the form of abstractions. They will be oversimplifications of reality. The real world of social encounters is sufficiently chaotic to make the detection of whether or not these criteria have been satisfied a correspondingly haphazard and often messy enterprise. Nevertheless if we make no attempt to specify criteria, we will be unable to assign value and worthwhileness to different activities. All educational encounters will then exist in some kind of moral vacuum, and we will be unable to judge whether a lecture in which a religious or political dogma is fervently and uncritically expounded is more or less educational than a discussion of the ethical assumptions underlying communism and capitalism.

If we are to wear the mantle of "educator," we must, at some minimum level, make explicit the criteria by which we determine the educational worth of our efforts. Not to do so is unthinking or dishonest, and it is to consign ourselves to being adaptive and reactive satisfiers of whatever consumer learning needs happen to capture our attention. But it is to the means for determining whether or not these criteria are actually being met in an educational activity that we must now turn our attention.

The preceding chapters have been concerned chiefly with matters of practice-facilitating adult learning through self directed modes, using and ragogical methods, teaching adults through discussion groups, developing programs for adult learners, and evaluating effective practice. Implicit in these discussion of practice, however, has been a concept of facilitation somewhat different from that held by many practitioners. In this final chapter it is important that the philosophical assumptions on which this concept is based be stated clearly. As has been repeatedly argued, practical expertise that exist in a moral vacuum can be a dangerous thing. Practitioners can become technically proficient but find that without a firm philosophical rationale to guide the application of their skills, they are devoting their efforts to programs and purpose that are morally dubious.

Contained in these characteristics are features that will be familiar to those who know the literature of humanistic psychology and psychotherapy- a respect for participants in the teaching-learning transaction, a commitment to collaborative modes of program development, and an acknowledgment of the educational value of life experiences.

Hence, effective facilitation means that learners will be challenged to examine their previously held values, beliefs, and behaviors and will be confronted with ones that they may not wnat to consider. Such challenges and confrontations need not be done in an adversarial, combative, or threatening manner; indeed, the most effective facilitator is one who can encourage adults to consider rationally and carefully perspectives and interpretations of the world that diverage from those they already hold, without making these adults feel they are being cajoled or threatened.

This experience may produce anxiety, but such anxiety should be accepted as a normal component of learning and not as something to be avoided at all costs for fear that learners will leave the group. There are forms of fulfillment that are quite unlike those produced by a wholly joyful encounter with a new form of knowledge of a new skill area. It is this dimension of increased insight through critical reflection on current assumptions and past beliefs and behaviors that is sometimes ignored in treatments of adult learning. One purpose of this book is to place the prompting of this form of learning at the heart of what it means to be a good facilitator.

It is important to state, however, that because teaching learning transactions are collaborative, the prompting of critical reflection may not always be done by the participant designated as the facilitator. In the most effective learning groups, facilitating behaviors are assumed by various members of these groups at different times. One features the leaderless groups discussed in Chapter Six—women's consciousness-raising groups, quality circles, political advocacy groups, and so on—is that the member who is responsible for the initial formation of these groups does not have to assume full responsibility for facilitating learning. As a group culture develops, various members will challenge others to examine their current ways of thinking and living, and this activity will be seen as wholly appropriate.

Critical philosophy of practice

The public articulation of a philosophy of effective practice is an activity viewed with apparent indifference or distaste by many educators and trainers of adults. Such educators might appear to an outsider to be bereft of any rationale for their practice. This is rarely the case. In reality, most practitioners accept employing agency mission statements as general definitions of purpose or declare good practice to be the satisfaction of felt and expressed needs. These positions in themselves exemplify a philosophical rationale-that of pragmatism. Acceptance of this pragmatic rationale is perhaps most evident in the tendency to equate the design of effective program-planning models with the sum total of effective practice.

According to this argument, the education of adults is a matter of designing, conducting, and evaluating educational experiences so as to meet the felt needs of adults. Hence, practitioner effectiveness becomes defined in terms of processes and activities-the ability to design, conduct, and evaluate programs for learners-rather than in terms of fundamental purposes or curriculum. But if we view effective practice solely as the improvement of ever more refined practice skills and regard facilitator roles and responsibilities as being primarily those of technicians of design, we denude practice of any philosophical rationale, future orientation, or purposeful mission. There exists no philosophical yardstick in terms of criteria of success, notions of purpose, or appropriate curricula against which the effectiveness of such facilitation can be judged.

Furthermore, if we accept the view that we should serve only felt needs, then our priorities, purposes, and primary functions will be wholly determined by others. Our curriculum will be devised in response to demands made by those who can best attract our attention and are most articulate in presenting their case. To counter this danger that facilitation will become solely a responsive, reactive activity, it is important that practitioners develop a philosophical rationale, or what Apps calls a belief system, to grant their practice order and purpose. They need to identify those characteristics by which the fundamental worth of any attempt to facilitate adult learning can be judged.

This does not mean that such a philosophy must be exemplified to its fullest degree in every educational encounter with adults. Such an insistence would be so intimidating to practitioners as to prevent any attempt to implement a philosophy. We should regard this rationale rather as a variable that can be realized to a greater or lesser extent at different times, in different settings, with different groups. Even within one class session the extent to which this philosophy is realized will vary with the nature of the individuals concerned, the exercises pursued, and the educator's conduct. Nonetheless, it is vital that a clear rationale be articulated so that practitioners may have a benchmark for judging the extent to which their activities exemplify fundamental purposes, principles, and practice. Without a coherent rationale, practice will be condemned to an adaptive, reactive mode. Practitioner activities will be determined by current curricular trends or by the ability of certain individuals and groups to make themselves heard and their demands felt. Several writers have indeed warned of the dangers of succumbing to a reactive and pragmatic rationale. Lawson and Monette have both condemned the insidious influence of the service rationale on programs for adult learners.

According to this rationale, practitioners are technicians whose function is to cater to the expressed needs of their clients in as effective a manner as possible. These writers point out that by responding to felt needs, the educator does not have to make value judgments concerning the relative merits of different curricular offerings. Only rarely is there any acknowledgment in the literature of the moral and professional requirement that the educator act in accordance with value choices.

Crabtree has also condemned the manner in which the idea of "customer service" comes to determine the form of the curriculum for adult learners. Similarly, Powell warned against the importing of a business rationale into adult education and expressed his concern at the growing tendency to let a preoccupation with needs assessments and marketing procedures replace the setting of fundamental goals for a program. Seduction of the programmer by evidence of a strong and immediate demand for a certain course offering was also recognized by Herring, who blamed the galloping mediocrity he saw in many programs for adult learners on the institutionally prescribed need to increase enrollments. Herring lamented the tendency of program planners to avoid social and political issues that they thought were too serious or too contentious to draw large numbers of participants. In adult education, however, we seem currently to be in danger of becoming preoccupied with refining techniques to the exclusion of any consideration of the rationale underlying those techniques. We are philosophically numb, concerned with the design of ever more sophisticated needs assessment techniques, program planning models, and evaluative procedures. It seems not to have occurred to us that the perfection of technique can only be meaningful when placed within a context of some fundamental human or social purpose.

Technique is, after all, only a means to broader ends. When technique is worshipped to the exclusion of the human or social purposes it is meant to serve, then it is easy for us to become dazzled by the convolutions of the latest shaman of procedure and by the pronouncements of those who flaunt commonsense ideas regarding teaching and learning under the guise of presenting a revolutionary paradigm of practice.

In contrast, this chapter attempts to comment on the fundamental nature and proper purpose of facilitating learning by outlining a philosophy of practice that comprises three fundamental elements. Finally, on the basis of this definition and its general statement of purpose there should be formulated a set of criteria by which the success of various practitioner efforts can be judged. Such criteria would allow us to reflect on our own practice and to examine the activities of others in terms of their effectiveness.

This definition, statement of purposes, and explication of criteria should be firmly and avowedly prescriptive. A philosophy of practice should, at the most fundamental level, be concerned with the resolution of second-order questions, that is questions that cannot be answered by recourse to the empirical world. In other words, we cannot conduct a survey to determine in some objectively empirical sense what should be the purpose of our efforts.

We can conduct assessments of present levels of competence and declare certain populations to be in states of educational need with regard to some previously defined standard. Such assessments are only objective, however, to the extent that they are based on a normatively defined standard of competence. Similarly, by conducting a Delphi survey of adult education professors, we can determine their views on the proper purposes of facilitation. This survey will not answer for us, however, the fundamental question concerning what should be the purpose of educating adults, for this is a question that is explored in a quite separate area of intellectual discourse.

The domain of discourse surrounding such a question is one of prescriptive preferences, moral commitments, and categorical imperatives. We will come to construct our philosophy of practice on the basis of the personal and social imperatives we feel to be most potent. In the course of this construction we will admittedly be cognizant of the opinions of those intellectual leaders we respect. Such opinions cannot grant to our philosophy its internal power and commitment, however, since this will be derived from our experience of the world and from our personal belief system concerning the most desirable and meaningful aspects of this experience.

A philosophy of practice should allow considerable scope for operationalization. In an activity such as facilitating learning, statements of fundamental purpose are of limited value if they cannot be realized in terms of practice. Concomitant with this outline of a philosophical rationale, therefore, should be some guidance in regard to teaching method, curriculum development, program planning, and evaluation. But such techniques will not exist in their own right; they will be grounded in, and derived from, a carefully explicated rationale. This rationale from which are derived various practical injunctions in terms of planning, teaching, curriculum development, and evaluation—will serve as a yardstick against which the effectiveness and worth of a particular effort can be judged. This philosophy and its concomitant operationalizations should serve as a benchmark and as a guide by which practice can be mapped. The philosophy of practice proposed within this last chapter centers on the notion of the adult's developing sense of control and autonomy.

Such autonomy is not to be equated with atomistic isolation; rather, it is realized in personal relationships, in sociopolitical behavior, and in intellectual judgment. The purpose of facilitation is to assist individuals to begin to exercise control over their own lives, their interpersonal relationships, and the social forms and structures within which they live. This is not to say that facilitation will enable adults to exert complete control over all aspects of their worlds. However, it is possible to envisage existences that are more or less meaningful and authentic to the individuals involved, according to the degree to which they feel they have some proactive role in creating their worlds.

It is proposed that all involved in teaching-learning transactions assist each other to identify the exernal sources and internalized assumptions framing their conduct and to be ready to assess these critically. Such critical awareness will involve an appreciation of the contextual, provisional, and relative nature of truth, public knowledge, and personal beliefs.

When a disjunction becomes evident between adults' individual aspirations and the socially received codes, value frameworks, and belief systems informing their behavior, then autonomy is reflected in a jettisoning of received assumptions. Occurring along with this abandonment of assumptions perceived as irrelevant and inauthentic will be the transformation of individual and collective circumstances. Teaching-learning transactions are no exceptions to this rule; indeed they possess an unusual degree of potency in that the facilitator's statements and comments are typically granted a high degree of credibility and significance by learners.

Learners grant authority to interpretations, generalizations, and statements of preference made by the facilitator, even though he or she may arow this equality of status with learners and emphasize that they are partners in a collaborative endeavour. Facilitators may profoundly dislike this role, particularly those of a democratic, egalitarian temper. To be the beneficiary of imputations of moral as well as intellectual superiority by learners is confining and often even embarrassing. However, inasmuch as most adults received an initial education that encouraged them to see teachers as authority figures, it is hardly surprising if they prove incapable, at least at first, of viewing the facilitator as partner and intellectual collaborator.

This ascribed authority places facilitators in an uncomfortable position, particularly if they subscribe to andragogical principles. It also makes the adoption of an ethical code of practice-a requirement of first importance in any profession doubly necessary. Any position of authority, whether ascribed or prescribed, carries within it the possibility of abuse. This potential will be reduced if facilitators seek, as rigorously as possible, to submit all assertions to critical scrutiny.

Facilitators will cite apporopriate evidence for any generalizations they make and will treat all theories, explanatory systems, standards of esthetic discriminations, conceptual constructs, and criteria of excellence as provisional and relative.

Aside from viewing theoretical systems or explanations as provisional, the ficilitator should also present alternative interpretations and possibilities to students. Such alternatives may be esthetic, cognitive, or sociopolitical. Hence, a course on craft skills should encourage inquiries into the origins of standards of excellence and not concentrate only on the development of psychomotor skills exemplifying those standards.

A similar requirement also holds for courses dealing with bodies of cognitive knowledge. These should submit central concepts and theoretical frameworks to critical review.

Criteria of intellectual excellence should be viewed as humanly contrived, not divinely ordained, and all statements and assertions should be regarded as provisional. With regard to those courses dealing with behavioral phenomena-for example, role training, interpersonal skill development, or counselling techniques-the twin canons of relativity and provisionality also pertain.

In fields such as health education, administrative studies, or personnel management, training courses can only qualify as examples of effective facilitation if the behavioral paradigms presented in them are subjected to critical scrutiny. Moreover, if such courses are to be seen as involving education and not simply training, they must incorporate a willingness to consider alternatives to the popularly prevailing norms governing correct professional behaviors. Participants in such courses would learn to be skeptical of definitive sets of principles of practice and to view conventionally accepted wisdom or apparently exemplary behaviors as relative and provisional.

The chief argument proposed here is that effective facilitation is present when adults come to appreciate the relative, provisional, and contextual nature of public and private knowledge and when they come to understand that the belief systems, value frameworks, and moral codes informing their conduct are culturally constructed. It is also evident when adults are enabled to create meaning to their personal worlds through a continual redefinition of their relationships with others.

Following on from this exhibition of personal autonomy and the realization that individual circumstances can be consciously altered comes the insight that it is possible, in concert with others, to change cultural forms, including attitudinal sets, role expectations, conventions, and folkways, as well as social structures.

This concept of facilitation is obviously prescriptive; that is to say, the outcomes identified in the preceding paragraph are given in the form of stipulative preference statements. This is not to imply that adults can become adept at critical reflectivity in some final, static manner. Rather, it is to say that adults should be encouraged to engage in the continuous critical analysis of received assumptions, commonsense knowledge, and conventional behaviors. The state of adulthood can never be fully realized, and it is not a question of an adult's acquiring a set of fixed competencies. Adult education as a transactional encounter is essentially a process. Central to this process is a continual scrutiny by all involved of the conditions that have shaped their private and public worlds, combined with a continuing attempt to reconstruct those worlds. This praxis of continual reflection and action might be accurately viewed as a process of lifelong learning. It is important to realize that philosophical prescriptions painstakingly derived from impeccably developed rationales are going to be contradicted daily in the real world of practice.

Teaching-learning transactions are, after all, dynamic interactions—psychosocial dramas in which unforeseen eventualities, serendipitious circumstances, and individual idiosyncrasies constantly distort our neatly planned visions of how our learning groups should function. Educators employed within formal educational institutions daily contradict their own prescriptions concerning how best to foster learners' freedom and individuality.

Very often, as the learning group reviews the curriculum, format of meetings, and evaluative procedures of the last few weeks or months, it becomes evident that a familiar dynamic has operated, despite all our best intentions to the contrary. According to this dynamic, I have begun by emphasizing the collaborative nature of the course and then, with the apparently unwitting connivance of course members, have proceeded to assume major responsibility for the most important decisions concerning course content and format.

Educators of adults, as much as learners, uncritically assimilate various assumptions, norms, beliefs, and values, and it is a genuinely humbling experience to ask participants in a learning group to point out the disguised authoritarianism in one's own practice.

What must never be lost sight of, however, is the need to develop a clear rationale for practice, even though that rationale may be contradicted or only partially realized in the day-to-day practitioner reality of facilitating learning. Without such a rationale we are little more than reactive automatons-ciphers through whom are channeled the latest curricular or methodological fads, irrespective of any consideration of their innate validity. While a healthy skepticism regarding the possibility of continually exemplifying such a philosophy of practice is essential to the sanity of facilitators, the necessity to develop such a philosophy should be regarded as fundamental to good practice. Educators of adults have grown accustomed to living with organizational and professional contradictions.

They probably became facilitators because they saw that as a way of increasing individuals' fulfillment, happiness, and sense of control, yet organizational criteria for their success are frequently antithetical to these motivations. In colleges and universities, for example, educators are encouraged to develop curricula and to arrange classrooms so as to attract the largest possible number of learners. The reason for this is not only to add to the sum total of human happiness and enlightenment, but also to make money.

Educational institutions, particulary in an era dominated by supply side economics, are viewed by politicians, trustees, administrators, and sometimes even faculty partly as educational enterprises partly as business operations. Hence, the greater the numbers of students that can be attracted, the greater the revenues for the educational institution. In business and industrial settings, these economic criteria are applied quite openly to determining the success of training initiatives. While trainers may hope that workshops and seminars will enable adults to make sense of themselves and their worlds, their success as trainers will be judged by whether or not productivity rises as a consequence of attendance at the training sessions. Furthermore, most educators and trainers of adults subscribe to a professional code that acknowledges the value of democratic collaboration and the inequity of forcing students to learn. Yet in their daily practice they repeatedly encounter a set of contextual constraints that force them into precisely the behaviors that they criticize in philosophical terms. Institutional timetables, economic necessities, standardized curricula, and unofficial norms of "what works in the real world" all conspire to nudge the educator into more didactic, authoritarian attitudes and behaviors than he or she might wish.

The conspiracy of contextual constraints becomes all the more compelling when learners repeatedly declare that they wish for more direction from facilitators or that they want facilitators to "put more of themselves" into the learning encounter. Learners, as much as facilitators, have been socialized into a view of education as an authoritarian-based transmission of information, skills, and attitudinal sets from teacher to taught. Under these circumstances, it will often be hard for educators to stand firm against the temptation to take more control over the learning encounter. Yet to give in to this temptation is to reaffirm precisely those patterns of dependency that prevent adults from becoming empowered, self-directed learners.

Given the force of these organizational constraints and professional expectations, it is not surprising that facilitators revert, with only an occasional twinge of conscience, to patterns of behavior they observed in their own teachers. How, then, can they break these patterns and begin to assume the kinds of facilitation roles outlined in this book? My answer is, only by developing a thoughtful rationale to guide their practice.

Possessed of such a rationale, facilitators are more likely to stand firm against organizational and professional imperatives that exert pressure on them to dominate learners under the guise of "providing structure' or 'clarifying ambiguities." Without such a rationale it is likely that most facilitators will sooner or later fall unthinkingly into patterns of facilitation that support structures of organizational convenience and confirm learners' patterns of dependency learned in the school classroom but have little to do with assisting adults to create, and re-create, their personal, occupational, and political worlds.

Central to the nation of discussion are two features that may be either complementary or contradictory. Discussion sessions can be judged successful to the extent to which they purssure certain cognitive ends or to the extent to which all members offer verbal contributions of approximately equal length. In a critique of discussion behaviors, I have examined the way in which discussion groups can become arenas of psychodynamic struggle and fields of emotional battle.

Many adults were schooled in competitive settings in which the pursuit of knowledge was obscured by the quest for grades and examination success. It is hard for such individuals to accept openness of discourse and to tolerate diverse opinions. Since discussion session are invested with emotional significance, any disagreement may well be interpreted as a personal assualt. Additionally, groups tend to place high value on cohesiveness and to exclude deviant opinions. But as Fawett-Hill maintains, it is important that groups tolerate deviant opinions. Such divergence guards against intellectual stasis. Bridges has specified certain epistemological underpinnings of discussion. All members should have respect for each other, and all should be septical of their own, as well as of others', authority.

Bridge also prescribes a moral culture for group discussion; it includes six ethical principles that participants should accept as the tacit assumptions underlying their discourse: reasonableness, peaceable orderliness, truth-fulness, freedom, equality, and respect for persons. Discussion conforming to the epistemological principles and moral culture outlined by Bridges would be characterized by openness of content, membership, and learning outcomes. Participants would set aside their own prejudices to entertain imaginative speculation.

Paterson proposes discussion as the educational activity par excellence. It is an educational end it itself, erquiring no extrinsic justification. To Paterson, adults commit and discover their whole beings in the process of presenting for group consideration their interpretations of their experience. He writes that "to adress others in discussion...is to bear witness to one's attempt to reconstruct ones, experience meaningfully, and it is at the same time to invite others to share this reconstructed experience". In this way participation in open discussion becomes a characteristically human activity of the most intimate and fundamental kind. Since openness is an essential characteristic for discussion, the concept of guided discussion must be discarded. In Paterson's words, "True discussion cannot be directed, or even guided, for to attempt to do so is in effect to opt out of the discussion, to close one's consciousness to alternative interpretations of the phenomenon under discussion before these alternatives have ever been stated"

To participate in this authentic form of mutual address, in this collaborative search for meaning, requires personal courage and analytic ability of a high order. It requires adults to be willing to examine the cultural orgins of many of their beliefs, to be aware of how many of the assumptions that inform their conduct have been acquired from external sources and authorities such as parents, schoolteachers, and peers, and hence to view their dearly held meaning systems as provisional and relative. In this sense to participate in discussion-in the collaborative externalization, exploration, and critical analysis of personally significant meaning systems is to realize one's adulthood to its fullest extent.

Four conditions can be identified that, if they are met, are likely to increase the chance that productive discussion will occur. The first of these is for group members to devise an appropriate moral culture for group discussions. This requires the group to arrive at a set of procedural rules for achieving equity of participation. Second, discussion leaders can give some thought to the materials that are to form the substantive focus of group discullions. The questions to be discussed should not be too factual or too uncontroversial, and they sould not be answerable in the course of preparatory reading by the group. Third, the leader should be well versed both in the subject matter to be covered during the discussion and in the principles of group dynamics. Only someone skilled at dealing with the problems caused by apperent isolates, pressures to silence deviants, and those adults who attempt to use the group as a means of bolstering their self-esteem can be said to be an effective discussion leader. Fourth, discussion participants should be prepared for discussion not only through the generation of a moral culture for discussion session but also through the development of reasoning skills and the improvement of communication abilities. In providing a forum for the pursuit and realization of these reflective analytical akills, as well as in requiring participants to evolve a democratic, moral culture governing group discourse, the discussion method is uniquely suited to facilitating critical adult learning.

Although collaborative discussion is now seen as an effective mode of facilitating learning, the literature that deals with instructional methods is still based mainly on the work of Tyler, and the task of teaching adults is frequently seen as a subcategory of the general task of program devolpment. Teaching is relegated to step three or four in different models of program development, including those of Houle, Knowles, Verner, Lauffer, and Boyle. In fact, teaching is generally not referred to as "teaching" at all, but rather as management of learning experiences, insturctional management, or implecmntation of the instruct-ional plan.

As will be argued further in Chapter Ten, however, this view is only one of a number of approaches to teaching adults. The Tylerian model of objectives-oriented program development in which learners acquire skills and knowledge specified in advance by the teacher and in which success is measured by learners performance of predetermined behaviors is often constraining and overly restrictive. The model does have some utility, but chiefly in the area of psychomotor skill acquisition. Tyler developed his work to assist schoolchildren acquire specific, predetermined skills and knowledge of an unambiguous, technical kind. In some training contexts where it is a question of acquiring technical skills, the sequenced, objectives-oriented nature of the model is highly satisfactory.

The problem is that some facilitators of learning have taken this model as the paradigm suitable for encouraging all kinds of adults learning. Much of the most significant adult learning, however, is of a nontechnical kind. It is concerned with the resolution of moral diffculties, with the development of self-insight, with acquiring the capacity to explore the world views of others, with reflection on experience, and with the evolution of personal ethical codes. One mode of teaching and learning highly suitable for these forms of learning is the discussion method. It is striking just how frequently the educational activities organized by adult learners themselves take this form.

For example, collaborative discussion is typically found in groups organized by single parents, the recently bereaved, divorcees, homosexuals, newly arrived immigrants, drug abusers, and feminists. These groups are composed of individuals who are seeking a reinforcement of their sense of self-worth. Their members are engaged in a redefinition of self and in a reinterpretation of their past actions and relationships from a newly realized psychological vantage point. They are also all seeking to set forth their experiences, to understand and explore others' experiences, and to heighten their self-awareness through this process of collaborative interpretation. The leadership of such groups is typically rotational. At different times, various individuals within these groups will take the responsibility for encouraging others to contribute to the discussion and will attempt some kind of analysis or interpretation of the experiences that have been voiced.

The adults in these groups are attempting to create new meaning systems. They are reinforcing each others' dormant, half-preceived feeling that there is some massive disjunction between their present ways of living and thinking, on the one hand, and the kind of existence they ideally envisage for themselves, on the other. At times these support and experience exchange groups transform themselves into activist groups that work to change oppressive external conditions. For some groups a common pattern will be a form of praxis in which analysis of common experiences alternates with public advocacy and demonstrations. The very act of participating in a public demonstration in support of gay rights or to demand changes in housing and welfare policies to benefit single parents will serve to strengthen and reinforce these adults' newly adopted and newly created identities. For groups of drug abusers, divorcees, newly arrived immigrants, or the recently bereaved, however, it will often be enough for members to meet regularly for support, for the presentation and analysis of typical problems, and for the gaining of practical assistance in negotiating the changed circumstances of their lives.

Teaching otucomes

We have emphasized that the concept of facilitation should be broadened to include activities in which adults are encouraged to consider alternative ways of thinking and living and in which they are prompted to scrutinize critically the extent to which supposedly universal beliefs, values, and behaviours are in fact culturally constructed. But if we prompt adults to consider these questions, are we not really engaging in a form of amateur psychotherapy? Asking people to reflect on their experience, to consider the motivations underlying their actions, and to try to appreciate the way in which their behaviors are perceived by others sound dangerously close to playing at therapist. This argument deserves to be taken seriously. There are many adults who suffer from clinically diagnosed conditions that range from schizophrenia to severe depression. For an educator to presume to treat them effectively is folly indeed.

There are, however, many adults who are troubled, frustrated with circumstances in their personal or occupational lives, insecure concerning their abilities, and seeking ways to develop more productive relationship with others. Such adults may be disturbed at certain aspects of their personal lives, but they are in no sense clinically "disturbed." There are very few readers of these words, I would venture, who are not disturbed at some aspect of their personal worlds or accupational lives, and it is precisely these adults who frequently form the clientele of adult classes. One of the great tragedies of contemporary life is the overprofessionalization of all aspects of human interaction. We are getting dangerously close to believing that we can engage in thoughtful self-reflection only if we are sanctioned by some professional to whom we pay a fee for the supervision of our self-reflection. Those who accept the argument that adults can undertake reflection on their past actions and current relationship only under the guidance of a skilled psychotherapist are doing nothing more than supporting the professional power and prestige of therapists.

One of the most valuable inquiries into methods of helping adults become critically reflective was intiated by Perry and pursued by Weathersby, Weathersby and Tarule, Boud, and Cameron. Instead of talking in a general wayu about the development in learners of critical awareness and the realization of the contextual, subjective aspects of the world, Perry sets forth nine intellectual stages, which he terms positions. These positions are not meant to be rigidly sequential nor to be mutually contradictory. Additionally, they do not include all the intellectual orientations possible in adulthood since they are derived from a series of intensive interviews with undergraduate students at Harvard. They do provide a useful analytical structure, however, that can be applied to understanding the development of critical reflectivity in adults, without in any way presuming them to be inevitably followed in every case. Indeed, with his undergraduates Perry freely admits that students became frozen at different stages of passive detachment of dualist absolutism.

Put simply, Perry's nine positions represent a move from an initial dualist perspective in which the world is percieved as comprised of black and white, mutually exclusive polarities to onen which the individual has come to a realization of the contextuality and relativity of the world and has then gone on to make a conscious commitment to one of many possible identities. In their exploration of these ideas on ethical growth and intellectual development as they relate to adulthood, the Syracuse Rating Group has also distinguished nine stages in adults' intellectual and ethical development.

The final stage of "developing commitments" is distinguished by an awareness of the effect that individual behaviors have on others and by a continuous search for new challenges. This search is undertaken with full knowledge that these challenges involve risks to one's self-esteem and that this final stage is never really "final". In leading up to this final stage, adults typically pass through stages in which they begin to view knowledge as contextual and become able to take on the perspective of others.

This recognition of the contingency of knowledge inevitably brings about an appreciation of the socially created nature of knowledge. Immediately prior to stage nine are those stages in which adults realize that only through making a commitment will a sense of individual meaning and responsibility for the creation of their personal worlds emerge.

As Boud has noted with regard to the Perry scheme, "It is helpful for the teacher to have in mind that within the same class there will probably be students with radically different outlooks on what is taking place, who will be reacting in very different ways". An early application of the earlier stages of this framework to a sample of adult students at community college identified dualist, multiplist, and relativist positions among the adults studied. The study noted that faculty in community colleges typically teach content in the same manner, regardless of the intellectual development of class members, and that faculty need to be more flexible in their pedagogic role to take account of the diversity of intellectual stages present in any class.

The Perry scheme ropresents an intersting area of future speculation for theorists of adult learning. Perry's contribution has been to posit an initial framework in which the transition from dualism to relativism to critically aware commitment has been clearly outlined. If these stages can be translated into specific ourcomes, with sufficient flexibility of interpretation so that widely varying settings can be included, this might provide adult teachers with a means by which they could recognize the diversity of stages reached by different members of learning groups. Alternatively, and in a more inductive manner, the frame work provides an analytical construct that one can apply to many different educational initiatives as a way of coming to understand the teaching- learning transactions occuring therein. There is little doubt that didactic pedagogic procedures in which learners are viewed as receptive repositories eagerly awaiting the deposits of experts are not likely to result in the development of critically aware commitment as outlined by Perry.

Rather than looking to concepts of teaching drawn from research on traditional teaching methods, therefore, it might be more fruitful to consult concepts and practices drawn from related fields such as community development or community action. The concept of the animateur is one such ides, and UNESCO has explored the manner in which training schemes to develop animataeurs might be established. At the very least, it is important to realize that between the authoritarian transmission of information to uncritically receptive automata and the nondirective, free-flowing realization of learner-defined activities lies a crucial facilitation role.

Facilitators have to be as wary of supporting every inclination, preference, or demand of learners as they are of forcing these same learners to follow a lockstep sequence of previously prescribed educational activities. In both instances learners are liable to develop an uncritical stance toward their own personal and intellectual development; in the one case because their opinion is never challenged or quesitioned, in the other because they are given no choice or chance to voice an opinion. Either option denies the essentially transactional nature of teaching-learning, and both options pretend that challenge, creative confrontation, and self-scrutiny have no place in adult learning. Without these elements, learners may find their educational encounters initially comforting but they will sooner or later come to suspect that such encounters are not really educational at all. When this awareness finally dawns, the resultant withdrawal from participation will have the same significance and result from the same kind of frustration as that caused by the learner's being allowed no voice in the educational transaction.

Profound changes of various types throughout the world have caused profound thinking regarding the role that education must play in helping people enhance the quality of their lives. Compton and Parish suggest that at least three concerns must be addressed in some way through educational efforts:

1 The increasing gap between the rich and the poor; the gap between rich nations and developing nations.

2 The disproportionate share of the world's resources now allotted to dominant world.

3 The increasing awareness in the Third World of the double standard of living.

Such concerns as these plus the constancy and rapidity of change, suggest to us a need to help people make the most of their individual potential. Boucouvalas describes a standing regulation in Greece that captures this notion of promoting individual ability: "The view of as a self-sufficient and independent personality and as the agent of development". It seems that learner self-direction and self-directed learning skills are crucial to the achievement of this human potential.

The study of self-directed learning appears to be primarily western in orientation and interest, with little relationship many parts of the world. In fact, the majority of recent research, writings, and language related to self-direction in learning have emanated from North America.

We thus believe that it is important to our success with adults as learners to take a more global approach in our understanding about self-direction in learning. We realize that not all our assumptions about learners and their abilities to accept personal responsibility will translate entirely from one setting or culture to another. However, this chapter's purpose is to present some reflections and understandings regarding the universality of self-directed learning principles and approaches.

We will present some background information before launching into discussions about self-directed learning in selected countries. Both of us have had many international students in our courses. Observing the successes and difficulties involved with facilitating their independent learning have provided us with some understanding of requirements across cultures in applying self-directed learning principles. We also have examined some of the international literature related to self-directed learning and have interviewed and talked informally with several people from other countries to obtain their views regarding such topics as autonomy, learner control, and instructor roles. Thus, what will follow is a summary of the literature we have studied regarding self-direction in selected settings ourside on North America. In addition, for two countries, we present a description of how indigenous adult educators believe that self-direction in learning would be possible in their respective countries.

We also need to say something about the nature of self-direction in learning in various cultures. Based on our reading and conversations with people from various countries, there seem to be many different ideas about what it means to study or plan individually. One country will have as an avowed policy the promotion of individual learning ability, while at the same time advocating participation in governmental sponsored programs to achieve such a goal. Another country will talk about self-education as a primary means for adults to learn, but the nature of the programs described would indicate to a North American observer that rew opportunities exist for individualized decision-making regarding the learning process.

Another problem stems from the structural design of certain approaches intended to promote independent study. For example, a correspondence course that requires strict adherence to a planned route of readings and testing procedure may offer little freedom to the learner other than pacing or sequencing of micro-learning components. Ljosa and Sandvold, on the other hand, make a case for the various ways by which learners can exercise freedom of choice within the didactical structure of correspondence education.

Moore describes how he thought about learner freedom in designing as Open University course. The course was based on: (a) a psychological climate that ecphasized learner decision-making and experience; (b) an emphasis on self-diagnosis; (c) a personally planned route of study; (d) a tutor seen as a resource person; (e) some learner-designed evaluation criteria; and (f) an emphasis on each student's personal learning experiences.

A wide range exists in interpreting and permitting freedoms such as these within the learning setting. As noted earlier in the chapter, some suggest that self-direction is primarily a middle-class, white phenomenon by its emphasis on the individual. Even though some research has demonstated that certain self-directed learning concepts hold across racial, economic, and social groupings, the concepts may not always directly apply in other cultural contexts. However, we firmly believe that as long as cultural context is recognized and respected, it is possible to apply many of the instructional and learning tips described in this book in any setting.

There are many countries that should be examined in terms of their self-directed practices, activities, or philosophies. However, that needs to be the subject of another book as we work toward a better understanding of various implications for the way in which adults are helped in their efforts to maximize their potential. In this section, we touch on just a few countries in order to highlight interesting aspects of self-direction in different cultural contexts.

Scandinavian countries have a long history of adult education. Grundtvig's pioneering work in Denmark with the folk high school movement began in 1844. Grundtvig, in developing the folk high school movement, wanted an educational experience for adults that was residential in nature but small in scope. He also wanted a mixture of practical and theoretical work, supported by lots of decussion. These institutions therefore stress work in the group setting, and are aimed at the individual development of each person. In fact, their methods and environment are designed to encourage individuals of all social classes to broaden their personal horizons. Folk schools have spread to many other countries in the past century and a half.

Sweden has make several efforts to promote education for adults that is self-directed in nature. One stated adult education aim of the Swedish government, for example, is to cater "to individual preferences and needs" 1977 governmental ordinance called for learning opportunities to increase awareness of personal capacity, to develop independence, to promote creativitym, and to foster critical reflectivity.

One of the most innovative approaches to adult education has been the study circle. These have been used to provide many citizens in Sweden with an opportunity to develop self-study skills.

While the group emphasis of the study circle at first glance may seem inconsistent with notions of self-direction. Oliver states that historically in Şweden: "study circles encouraged self-directed learning and full participation, blending the intensive small group format with traditional Swedish culture-particularly small-town life and the face-to-face conversations of friends and neghbors". Svensson notes that more than 2.5 million people are involved in Swedish study circles each year, with 1.5 million of these women.

While not quite as popular, another important Swedish form of individualized learning is correspondence study. The country has three such organizations: "one that is authorized to hold examinations for formal educational institutions, one that provides study materials that do not lead to any formal qualification, and one that provides agricultural correspondence materials". Nearly 20,000 people each year enroll in correspondence study.

In Norway, correspondence schools have long played a very important role in educating adults. In fact, Norway's Adult Education Act of 1976 was intended to influence learning throughout life and "should give the core ingredient for elf-managed learning throughout the rest of life". Finland, too , has several correspondence institutes that offers expert aid through study centres to assist individual students in their educational efforts.

United Kingdom

The United Kingdom is perhaps most well-known in the area of self-directed education for its pioneering work with the open university concept. There are also many other opportunities for the learner interested in independent study. For example, the number of adults studying by correspondence in the UK is estimated to "range from 500,000 to 750,000 a year".

Another imaginative attempt to foster independent learning took place at Malvern Hills College, the center for adult education in the rural English counties of Hereford and Worcester, Several adult students were having difficulty attending a regular college class. Thus, a Correspondence Tution Service was established, to "provide individually oriented programmes of home study supported by personal tutorials". An initial diagnostic interview between a tutor and the student, tutorial assistance with learning projects, and home study correspondence courses are some of the avalable resources.

Brookfield also describes his research, which examined the self-directed efforts of individuals not associated with any formal organization or institution. He chose twenty-five working-class individuals whose formal education had ended at age 16, and whose expertise stemmed from extenxive study of, or involvememt with, a hobby or perosnal-interest area.

His research helped to advance earlier work, primarly in North America, related to learning projects. It also dedonstrated that independant efforts to obtain mastery over some area of study can take place across a wide rage of cultural and educational backgrounds. He concluded that many adult learners will look to to other learners for information and support rather than to societies, organizations, and professional educators. He noted: "subjects would mention influential books and magazines but would preface these comments by declaringtheir `real'source of information was their fellow enthusiasts".

Japan

Japan's progress in industrialization since the Second World War, coupled with its more recent emergence as a world leader in various ways, has prompted a varyety of changes within the country. These range from a growth of pizza parlors and fast-food restaurants, to increasing disposable income for most people, and a constant contact with oither nations. Such changes have also affected education in many ways, including the education of adults. As one example, open-university-type programs reach adults throughout the society.

The pressure to be part of a societal group remains, but subtle changes are taking place in education. A Jaamese, Seiichero Miura, who works sith adult education activities, was interviewed about adult education in his country. He describes the change as follows:

One thing I might mention is the use of groups in adult education practice. I recognize the heavy emphasis in the United States on the self-directed learner. But form looking at human nature I suggest it is not easy for some to be self-directed. In Japan, we would organize a self-directed. In Japan, we would organize a self-directed group, kind of a mixture between group study. Subtle group pressure and a Japanese sensitivity to groups promote a kind of invisible network forcing you to be there, to participate even when you may be reluctant to attend. Thus, you sacrifice your individual desire to the group. I call theis interdependent learning rather than independent learning.

Professor Miura was also asked how he would introduce learning contracts, frequently used in self-directed learning efforts, into the Japanese culture: "I will introduce the idea of the learning contract but it will be utilized within a group setting. I will need to introduce it slowly and find the ways it can work".

Thus, Japan appears to be in a transitional state where the sanctity of the group is being reevaluated in terms of individual needs and wishes. This may be most clear in adult education effort with older Japanese. Sekiguchi describes a 1981 Recommendation Paper by the Central Committee on Education. Among the Paper's recommendations is a call for the older person's self-education. As a method of study, "learning in a large group or in a classroom will not be adequate since there is a great difference between individual learners. Instead, individual learning methods are recommended as a more suitable way". Facilities such as libraries, museums, and similar institutions are suggested as organizations which need to play a more active role in meeting older adults' needs. Study courses on radio and television and correspondence courses are recommended as effective methods for the older person.

China

The changes that have taken place in China during late 1989 and on into the 1990s make it difficult to comprehend fully what the future holds. However, the last several years have been marked by some important changes relative to adult learning: "Since 1977, when the expansion and restructuring of adult education began after the Cultural Revolution, important changes have taken place in many sectors of adult education". For example, current radio and television delivery methods are patterned after Great Britain's Open University. The Chinese Telivision University opened in 1979 and provides several degree opportunities. In fact, TVUs operate at the national and municipal levels. Telievised instruction is also used at factory colleges, spare-time colleges, and regular universities. Municipal television universities and corresponding study centers in a variety of settings cooperate with centralized programming efforts. They serve some 800,000 registered students and many more casual viewers whdo do not enroll credit.

There are other forms of adult education in China that offer some opportunities for individualized learning.

Correspondence courses are avaliable, and individual tutoring is sometimes available. In 1980 factory universities set up correspondence courses that enrolled 240,000 students. Zhou reports that there are some 32,000 people enrolled in independent correspondence colleges, and another 150,000 students enrolled in 148 evening college correspondence divisions.

The "visiting teacher" program also offers opportunities for a leaner to work individually after the teacher provides some initial assistance: "In this program, literacy is taught by a teacher who visits the peasant, with home and labels common household objects the appropriate Chinese characters. The learner thus learns the characters as the items are used"

Indonesia

Traditional beliefs and expectations in Indonesia regarding learning have placed the instructor in a role as authority figure. In fact, learners have not been given many opportunities to assess personal needs as a basis for learning. These learners aslo usually expect the teacher to be an authority on whatever subject matter is being discussed. Furthermore, they view experiential learning activities, such as using various community resources outside the classroom, as a waste of time. They would believe that such time could more appropriately be spent in the classroom listening to an instructor. However, increasing levels of education among the population and a better understanding of teaching approaches outside of Indonesia among educators are indicators that self-direction in learning is possible with appropriate modifications.

For example, one Indonesian educator studying adult education in the United States told one of the authors how he would apply various self-directed learning techniques in introducing family planning to community leaders when he returned home. During his initial contact with the leaders he would discuss the importance for the country of the content to be covered. He would also discuss with them their learning needs, based on their roles, tasks, and functions as community leaders. Because he would be viewed as the authority, he would come well prepared and make the initial presentation with the use of various audio-visual aids.

The participants would then complete a pre-designed, needs-assessment from, and come to some initial conclusions regarding personal needs. This educator would then lead a general discussion to determine needs, strengths, and weaknesses among the group. He would begin by listing learning needs on a chalk board or on poster paper, and ask participants to help him rank them. He would conclude with a summary of the needs, strengths, and weaknesses. Then a description sheet of the content areas that could be covered during subsequent session would be distributed and discussed. He would make every effort to accommodate the uncovered needs, but would be very specific in describing those content areas that he believed must be covered because of official requirements of his own personal convictions, even if they did not match well with the rankings.

After that initial session, he would spend time putting together the plans for remaining sessions. This would include determining who would be responsible for various content areas, what learning aids would be needed, what teaching and learning technique would be used, and what arrangements were needed for outside resources or resource leaders. Passive learning activities would be expected, although small group discussion could be designed for occasional use. If any individualized or experiential learning activities were desired or necessary, special efforts would be needed to make clear the importance of such experiences. As evaluation in the form of testing would be the normal expectation, some efforts would also be needed to design the procedures and instruments.

Thus, some of the self-direction procedures described in this book would be possible, but the instructor or trainer would need to explain such procedures very carefully and help participants understand how they would enhance the learning. Cultural traditions and expectations regarding the role of the instructor do not rule out more individualized approaches, but adaptations based on an understanding of prior expectations of students and teacher roles would be required.

Even the small group discussion typically will center on questions posed by the instructor, although students feel they have some latitude in discussing areas beyond the instructor's question.

Experiential learning activities will be looked at by most learners and instructors as a waste of time. They fear that such activities will take time away from the instructor's lecturing. Although a few learners would thrive probably believe that an instructor using such approaches did not know the probablybelieve that an instructor using such approaches did not know the subject matter and was employing them to cover up for inadequacies. One Tanzanian adult endeucator studying in the United States felt that back home his biggest hurdle would be the unwillingness of his university administrators and fellow teachers to accept teaching approaches that placed considerable responsibility on the learner

Another problem area revolves around evaluation and grading. Many of the current traditions of grading were inherited from the British, and the result is usually a highly structured process. For example, many teachers are expected or even required to give a certain number of lower grades. The Tanzanian adult educator mentioned above, who by the time of the interview had considerable experiences with self-directed learning in the classroom from his United States graduate training, felt that the use of a learning contract in his country would be problematic.

The above points suggest that the employment of self-directed learning principles in Tanzania would be difficult, at least initially, because of traditional expectations about education. However, one of the authors spent some time in Tanzania and observed some self-directed adult learning taking place at the village level. In fact, the country supports a national policy of "self-reliance," in which elected village leaders take on primary responsibility for local development. The policy has worked only coderately well in some parts of the nation and not well at all in others.

Eastern Europe

In most Eastern European countries, a varity of independent study opportunities exist. Correspondence study seems to be quite popular for the learner who, out of preference of necessity, selects individualized approaches. Albanian workers are encouraged to educate themselves through various forms of education, including correspondence study. Correspondence is also one of the favored delivery methods for adult learning in Bulgaria and Poland.

In Germany, correspondence education is recognized as equal in value to other forms of adult study: "Those who acquire education in this manner are offered special facilities and encouragement, such as leave from work amounting to seventy-seven days per year while retaining the right to a full income". In Hungary, combining both correspondence study and evening courses, according to a 1975 study, "those who acquired a degree in this manner were 45.2% of the total number of people who received a university degree. In Rumania nearly 30 per precent of all adult students study either at evening school or through correspondence.

Yugoslavia is perhaps the most progressive of these countries. It has schools of self-guided learners, developed through federal legislation, and other institutions through which the individual learner uses various enducational resources, such as cultural centres, museus, and liabraries. The country also was among the first nations to provide special study on the conception of andragogy, including both graduate and undergraduate study.

Obviously, the events that have taken place throughout eastern Europe in the dawn of the 1990s will have an impact on the education of adults. While it is too early to speculate with any high degree of confidence, we believe that these changes signals potential for positive developments on the self-direction front. Only time will tell, through, what specific impact may take place.

The issue of wider access is but one of many driving forces putting the impact and process of higher education under scrutiny. The followinng kinds of questions are now the subject of frequent speculation and, more recently, research:

What are students learning and why?

- In what kinds of learning processes are they engaging?
- What is the quality of their experience?
- How effectively and efficiently are resources being deployed to develop tthe potential of new kinds of students?
- What kinds of qualities and competences are being developed and assessed, and for what purposes?
- To what extent do flexibility, openness andd choice obtain with regard to learning struictures and oppertunities?
- Do different kinds of students experience the education offer as 'relevant, useful and enabling'?
- Are students being helped to 'learn how to learn', for a changing world in which social relations are more complex, professional athority and the effectiveneess of traditional structures are being challenged, and knowledge and information increase at a rapid pace?

Students, an increasingly influential group of stakeholders but heretofore often invisible in such debates, consider the impact, process and structures of higher education. Their reflections on issues such as quality and responsiveness derive from their experiencee of having returned to academic learning programmes. The voices represented in this chapter come largely from those adults who are often at issuee in access debates. The literature on adults as learners in higher and continuing education tends to reflect the experience of largely white middle-class adults, often North American, who as students or educators have experienced a great deal of previous formal education. In this, they may be similar to other younger adults who have spent most of their school years feeling like this, and who remain under-represented in British higher-education institutions.

The views represented here come from a multi-site qualitative research study. We have investigated the perspectives of adults who have returned to do some kind of higher or continuing education course after an interval of generally at least five years following the end of their initial learning, within and outside formal education, had a bearing on their expectations and experiences of returning to a formal learning context. Through largely individual depth interviews, supported by participant observation and group interviews and discussions.

Broadly, 32 different kinds of learning situations provide the basis from which these adults reflect on their experiences as learners. Overall, 48 learners participated in the study over the course of 8 research cycles, each involving a different formal learning context. Twenty-three of the total 32 who were interviewed individually, and who therefore provided in-depth learning histories, left school with few or no qualification. Only 7 in the study had experienced higher education previously.

Thirty-seven in the study were women: 6 were black. Thirty identified themselves as clearlyy working class, 12 as clearly middle class with 3 unknown. Nine found it difficult to make a distinction, but of this group, felt more working class than middle class.

Six women were followed up, after they completed the diploma at Hillcroft College about which they were first interviewed, and had moved on to university or polytechnic degrree courses. At the end of these second interviews, they had the opportunity to reflect upon the transcript of our previous meeting at which they had anticipated their experiences of higher education.

Disjunction refers generally to sense of feeling at odds with oneself, as a learner learning in a particular set of circumstances. It is not the result of a cause-and-effect relationship but rather emerges out of mutually interacting influences, as well as past and present experiences of being a learner in different kinds of learning contexts. A sense of disjunction can be felt to be associateed with who one is, where one is, and how one's present experience as a learner relates to previous or concurrent experiences, within and outside the formal learning context.

Disjunction can be associated with feelings of alienation, anger, frustration and confusion. In this study it always refers to a sense of fragmentation and involves issues of both personal and social identity. Disjunction sets up the potential for education and for miseducation depending upon mitigating circumstances from the past and in the current situation. When miseducation results, thus 'arresting or distorting the growth of further experience', the overall sense of identity as a learner can be fundamentally undermined. Certain kinds of social conditions can lead to the damaging efffects of such an experience becoming internalized.

Alternatively, by chance, design or conscientious planning on the part of educators, disjunction can be constructively 'made sense of' and managed. This is especially true when various partners in the learning context become more responsible and accountable for what is occuring. This creates the possibility of future actions that can simultaneously compensate for, anticipate and manage disjunction.

There are, however academic learning situations that, by design, intent, or tradition, afford little or no possibility for individual of collective structured reflection on what it means to learn in that situation or on how the situation might be made more effective. The management of disjunction under such circumstances may be more challenging for some learners. The extent to which adults feel able and willing to cope with disjunction, and the concomitant feelings of isolation and lowered self-worth that can be generated, seems to be tied up with many factors.

These include the inflences of previous learning and presumptions about education at home and school; experiences of learning and being a learner as an adult within and outside higher education; one's self-concept and overall sense of self-esteem at that time in one's life; the quality of the support and relationships available within and outside the education situation, and the kinds of compensating experiences available at the time in the overall learning environment.

In this study, adults described experiences characterized by a sense of disjunction in relation to the following:

- their expectations of and their initial encounter with the formal learning context;
- the degree of continuity between the new learning experience and prior ones, both within and outside formal education;
- their experience of the assumptions and approaches operating with regard to teaching and learning, and

the extent to which these hard with prior expectations and assumptions about learning, based on experience elsewhere;

- the ways in which social differences and power relations were experienced and managed in the learning environment;
- the extent to which core aspects of their personal and social identity felt threatened or at risk in that environment;
- the management of multiple and often conflicting roles;
- the impact of contradictions between tutors'private and public stances; for critical reflection and analysis;
- the ways in which it was expected that knowledge and knowing could be legitimately explored in that learning situation:
- the nature of the dialogue, relationships and learning processes experienced in the formal learning context;
- the ways in whicch personal defelopment and change were occurring:
- in spite of or because of what wass occurring in a particulasr learning situation.

Integration as equilibrium

On the other hand, integration within this conceptual formulation implies that one's sense of personal and social identity does not feel itself to be fundamentally at issue, of at risk, in a particular learning environment. Integration tends to be associated with a sense of equilibrium, or an 'all of a piece feeling'. Integration does not necessarily give rise to learning itself, but rather helps to create the conditions conducive to an individual learner being able and willing to learn in a particular learning situation. In other words, there is potential for benefit, and for education. Integration thus need not be associated with intensely positive feelings.

Integration can also refer to heightened feelings of self-validation, arising out of the extent to which a new situation compensated for prior experiences of disjunction elsewhere. Alternatively, it emerged as a resolution to disjunction involving some kind of invalidation of previously held beliefs, ideas or meanings. It is within this context that disjunction can be experienced as a constructive starting point for learning. The critical difference between the experience of disjunction as an enabling rather than a disabling experience lies in the kinds of values, purposes and relationships which obtain in the learning situation.

A critical factor is the nature of the support available to guide the learner through the sense of confusion and fragmentation generated by the experience of disjunction and which enables him, or her to steer a path through it towards significant learning and change. In this study, such situation tended to be characytrized by the adults concerned as feeling valued for who they were as people, and for their prior experience. Learning entailed active involvement and interrelating.

Conditions asso-ciated with cycles of disjunction and integration, and indeed an overall sense of integration itself in connection with academic learning programmes, included the following: the active used and appreciation of different forms of knowledge, the making of connection across disciplinary boundaries, and a positive valuing and use of personal and social differences within a group. For many learners in this study, to experience learning situations characterized by such conditions and an overall sense of integration, often served to repair severely damaged confidence and self-esteem, and to compensate for prior experiences of education.

Alternatively, a relationship with a particular tutor could positively mediate an overall sense of disjunction with regard to that course or learning context as whole. Others found that experiences of disjunction on a course could be positively mediated by prior experiences in which confidence had been built, and self-esteem with regard to one's learner identity and potentiality began to develop. Relationship with peers and spouses also played a vital role in enabling learners to make sense of and manage experiences of disjunction. None the less, many of the learners in this study seemed to have required repeated experiences of integration to enable them to feel sufficiently resilient and able to withstane and indeed manage forces which could otherwise damage them. Even then, the path of the development of such resilience and confidence was by no means linear.

Certain situations could spiral the learner back into feeling the scars of prior experiences, although in this study no one experienced the feeling of going back to 'square one': earlier experiences that had given rise to a sense of integration had created an internal store upon which to draw when necessary. To survive, and thrive, in academic contexts, however, it seemed that some of these experiences needed to have occurred within formal education.

Learning as 'all of a piece'

It would be well beyond the scope of a single chapter to illustrate the many ways in which the concepts of disjunction and integration are grounded in the data. Here, however, I shall draw upon a specific block of material from the study, which was generated in one of two ways. During the course of the initial researh cycles, would often ask participants directly about what they wanted and needed from teachers in higher and continuing education.

Each of these approaches involved participants in a particular kind of imagining process in relation to their needs and previous expectations. In undertaking it, they teased out the kinds of learning situations and relationships that they saw as conducive to integration and thus to the possibility of education rather than miseducation. The role-play approach, especially, helped to draw out issues which most mattered to these adults if they were to feel willing and able to learn in academic learning situations.

The following main themes emerged from the data elicited by these two techniques: the notion of personal stance in teaching and learning; recognizing and respecting differences; 'unlearning to not speak'; the role of relationship in mediating disjunction; and 'learning-in-relation'. Each of these is dealt with below, illustrating from a particular angle various aspects to the disjunction-integration formulation.

We often speak about teaching and learning as if they were simply a function of subject expertise, skill and method. These adults' accounts, however, illustrate the extent to which for them, the quality of teaching, and indeed of learning, is mediated by the 'personal stance' of the teacher. I used this term in the sense of Salmon who suggests that 'the material of learning has traditionally been viewed in different terms from those that define the learner'. For Salmon, the metaphor of personal stance lay emphasis on the personal positions of teachers and learners, and how they give meaning to their learning:

> How we place ourselves, within any learning context, whether formal or informal, is fundamental. This is not just a matter of 'attitude', in so far as it defines our own engagement with the material; it represents the very stuff of learning itself...how we position ourselves towards [each other] in any educational setting... is what governs the limits and possibilities of our engagement together, what shapes and defines the material we construct out of that engagement.

In the accounts which follow, these adults' perceptions and experiences of teachers' personal stances towards them as adult learners are seen as vital to their feeling able to enter into the possibility of education. For example, Gaynor was a working-class woman in her mid-fifties who returned to do an academic diploma which would enable her to go on to a degree course. She had worked largely inside her home for many years and had little confidence and low self-esteem when she entered Hillcroft College. Speaking within the contexxt of the role-play describeed above, she implores me to remember what it is like to bave no knowledge of that subject at all. Rhoda, long unejoloyed and with little sense of self-esteem or direction, stresses the negative impact of tutors who position themselves towards their material, rather than towards the student. She is describing here the extent to which she had felt progressively silenced by what she had experienced from certain tutors.

Rhods: They have to be hearing what they have to say. I constantly get interruptions which makes me feel, 'Should I be here?'... And they are always so busy. I always feel I'm taking up his time.

SWW: What about attitudes?

Rhoda: I always have the feeling with my tutor that he's 'in the know'. He soes most of the talking. He should be more laid back and draw me out more.

Frank was a lower working-class man and previously a labourer who read 12-15 books a week, across at least six subject areas. He re-encountered a former teacher whose previous attempts to encourage him at school had been 'too little too late'. She persuaded him to return as a mature student to an FE college to do O-levels. He did A-levels there also and, after an interval, went on to a polytechnic course. He had, however, condistently encountered structural and attitudinal barriers in his attempts to engage with formal learning contexts. He felt that, during those years of struggle, It was only in political groups that he was able to find the intellectual stimulation and dialogue that he actively craved. Here, he too emphasizes the importance of a personal and social dimension in his interactions with teachers. Unlike many of the women in the above acconts and those that follow, however,, he communicates a certain resilience and autonomy in his expressed wish for confrontation and challenge.

Frank: Their responsibility is to point out the central core of the basic theory, to confront you as an individual. You can then decide if you agree or not ... But they must draw people out. Reach for their potential. Help you to engage with central theory. It is an interactive relationship. This requires knowledge, skills and personal qualities. Also, they must be sensutive to personal problems because these will distort the learning preocess.

SWW: What skills?

> Frank: An intellectual grasp. A degree of lucidity with which they can ecplain. Must be evaluated on the extent to which they can facilitate people's interestin and ablity to deal with knowledge and their capacity incorporate within te learning situation the vviews of the students. Especially the older ones. Which may be in direct contradiction and which may not be supported with six million academic references, but practical experience.

Fran was a working-class woman who throughout her initial schooling aimed to be a hairdresser. She eventually became a llecturer and teacherin this field, to the amazement of her family, since they had always seen her sister as the 'academic one' and Fran as the 'practical one'. The ways Fran strived to use her intelligence and creativity in each work situation, however, often seemed to put her at odds with colleagues. One summer, after she had left an unsatisfactory work situation, by chance she came upon information about the local polytechnic's willingness to accept adults without A-levels. She enquired, out of curiosity, and was offered a place. She describes running all the way home, in panic and disbelief. She spent the entire summer trying to persuade officials that, if they were willing to give her a grant to study for three years, they could give her one-third that money to set up her own business as a hairdresser. Failing in this, she began at the local polytechnic in the autumn.

Fran speaks about the need for someone 'with communication skills, and for tutors who can 'break into a language that you can understand.'

> Fran: I could understand what they were saying it would be lovely. They need to talk to me and explain it to me. I would expect them to be positive and

encouraging. Usually, if you ask a question, yuo end up with a negative ... They don't use a reinforcing way of learning. They just sit there and rub up their own ego... One thing they need to know is how to be a teacher. That's the one thing they don't know.

SWW: What does that mean to you?

Fran: If I have so sit and take notes for an hour, which is far too long, I need something that is constructed in a sane pattern. So when I read my notes afterwards, they make sense to me... They ought to be able to use experience, and break into the lecture, without feeling you are taking them off at a tangent... They can't convey what they know...They don't connect it with anybody else's subject matter.

Moreover, her own experience as a hairdressing lecturer, after years of apprenticeship and training, led her to feel incredulous that teachers in higher education had preparation only in their subject area.

Adults in the study continually spoke about the importance of being acknowledged and respected for their differences. The interview questions constantly revealed ways in which a failure-in actions, not just words-to recognize and respect their differences could prove a source of disjunction.

Connie was a middle-class woman who had worked entirely inside her home and had taken primary responsibility for parenting. She reached a point where she bought an IQ book, because she felt no better than a 'cabbage'. She returned to higher education via an FE college that catered particularly for mature women returners. This experience had been characterized largely by integration, with continual discovery and challenge emerging out of the quality of the relationships with peers an tutors. She found her transition to the polytechnic unsettling in many ways. Here she emphasizes the effect of different kinds of personal stances of tutors upon her as a learner. In particular, she highlights a confusion she elaborates in other parts of our interview: namely, that tutors are adult learners too, and therefore how can they not understand differences? She speaks sbout the need for tutors to remember that they too are mature students and to use that as a way of relating to mature students. They come with experience. How they see us affects how they interact. They must be helped to see that., 'If you're motivated, you'll get it.' Your pressures are seen as a testing ground. For example, 'You'll be a good rather than realizing the pressures you are under. I wouldn't want the structure and the knowledge to be changed. Just to have more time, and more emphasis on motivation. But sometimes, I just cannot cope. There must be a positive discrimination towards older people.

Todd, a working-class man, had struggled all through initial schooling, feeling out of place in terms of his artists interests. Throughout his education he had felt pressured to be someone he was not, symbolized by the efforts of teachers to turn him from left-handedness to righthandedness. He left school with no qualification and went to work in the markets.

Before returnintg to do a degree, he had been both unemployed and a musician, having discovered a relationship with another musician through which he could develop these interests and talents. Here he elaborates on the differences cited by Connie and, like her, stresses the pressures on him in terms of the complexity of his life: in this case, as a musician, as a parent, as one of many in this situation who were not well-heeled financially, and who had anything but the prior learning and life histories of more traditional students. He asserts the need for tutors to recognize.

> That we're not just students. We have an outside life too. We suffer the same problems. We're not purely a brain. We're human beings. That's the way it is with normal education. It's not right. But they think they can group us in a lump. Shows a lack of responsibility. Here, they still teach you like you were secondary school. It's the same process: socialize, work, see tutor. But they must know about people like when they are starting to flag. Like this guy who was living in a squat and had to take casual work for four weeks. They have to have skills of working with people: diverse people. People who were delinquent, mentally ill. It's not so much they are misfits. There are lots of really clever people. It's just that they should not be treated as if they were academics...No one here has asked me what I am going to do, much less what I have done.

Recognizing differences for a number in the study also meant recognizing previous damage and actively repairing confidence, particulary in the case of women. Sally is another working-class woman who experienced redundancy and separation before her return to study at Hillcroft. Initial education for her had been fraught with one trauma after another. Here she speaks out of her experience of returning to formal education in a women's college where small groups were a key feature of the learning environment.

Index